THE HOUSE FLIPPING FRAMEWORK

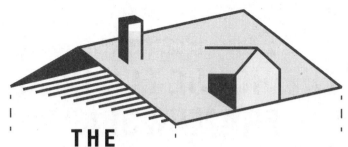

THE
HOUSE FLIPPING
FRAMEWORK

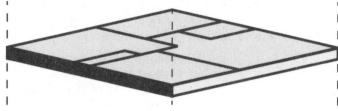

THE TACTICAL PLAYBOOK TO
SCALE YOUR REAL ESTATE PORTFOLIO
AND REINVEST YOUR PROFITS

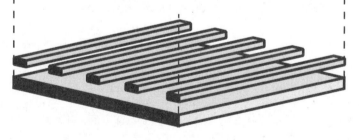

JAMES DAINARD

BiggerPockets®
PUBLISHING
Denver, Colorado

Early Praise for
THE HOUSE FLIPPING FRAMEWORK

"James Dainard is seriously one of the most successful investors that I've personally, and I'm continually blown away by the systems and efficiency he's created in his flipping business. This book takes years of experience and lessons learned and boils it all down to an easy-to-understand yet extremely powerful framework that anyone can follow. It's a *must read* for anyone who wants to shortcut their way to wealth through flipping."

—Tony Robinson, cohost of the BiggerPockets *Real Estate Rookie* podcast, founder of Robinson Equity, coauthor of *Real Estate Partnerships*

"A lot of people can speak the language of real estate, James lives it. Better yet, he's lived in for 20+ years now. He's one of the few people who can speak to every facet of real estate, and we're all lucky he's decided to put his brain on paper for us. He's spent years helping other investors behind the scenes, now he's doing it at scale. This is a must-read!"

—Cole Rudd-Johnson, founder Hello Pad, host of the *Off Market Operator* podcast

"*The House Flipping Framework* is an invaluable guide for anyone interested in the real estate industry, particularly in the niche of house flipping. This book stands out not just for its insightful advice but for the depth and clarity with which it addresses the often overlooked technical aspects of fixing and flipping homes. James has been a mentor to me for over a decade and I have had the pleasure of learning from him first-hand! His teachings have helped me make millions in revenue through my house flips and create a multi-million dollar rental portfolio."

—Leka Devatha, president of Rehabit Homes, Inc.

"*The House Flipping Framework* is packed with actionable advice from one of the best in the business. James's dedication to helping others become better operators shines through every page. His book is an invaluable tool for anyone in the house flipping game."

—**Henry Washington, cohost of the BiggerPockets** *On the Market* **podcast, author of** *Real Estate Deal Maker*

"The opportunity to learn from James should not be missed. He's probably the most knowledgeable investor in the industry and is a great teacher. His book is a must read for anyone interested in house flipping and value add investing."

—**Dave Meyer, host of the BiggerPockets** *On the Market* **podcast, author of** *Start with Strategy*

"Dainard's clear, step-by-step approach ensures that readers not only learn how to maximize profits but also minimize risks, making this an essential read for anyone serious about building wealth through real estate. This book is practical for new and experienced investors looking to start in flipping or to continue to scale their business. Packed with real world insights from Dainard's experiences and practical strategies that you can implement to give you the tools you need to navigate the world of house flipping, from finding deals to managing rehabs."

—**Ashley Kehr, cohost of the BiggerPockets** *Real Estate Rookie* **podcast, author of** *Real Estate Rookie*

"*The House Flipping Framework* is a comprehensive roadmap that provides invaluable insights for both novice and experienced real estate investors. His straightforward approach, combined with real-life examples and actionable strategies, makes the complex world of house flipping accessible and engaging. Dainard's expertise shines through, making this a must-read for anyone looking to succeed in building a business flipping houses."

—**Ashley Wilson, cofounder of Bar Down Investments and HouseItLook LLC, author of** *The Only Woman in the Room*

The House Flipping Framework: The Tactical Playbook to Scale Your Real Estate Portfolio and Reinvest Your Profits
James Dainard

Published by BiggerPockets Publishing LLC, Denver, CO
Copyright © 2024 by James Dainard
All rights reserved.

Publisher's Cataloging-in-Publication Data
Names: Dainard, James, 1983-, author.
Title: The house flipping framework : the tactical playbook to scale your real estate portfolio and reinvest your profits / James Dainard.
Description: Denver, CO: BiggerPockets Publishing, LLC, 2024.
Identifiers: LCCN: 2024942532 | ISBN: 9781960178725 (paperback) | 9781960178732 (ebook)
Subjects: LCSH Real estate investment. | House buying | House selling. | Real estate business. | Personal finance. | BISAC BUSINESS & ECONOMICS / Real Estate / Buying & Selling Homes | BUSINESS & ECONOMICS / Personal Finance / Investing | BUSINESS & ECONOMICS / Industries / Construction
Classification: LCC HD1382.5 .D35 2024 | DDC 332.63/243--dc23

Published in the United States of America
FR 10 9 8 7 6 5 4 3 2 1

Printed in Canada

DEDICATION

This book is dedicated to my wife, Clair: You have been there for two decades. You believed in me during the toughest parts of this journey and built me back up when I wanted to quit. You are my greatest supporter, my best friend, and my why.

TO THE READER

I want to thank you for taking the time just to pick up this book. There's a ton of different routes to learn about flipping houses (some good, some not so good), and I want to sincerely thank you for trusting me.

TABLE OF CONTENTS

PART 1
GET STARTED FLIPPING

PART 2
FINDING & FUNDING
FLIPPING DEALS

PART 3
MANAGING YOUR FLIP FROM START TO FINISH

PART 4
SCALING YOUR FLIPPING BUSINESS

INTRODUCTION

Each person holds so much power within themselves
that needs to be let out. Sometimes they just need a little
nudge, a little direction, a little support, a little coaching,
and the greatest things can happen.
—PETE CARROLL, FORMER SEATTLE SEAHAWKS COACH

PERSONALLY, I'VE BEEN a real estate investor since 2005, back when everybody was listening to their favorite songs on a colorful iPod Nano or scrolling YouTube for the first time. I was in my last year at the University of Washington, and I wanted to get ready for a professional career, something in sales and finance. School was great, but I wanted real-world, hands-on experience to teach me how to communicate with clients, follow up with leads, and, of course, how to close deals. So I had started looking for an internship or part-time sales position when my roommate and future investment partner, Will Heaton, took a job with a real estate investment company. The job was basically just knocking doors to find off-market deals.

In the world of wholesale real estate, an **off-market deal** refers to a property that is not listed on the open market, or the Multiple Listing Service (MLS). Wholesalers and investors seek out these off-market properties to acquire them at a discounted price. Back then, door-knocking was one of the primary methods for sourcing off-market real estate deals. It still works today, but it's a bit primitive when compared to all of the technological ways to find leads, such as mailers, online advertisements, cold-calling, and everything in between. They all serve the same goal, which is to find an off-market deal.

Door-knocking in wholesale real estate is a unique form of sales that requires not only the tenacity and resilience of traditional sales but also a heightened sense of empathy. When engaging with homeowners, wholesalers are essentially asking to purchase their home, which can be a sensitive and emotional topic. To initiate a conversation, wholesalers often look for signs of distress on the property, such as overgrown lawns, abandoned vehicles, blue tarps on the roof, or broken windows. These suggest that the property may be abandoned, unwanted, or simply burdensome for the current owner, making that owner more likely to consider selling.

When Will took that job, I saw a clear path to get more sales training in less time, while making some real money. Better still, I might actually learn how to invest in real estate. Knocking on doors will train you how to handle rejection, how to deal with failure, how to close customers, and it gives you nerves of steel. It's a hands-on strategy that can literally work in any area, as long as those knocking have the courage and mindset to stick with it. I've never been one to back down from a challenge, so I was excited to give it a try.

I believe I had the right intentions and the right goals, but it just didn't work out for me. (In other words, I was a complete failure.) I would knock doors for four to five hours a day after my university classes and before my bartender job, but the closest thing I had to success was a door opening for a brief moment then slamming shut. I did this for twelve long months, spent thousands of dollars on a new laptop, thousands more on gas and car maintenance, and earned a measly $1,200 bucks on a single deal. If you're keeping score at home, I was financially in the red, but I was mentally hooked by the idea of becoming a real estate investor.

Around this time, I was coming up on graduation, and I had offers from medical device companies that were going to pay me about one hundred times what I made as a wholesaler. I was really questioning if real estate was for me. I talked it over with my girlfriend at the time, Clair (who is now my wife). She saw that I was discouraged, but she also saw that I had a genuine passion for real estate and encouraged me to stick it out for another six months. I read everything on real estate training I could find, quit my night job as bartender, and forced myself into a sink-or-swim situation. I cut the safety net, turned it up a notch, and somehow, someway, something did truly change. It was like the lights turned on. I went from doing one deal per year to closing about ten deals per month!

My passion to be an entrepreneur was growing despite the initial setbacks and learning curve. I knew I was on the right path and that wholesaling could teach me the basics of real estate investing: how to find a good deal, how to evaluate the property, and how to network with other real estate investors and lenders and find resources for when I wanted to make my first purchase. That said, while you learn the fundamentals as a wholesaler, you don't necessarily learn the skills and tool kits to actually flip a house, run a team, or close deals with more complex methods—all of which we'll discuss later in this book. Sourcing a deal and renovating a home are two very different skill sets.

For starters, wholesaling is generally more about quick cash with low risk, because you're passing a deal to someone who has a team, knows how to run their numbers, and is taking less of a risk purely because of their experience and their crew. As a wholesaler, in basic terms, you find the deal, pass along the deal, and profit from the deal.

But, as good as that sounds on paper, you're not *maximizing* the deal. In order to scale, and if scaling is in your future, you have to understand how to maximize your deals. Flipping gave me the capital to scale and grow to where I am today. As a real estate investor with nearly two decades of experience and involvement in over 3,500 transactions, I have navigated the ups and downs of the fix-and-flip industry. My journey began in 2005 as a wholesaler, and since then, I have grown my business to encompass eight different real estate investing ventures, generating over $50 million in annual revenue and achieving a passive income of nearly $1 million per year.

Flipping properties, also known as "house flipping," is one of the most effective ways to generate capital and achieve financial freedom in real estate investing. House flipping involves purchasing a property, renovating it, and then selling it for a profit. Whether you're just starting out or you're an experienced flipper looking to scale your business, this book is designed to help you navigate the complex world of real estate investing and maximize your returns on every deal.

Real estate investing has long been recognized as a powerful vehicle for building wealth and achieving financial security. One of the primary benefits of real estate investing is its potential to generate passive income. By acquiring rental properties (as one example), investors can enjoy a consistent stream of revenue without the need for active involvement in day-to-day operations. This supplemental income can be used to pay down debts, save for retirement, or reinvest in additional properties, further accelerating wealth.

As investors expand their portfolios and optimize their rental income, they may even reach a point where their real estate investments can replace their traditional full-time income. In addition to providing supplemental income, real estate investing can also serve as a powerful tool for early retirement. By strategically acquiring properties and managing them effectively, investors can create a self-sustaining portfolio that generates enough income to cover their living expenses. This financial independence allows investors to step away from traditional employment and enjoy a more flexible lifestyle.

Perhaps most importantly, real estate investing has the potential to create generational wealth. By building a substantial portfolio of appreciating assets—thanks to proper scaling techniques—investors can establish a financial legacy that benefits their children and their children's children. This wealth can provide educational opportunities, support entrepreneurial ventures, and ensure a level of financial security that spans generations. Plus, by teaching their heirs the principles of real estate investing and responsible asset management, investors can empower future generations to continue growing and preserving the family's wealth. Real estate investing, when approached with due diligence and a long-term perspective, is one of the most effective ways to turn this dream into a reality.

But this doesn't mean there aren't inherent risks in the business. When you're trying to make anywhere from 30 to 100 percent return on investment (ROI) as a flipper, risk is obviously involved. It's within the risk that lies the reward. But the goal is to walk the tightrope of reducing risk while also maximizing each individual deal. This not only creates short-term revenue but also long-term success.

Throughout my career, I have gained invaluable insights into finding deals, securing financing, managing renovations, and scaling a profitable business. I have also developed a deep understanding of various financing options, including hard-money, soft-money, and private-money lending, as well as the art of building and managing a reliable construction team. My success is not solely measured by financial gains but also by the positive impact I have had on the communities in which I invest.

By transforming distressed properties into desirable homes, I have been able to contribute to the revitalization of neighborhoods and the creation of affordable housing options. In sharing my knowledge through this book, I aim to empower aspiring and experienced investors alike with the tools, strategies, and mindset needed to succeed in the dynamic world of fix-and-flip investing. By providing actionable advice, real-world case studies, and a step-by-step road map for success, I hope to inspire and guide others toward achieving their goals and building lasting wealth through the power of real estate. Flipping built that foundation for me. With this book, I want you to learn what flipping can do for you.

No matter where you are in your real estate journey, you don't know what you don't know. It's important to set realistic expectations. Can you make a ton of money flipping houses? Yes, but you can also lose a ton of money, and it could take longer than you expect.

So how do you set realistic expectations? Invest time in learning about real estate investing through books, courses, and webinars. You can find a number of resources from BiggerPockets at www.BiggerPockets.com/BookResourceHub. Understand the various investment strategies, market trends, and responsibilities of being a property owner. This knowledge will help you make informed decisions and avoid unrealistic assumptions about the industry.

Real estate investing is not a get rich quick scheme. It requires significant time and effort to research markets, find profitable deals, manage renovations, and handle tenant issues. Be prepared to dedicate substantial time to your investments, especially in the early stages, and don't expect immediate passive income. Begin with smaller, more manageable projects, such as single-family homes or small multifamily properties. This allows you to gain hands-on experience, build confidence, and refine your skills before taking on larger, more complex investments. Starting small also helps to minimize financial risk as you learn the ropes.

Investing also comes with its share of challenges, such as unexpected repairs, vacancies, or difficult tenants. Anticipate these potential obstacles and build contingencies into your plans. Maintain a financial buffer to cover unexpected expenses, and be prepared to adapt your strategies as needed. While real estate can be highly profitable, it's essential to set achievable financial goals based on your available capital, market conditions, and investment strategy. Don't base your expectations on exceptional case studies or unrealistic promises of overnight success. Instead, focus on steady, incremental growth, and celebrate small victories along the way.

Connect with experienced real estate investors through local meetups, online forums, or mentorship programs. Learn from their successes and failures. Seek advice when facing challenges. Understanding the real-world experiences of others can help you maintain a realistic perspective on the industry and avoid common pitfalls.

Real estate investing is a marathon, not a sprint. Understand that building a successful portfolio takes time, patience, and perseverance. Focus on making strategic, informed decisions that align with your long-term goals rather than chasing quick profits or trending investment fads.

As you gain experience and navigate changes in the market, be prepared to reassess your expectations and adjust your strategies accordingly. Regularly review your portfolio's performance, seek feedback from trusted advisors, and be open to adapting your approach as needed to maintain realistic expectations and achieve your goals. By following these strategies, new real estate investors can set realistic expectations that align with their skills, resources, and market conditions. This grounded approach will help them navigate the challenges of the industry, make informed decisions, and build a sustainable, profitable real estate investing career over time.

Taking on too much at once can have detrimental effects. This includes handling multiple renovation projects simultaneously, investing beyond your financial means, or setting overly ambitious timelines without considering potential obstacles. (It's all about being realistic and using data to predict outcomes.) Such actions can result in financial strain, compromised quality, project delays, and damage to one's reputation. It's crucial for entrepreneurs, especially those in real estate, to accurately assess their resources, capabilities, and limitations before embarking on new ventures. Setting realistic goals, managing risks effectively, and prioritizing tasks are essential strategies to avoid overcommitment while pursuing sustainable growth.

In real estate and many entrepreneurial ventures, a lot of failure comes when you bite off more than you can chew, meaning you take on more responsibility, work, or commitments than you can effectively manage or handle. This often entails overestimating one's capabilities or underestimating the complexity or scale of a task or project. When this happens, you may find yourself overwhelmed, stressed, or unable to fulfill your obligations adequately.

WHAT TO EXPECT FROM THIS BOOK

This book is your framework to learn everything you need to get started flipping houses, without making many of the mistakes I made earlier in my career. As such, here's the framework for the pages to follow. This is simply a quick overview, but all of these sections will be established later in the book, so you can feel confident in your flipping business.

Part 1: Let's get started flipping! These first two chapters will lay the foundation for your knowledge and understanding of the factors to consider before you decide flipping houses as your real estate strategy of choice. You'll learn how to conduct a thorough analysis of your income, expenses, assets, and liabilities, enabling you to determine the amount of disposable income you have available for investment purposes. Wondering how to set realistic goals that align with your financial circumstances? You'll discover how establishing clear financial objectives will serve as a guiding light in your decision-making process and help you determine the appropriate level of risk to undertake. Next, you'll use those goals to create your buy box, which will serve as your criteria when searching for and purchasing deals.

Part 2: Next, you'll need to know where to find and how to fund your flipping deals. These chapters will cover the full gamut of how to find deals, from building your deal-finding team to finding deals and analyzing them with your flipping criteria in mind. I will lay the foundation for flipping costs and how you can build a budget in these early stages to set yourself up for success after closing. Calculating expected returns on your first house flip can be a daunting task, but these chapters will teach you a practical approach to tackle this challenge by working backward from your desired income to determine the necessary returns. You'll also learn about the concept of annualized return, which will enable you to compare the profitability of investments with varying holding periods on a consistent, annual basis.

You will learn valuable underwriting considerations to help you understand what costs you will need covered by a lender or equity partner. Next, you'll learn how to make offers on flipping properties, using various negotiation strategies. Finally, you'll learn how to fund your flipping deals through various lending options, or through equity partnerships.

Part 3: You've purchased a flipping property; now what? Building a strong construction team is the key to success, and in these chapters, you'll learn why having local expertise on your team can save you significant time and money and how to build a bench of professionals who will help you tackle any project with ease.

If you're new to house flipping, you'll learn why hiring general contractors for your first few projects can be a game changer. Not only will you gain valuable insights into their systems and processes, but you'll also learn how to break down construction costs into different categories, giving you a better understanding of your direct costs for future projects. Plus, you'll discover how working with general contractors can help you flip houses while still maintaining your nine-to-five and working toward your financial freedom goals.

You'll also learn how to build a trade bench with direct relationships with subcontractors, including demo crews, electricians, plumbers, roofers, framers, HVAC specialists, and more. By having multiple options for each trade, you'll be able to control costs and avoid overpricing when a contractor is fully booked. And don't forget about the finish contractors —from drywallers and millwork teams to painters and cabinet installers, you'll discover how to build a team that can complete any project with precision and skill.

Last, I will discuss design considerations as you add those finishing touches to your flip. You'll learn how to properly stage and list your flip for a successful sale. Get ready to take your real estate flipping business to new heights with the knowledge and strategies you'll gain in this section.

Part 4: Let's scale. Curious about how to manage your team more efficiently as you scale your fix-and-flip business? We'll delve into the advantages of implementing robust reporting systems, including weekly budget updates, monthly P&L statements, regular CMAs, photo documentation, and detailed project manager reports. You'll discover how these reports can keep you informed without requiring constant site visits and highlight potential issues that may need your direct attention. We'll also explore essential reports such as year-to-date profit and loss (P&L) for closed properties and works in progress, real-time budget sheets, detailed project schedules, and cost spent to date versus completed work ratio.

Eager to learn how to expand your operation without proportionally increasing your time investment or financial risk? We'll discuss the importance of maintaining rigorous reporting and how this approach allows you to leverage the expertise of your contractors while maintaining control through data-driven management. By the end of this section, you'll have a better understanding of how to take on more projects and grow your business more effectively, ultimately enabling you to achieve your goal of scaling your fix-and-flip business.

WHAT CAN THIS BOOK DO FOR YOU?

For new investors, this book provides a solid foundation in the fundamentals of real estate investing. You'll learn how to find good deals, evaluate properties, and network with other investors, lenders, and resources. You'll also gain an understanding of the different investment strategies available and how to choose the one that best fits your goals and risk tolerance.

For advanced flippers looking to scale their businesses, this book offers expert advice on running a team, closing complex deals, and systemizing your income streams. You'll learn how to maximize your profits on each flip while also building a sustainable business that can weather inevitable market fluctuations.

Whether you're looking to generate low-risk cash as a wholesaler, build a portfolio of rental properties, or become a full-time house flipper, this book has something for you. Inside, you'll learn how to walk the tightrope of reducing risk while maximizing rewards and building the real estate business of your dreams. With the right knowledge and strategies, you can turn your passion for real estate into a profitable and fulfilling career.

Let's get started . . .

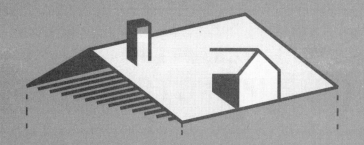

PART 1
GET
STARTED
FLIPPING

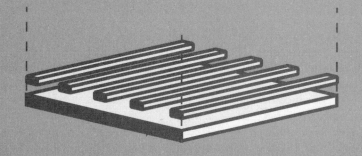

CHAPTER 1
THE FLIPPING FOUNDATION

The man on top of the mountain didn't fall there.
—**VINCE LOMBARDI, COACH, GREEN BAY PACKERS**

FLIPPING HAS BUILT the foundation of all of my real estate business, allowing me to create multiple streams of income for myself, my family, and my team. It has taken me from being broke and on the verge of quitting the business to a company that has been involved in nearly 4,000 real estate investment transactions, both on and off market. We currently have 1,000 properties in our portfolio, along with eight multifaceted real estate businesses, and we average fifty units per year and 200–250 fix-and-flip transactions annually.

Because of this flipping foundation, our other real estate businesses include:

- A real estate brokerage, Heaton Dainard Real Estate, that sells over 200 homes per year to investors.
- A wholesale business that generates over six figures annually.
- A hard-money lending business to help other investors with local financing.
- A property-management company that services our clients and our portfolio.
- A development company that builds over forty units a year.

To get started with your own flipping business, you need to have a basic understanding of the flipping world. **The foundation of these businesses lies in a fundamental principle: the art of identifying undervalued assets, enhancing their value, and subsequently generating wealth or income from them.** This principle forms the cornerstone of entrepreneurial endeavors, where the cycle of business perpetuates itself. Beginning with real estate investments, investors learn to discern opportunities where others may overlook potential value.

Through strategic rehab plans and innovative approaches, these assets are transformed, forcing a value increase and yielding profitable returns. As flippers delve deeper into the realm of real estate, they develop an awareness of the local landscape and its unique challenges. An understanding of market dynamics allows investors to identify unmet needs and gaps in services.

Whether it's creating innovative solutions to housing shortages, revitalizing neglected neighborhoods, or offering specialized services tailored to the community, the flipping journey evolves organically, driven by the desire to capitalize on untapped opportunities. The success achieved in one project often serves as a springboard for the next, which will eventually lead to expansion into new avenues of the flipping business. As you begin to accumulate wealth and expertise, you gain the confidence to pursue larger-scale projects or diversify your portfolio. This diversification not only mitigates risk but also amplifies potential rewards.

The journey of entrepreneurship embodies a continuous cycle of innovation, adaptation, and growth. It's a journey fueled by the relentless pursuit of value creation and the commitment to making a meaningful impact. As you grow in your flipping endeavors, you begin to leverage your experience and insights to find new pathways to success.

CAREER UPS AND DOWNS

On average, a typical house flip can take anywhere from a few months to a year, from acquisition to sale. This timeline includes the time needed to find and purchase the property, obtain necessary permits, complete renovations, and market the property for sale. The more extensive the renovations, the longer the flip will likely take.

In terms of personal time investment, the amount of time you'll need to dedicate to a flip will depend on your role in the project and the size of your team. If you are acting as the general contractor and managing the day-to-day operations, you can expect to invest a significant amount of time, often equivalent to a full-time job. This includes coordinating with contractors, overseeing renovations, and handling any issues that arise.

However, if you have a trusted team in place, including a reliable general contractor and experienced subcontractors, you may be able to take a more hands-off approach. In this case, your time commitment could be reduced to regular check-ins, decision-making, and project oversight, which may be more manageable as a side hustle.

While flipping can be done as a side hustle, it requires a significant amount of planning, organization, and dedication. Balancing a full-time job with the demands of a flip can be challenging, and it may limit the number of projects you can take on simultaneously. It's crucial to have a strong support system, both personally and professionally, to ensure that you can successfully manage the responsibilities of both your primary job and your flipping ventures.

For those considering flipping as a means to generate capital for long-term holds and financial freedom, it's important to approach it as a business and reinvest a portion of the profits strategically. By consistently allocating a percentage of flipping profits toward long-term rental properties, investors can build a substantial portfolio over time. This approach allows for the explosive growth potential of flipping to be harnessed and directed toward the creation of lasting wealth and financial freedom.

Ultimately, the decision to pursue house flipping as a side hustle or a full-time endeavor will depend on your personal goals, risk tolerance, and available resources. It's essential to conduct thorough market research, build a reliable team, and have a solid business plan in place before embarking on your first flip. With dedication, hard work, and strategic reinvestment of profits, flipping can indeed serve as a powerful catalyst for achieving financial freedom through real estate investing.

For myself, when I finally achieved a level of proficiency in wholesaling real estate, I discovered that I could earn between $2,500 and $10,000 per wholesale deal. This compensation was essentially a finder's fee for presenting a lucrative investment opportunity to an investor. However, I soon realized that I was leaving a substantial amount of money on the table. I would watch with frustration as the investors to whom I had sold these deals would then flip the properties and generate profits ranging from $60,000 to $100,000 on each property that I had assigned to them just months earlier.

Determined to transition from being a mere middleman to a true investor, I diligently saved every dollar I could to amass the necessary capital to take the next step. I developed a clear plan and adhered to it with unwavering discipline. My first foray into investing on my own came in the form of an off-market condominium that required a light cosmetic renovation. Although I had honed my skills as a wholesaler, I lacked hands-on experience in construction. I chose to begin with condos because they are relatively straightforward to flip, as the work is primarily focused on interior improvements. The typical scope of work for these projects included replacing carpets, repainting, upgrading appliances and countertops, and then listing the property back on the market.

By starting with condos, I was able to gain valuable experience in project management, budgeting, and overseeing construction without the added complexities of exterior work or structural renovations. This approach allowed me to build confidence in my abilities as an investor while minimizing the risk of costly mistakes. As I successfully completed more condo flips, I gradually expanded my investment portfolio to include single-family homes and larger multifamily properties, applying the lessons learned from my initial experiences to each new project.

RENOVATIONS 101

When it comes to house flipping, there are various levels of renovation projects you can take on, ranging from light rehabs to more extensive, studs-down renovations. As a new investor, it's crucial to have a clear understanding of the types of projects you and your team are capable of handling, as this will determine the kinds of deals you should pursue. Wholesalers and brokers typically won't advise you on the specific types of deals to buy unless you communicate your capabilities and preferences clearly. This is why it's essential to have a well-defined **buy box** (or a set of criteria that you use to guide your property selection) and a clear understanding of your team's skills and experience. When you're just starting out, focusing on light rehabs can be an excellent way to gain experience and minimize risk.

Light rehabs often involve cosmetic updates, such as painting, replacing flooring, updating appliances, and installing new countertops. These projects are typically less complex and require fewer specialized skills, making them more manageable for new investors. Condos can be particularly attractive for light rehabs, as they often involve working within the existing walls and don't require extensive structural changes. Additionally, condo associations typically handle exterior maintenance and repairs, such as roof work, further simplifying the renovation process for investors. As you gain experience and build a reliable team of contractors, you can gradually progress to more extensive renovations.

A mid-level flip might involve updating the layout of a property, such as removing non-load-bearing walls to create an open floor plan or adding a bathroom or bedroom. These projects require a higher level of skill and coordination, as they often involve electrical, plumbing, and structural work. At the highest level of renovation, you have studs-down rehabs. These projects involve stripping the property down to its bare bones—often removing all interior walls—and essentially rebuilding the home from the ground up. Studs-down renovations require a significant amount of capital, time, and expertise, as they involve a wide range of specialized trades, such as framing, HVAC, electrical, plumbing, and more.

Taking on a studs-down rehab is not a decision to be made lightly, as these projects come with substantial risks and challenges. However, they also offer the potential for significant rewards, as a completely renovated home can command a much higher sales price than a lightly updated property. Progressing from light rehabs to studs-down renovations is a journey that takes time and experience. As a new investor, it's essential to start with projects that align with your team's current skills and resources and gradually take on more complex projects as you build your knowledge and network.

Starting modestly with condo flips allows you to develop relationships with a core group of contractors, including painters, carpet installers, appliance specialists, countertop fabricators, and others. By starting with these manageable projects, you will be able to gain valuable experience and build a strong foundation for future growth. As your business evolves and your team's capabilities expand, you can begin to take on more extensive projects, such as single-family homes or even multiunit properties. However, it's crucial to approach this growth strategically, ensuring that you have the necessary skills, resources, and support in place before taking on more complex renovations.

While simultaneously flipping condos and wholesaling, I accumulated quite a bit of cash. I went from having less than $5,000 to my name, as a broke college grad, to $500,000 in my bank account in just a few years. This is when I decided I was ready to go to the next level. It was time to expand my buy box and start maximizing larger deals (or so I thought). I found a great buy at $250,000, where the new after-repair value (ARV) was going to be closer to $499,950! But, as many investors will warn you, I bought a property I had no business buying.

On paper, it was honestly a great buy.

I basically found a house worth $500,000 dollars that I could buy for $250,000 dollars. From my perspective—someone who had really only done simple condo flips at the time—I thought I could get it ready for market with just an additional $100,000 in renovation repairs. I soon found out that you can buy the best deal in the world, but it's only a good deal if you know how to execute it.

There were three main mistakes I made.

- **Lack of knowledge:** I created a budget based on what other people thought it would cost (rather than doing my own research to determine a more accurate cost)
- **Lack of systems:** I had no management system (I guesstimated with my general contractor friend that it would take five months, but it took fourteen!)
- **Lack of resources:** I reached out to a friend of mine (instead of a general contractor) who could work on the renovation for time and materials. (With the extra time, we easily took a $100,000 budget to a $200,000 budget.)

The result? I spent too much, took too long, and, to top it off, ran into a brick wall when the 2008 market crashed. The home's value went into a free fall, and I chased it all the way down to a sales price of $280,000. It was terrible. I went from having more money than I had ever seen to, once again, being flat broke, starting over again. This too-good-to-be-true deal completely wiped me out.

If I had had the right steps and processes to get through the deal in a timely manner, much of this headache could have been avoided. It's a lesson I had to learn the hard way, so I can pass it along to readers like you to learn the easy way (or at least the less hard). The lessons in this book will provide fundamental steps and real examples, so you don't have to make the same mistakes I made in the beginning of my career. This book will show you how to set up the right practices and procedures to help reduce inefficiencies to avoid nightmare scenarios. The right system doesn't guarantee zero risk, but it will reduce your risk and make sure you get through projects in the most profitable way possible.

CHASING FINANCIAL FREEDOM

Real estate can be a powerful wealth-building tool, but it is rarely a quick or easy path to replacing a full-time income. Successful investors often build their portfolios gradually, reinvesting profits and leveraging experience to acquire additional properties over time. Before investing in real estate, investors should prioritize building a strong financial foundation, including a stable income, healthy emergency fund, and understanding of the risks and responsibilities of owning properties. Seeking education and guidance from experienced professionals can also help navigate the challenges and opportunities of real estate investing.

The concept of achieving financial freedom through owning rental properties has gained popularity, but the reality is often more complex than it seems. While purchasing a rental property can provide passive income, the amount generated may not be sufficient to replace a full-time salary, especially when considering potential risks and expenses. Investors typically run financial projections to determine the expected cash flow and return on investment. Even if they achieve their target rental rate and occupancy, they may only generate a modest monthly income of around $250 or less per unit.

That said, flipping can scale your purchasing power, and the more capital you have, the quicker you can reach financial freedom. My team has been able to reinvest 20–30 percent of our profits into long-term holds over the past two decades. From doing so, we went from eight properties to over 1,000 and from a $600,000 portfolio to a $45 million portfolio. In essence, flipping is the catalyst for explosive growth. It arms you with the firepower to obliterate financial barriers and propel you toward unimaginable success.

When considering house flipping as a means to achieve financial freedom, evaluate the time commitment required and determine whether it can be done as a side hustle. The duration of a house flip can vary greatly, depending on factors such as the property's condition, the extent of renovations needed, and the efficiency of your team.

LIQUIDITY AND LEVERAGE

As investors, liquidity is the biggest key for real growth. In the context of real estate, liquidity refers to how quickly and easily an asset, such as a property or real estate investment, can be converted into cash without significantly affecting its market price. A highly liquid asset can be sold rapidly with minimal impact on its value, while an illiquid asset may take longer to sell and may need to be discounted to attract buyers. Several factors influence real estate liquidity, including market conditions, property type, location, price point, and financing availability. In a strong real estate market with high demand, properties tend to be more liquid, as there are more potential buyers, and transactions occur more frequently.

Some property types, such as single-family homes or condominiums, are generally more liquid than others, like specialized commercial properties or land, due to higher demand and broader buyer pools. Properties in desirable locations, such as urban centers or areas with strong economic growth, tend to be more liquid than those in less-sought-after areas. Properties priced at or below the market average are usually more liquid than high-end or luxury properties, as there is a larger pool of potential buyers. The availability of financing options, such as mortgages, can also impact liquidity.

When financing is readily available, more buyers can enter the market, increasing liquidity. Real estate investors must consider liquidity when making investment decisions, as it can affect their ability to sell the property quickly if needed or access capital for other investments. Investors seeking greater liquidity may opt for real estate investment trusts (REITs) or other more liquid real estate investment vehicles rather than directly owning physical properties. Understanding liquidity is crucial for investors to make informed decisions and manage their portfolios effectively.

In the context of real estate investing, **leverage** refers to the use of borrowed capital, such as loans or mortgages, to finance the purchase of a property. Leverage is a powerful tool that allows investors to control a larger asset base with a smaller amount of personal capital. So why is leverage so important? It allows you to maximize liquidity. Leverage allows you to reduce your deployment of cash that you have to invest. It also allows you to keep more cash on hand, which is your gunpowder to get into more deals and therefore scale faster. Here's how leverage can help maximize liquidity and returns.

- **Maximizing liquidity:** Leverage allows investors to reduce the amount of cash they need to deploy for each investment property. By using borrowed funds, investors can keep more of their own cash on hand, which can be used for additional investments or to cover unexpected expenses. This increased liquidity enables investors to be more nimble and take advantage of new opportunities as they arise.

- **Scaling faster:** When an investor can only purchase one property at a time using their own cash, their growth potential is limited. However, by utilizing leverage, investors can acquire multiple properties simultaneously, as they are not restricted by the amount of personal capital they have available. This ability to scale more quickly can lead to a more robust and diversified real estate portfolio.

- **Maximizing returns:** Leverage can significantly enhance an investor's returns on a property. For example, in the Seattle market, the average **cash-on-cash return** (CoC), which measures the annual return on the actual cash invested, is around 15 percent. However, when an investor utilizes leverage, their CoC returns can increase to 35–40 percent. This is because the investor is earning returns on the entire value of the property, not just the portion they paid for with their own cash.

When an investor has access to leverage, they can use borrowed funds to finance a larger portion of each property purchase. This means they can spread their available cash across multiple deals rather than tying it all up in a single property. For example, if an investor has $100,000 to invest and they use it to purchase a single flip property without leverage, they may stand to make a $50,000 profit upon selling the renovated property. This represents a 50 percent cash-on-cash return, which is the return on the actual cash invested.

However, if the same investor can access leverage and borrow a portion of the purchase price, they can potentially acquire two flip properties with that same $100,000. Let's say they put $50,000 down on each property and borrow the rest. If each property generates a $50,000 profit, the investor stands to make a total of $100,000 on their initial $100,000 investment. This doubles their cash-on-cash return to 100 percent, as they've effectively leveraged their available funds to generate greater profits.

The **"velocity" of money** refers to how quickly an investor can reinvest their profits into new deals. By using leverage to get into more deals simultaneously, investors can accelerate this velocity and grow their portfolios more rapidly. As they complete each flip and realize profits, they can reinvest those funds and any additional borrowed capital into new opportunities, creating a snowball effect of growth. For new flippers, it's essential to understand that while leverage can amplify returns, it also magnifies risk. If a flip project goes over budget, takes longer than expected, or sells for less than anticipated, the investor may struggle to repay their borrowed funds. New flippers need to thoroughly analyze each deal, maintain conservative budgets, and have contingency plans in place.

Leverage will grow you twice as fast—if not three times as fast—when used correctly. And if you save your money, it can compound and you can explode the returns. At the end of the day, leverage in debt is your foundation for scaling.

Leverage is the foundation for everything, but you must use it correctly. One of the biggest pitfalls investors can encounter is **overleveraging**, which means borrowing too much money relative to the value of the property or one's ability to repay the loans. When investors overleverage, they put themselves at risk of "bleeding out money" if the market shifts, rental income decreases, or unexpected expenses arise.

To use leverage effectively, investors should thoroughly analyze each deal and ensure that the property can generate sufficient cash flow to cover all expenses, including debt service. They should maintain a healthy debt-to-equity ratio, meaning the amount borrowed should be proportional to the investor's own capital contribution and the property's value.

Securing financing with favorable terms, such as lower interest rates, longer repayment periods, and non-recourse loans (where the lender can only seize the collateral property in case of default, not the investor's personal assets) is also crucial. Additionally, investors should have exit strategies in place, such as the ability to refinance or sell the property, in case market conditions change or the investment doesn't perform as expected. By using leverage judiciously and building a strong foundation based on sound principles, investors can maximize their returns while minimizing their risk.

THE RISKS OF FLIPPING HOUSES

I would be remiss if I didn't include some words of caution to consider as you begin your flipping journey. While I will be digging into how to avoid these risks later on in the book, I want you to have an idea up front of what problems may come up during a flip.

A major risk in flipping houses is that you're subject to market conditions. You can lose money quickly if you purchase a property and then the market takes a downturn. The expected return you considered at the start of the project may not happen if the prices drop suddenly. When the market comes down, it can do so in a short amount of time, and you might be in the middle of a flip when this happens.

We had some properties we flipped and sold in 2023 that if we had been able to sell them just one year earlier could have made hundreds of thousands more per property because the market was so high at the time. That's how fast it came down.

Another risk to consider when flipping property is the season in which you will sell the property. If you can target a spring season, you'll make more money on the deal (this is actually something we discuss on the BiggerPockets *On the Market Podcast*, so stay tuned into the podcast for up-to-date analysis on market conditions at www.BiggerPockets.com/BookOTM).

Finally, there are other risk factors to consider when flipping houses. There is inherent risk when hiring a general contractor to execute your property flip. If they make a mistake or their business fails, that's obviously going to impact you. (I'll discuss how to effectively manage your renovation in Chapter 12 to help minimize this risk.) You'll also need to consider the jurisdiction in which you are flipping. Different cities operate in different ways, and there are certain nuances you'll need to learn about the location you are flipping houses in. Additionally, you will likely come into contact with certain stigmas around house flipping. Not every local loves a flipper, and some really want to keep their neighborhood as-is. A flipped house could affect a neighbor's resale value or property taxes, so it's possible you'll run into some negative local feedback.

HOW TO LOSE MONEY FLIPPING

As a novice investor, there are many potential pitfalls that can lead to losing money in house flipping. By learning from the mistakes of others, you can make informed decisions and increase your chances of success. One of the most common mistakes is **overleveraging**, which means borrowing too much money relative to the value of the deal. When you're undercapitalized, you may feel pressured to make hasty decisions, leading to costly errors. To avoid this, it's essential to carefully analyze your numbers and stick to your budget, even if it means passing on a deal that doesn't meet your criteria.

Another pitfall to avoid is automatically choosing the cheapest house available. While it may seem like a bargain, there's often a reason why a property is priced significantly lower than others in the area. Before making an offer, thoroughly inspect the property and consider factors such as location, condition, and potential resale value. The goal is to find a property that offers the best potential for profit, not just the lowest price tag.

When purchasing a property from a wholesaler or another investor, it's crucial to verify all the information provided. Don't simply take their word for it when it comes to budgets, timelines, and potential profits. As the investor, it's your responsibility to conduct your own due diligence and run your own numbers. Wholesalers, especially those with limited experience in flipping, may not have accurate information or may not account for all the costs involved. By taking the time to verify the details, you can make an informed decision and avoid unexpected expenses down the line.

Finally, it's essential to structure your deals correctly to maximize your potential for profit. This may involve negotiating with the seller to find a mutually beneficial arrangement. For example, if a seller is asking for a price that would make it difficult to profit using traditional financing, consider proposing alternative terms. This could include a longer closing timeline or a different financing structure that allows you to offset the higher purchase price. By being creative and flexible in your negotiations, you may be able to secure a deal that works for both parties and sets you up for success.

One of the most common ways I have lost money or seen investors get into trouble on flip projects is because of the contractor hired. When flipping homes, flippers are dependent on third parties to help facilitate the plan. Investors hire permit teams, contractors, designers, and suppliers. If any of these resources fails to complete their job, it can be detrimental to the profitability of the deal. On every flip project I do, any contractor and subcontractor must sign a construction contract. This does not mean a contractor bid supplied by the contractor but rather my own internal document that gives a clear understanding of how the project will go. The purpose of a construction contract is to have all timelines, responsibilities, and costs clearly defined for each trade. Payments, change order processes, and how communication will happen are all clearly defined. It additionally gives me the power to charge late fees for work delays and protects me from having to pay for poor workmanship.

The same is true for not controlling your jobsite. Often, I'll talk to new investors and they'll tell me about overages, issues, or problems, but they haven't been to the property in weeks or months. If you're not at least occasionally visiting the site or speaking directly with someone you trust to run the site, this is going to lead to problems. If your contractor is running a sloppy jobsite, this is a problem that will eventually catch up with you. It could bring in neighbors, inspectors, and cause delays. On every jobsite, we have a key box, so contractors can access the property as needed. All permits, floor plans, designs, and the scope of work are posted to the jobsite. The answers to most installation questions are posted and available to access at any time. If the contractor installs something wrong, the clear plans are on-site, and they will need to correct it on their dime.

In the real estate investing industry, two common pitfalls that can hinder the success of a project are investors who become nervous Nellies and those who "fall in love" with a property. Both of these mindsets can lead to costly mistakes and ultimately undermine the profitability of a flip.

A nervous Nellie is an investor who becomes overly anxious or indecisive when faced with challenges or decisions throughout the project. This type of investor may struggle to make timely, confident choices, often second-guessing themselves or hesitating to take action. The problem with this approach is that indecisiveness can lead to significant delays, which translates directly to lost profits. In the world of real estate investing, time is money, and every day that a project is held up due to indecision is a day that carries additional holding costs and lost potential revenue.

An investor's indecisiveness can have a ripple effect on the entire project team. When an investor frequently changes their mind or fails to provide clear direction, it can create confusion and frustration among contractors, suppliers, and other stakeholders. This confusion can result in further delays, miscommunications, and potentially even subpar work, all of which can eat into the project's bottom line.

On the other end of the spectrum are investors who "fall in love" with a property. These individuals become emotionally attached to a project, losing sight of the primary goal of a flip: to generate a profit. When an investor becomes too personally invested in a property, they may make decisions based on their emotional connection rather than sound financial judgment. This can manifest in over-improving the property, spending too much on high-end finishes or unnecessary upgrades, or holding onto the property for too long in hopes of achieving an unrealistic sales price. The key to success in real estate investing is to approach each project with a business mindset. Once you have thoroughly evaluated a property and decided to move forward, stick to that decision and execute your plan efficiently. This means setting clear goals, establishing realistic budgets and timelines, and making swift, informed decisions when challenges arise.

Ultimately, a successful flip is one that is completed on time, within budget, and sold quickly for a healthy profit. By avoiding the pitfalls of becoming a nervous Nellie or falling in love with a property, investors can maintain a focused, disciplined approach to their projects. In the world of real estate investing, properties are assets to be acquired, improved, and sold for a profit—not lifelong love affairs. By keeping this perspective in mind and making decisions based on sound financial principles, investors can maximize their chances of success and build a thriving, profitable business in the exciting world of house flipping.

CHAPTER 2
ASSESSING YOUR FINANCIAL SITUATION AND BUILDING YOUR BUY BOX

To the young: work, work, work,
and then work some more.
—ED REED, SAFETY, BALTIMORE RAVENS

WHEN CONSIDERING INVESTING in house flipping or any other venture, you need to have a clear understanding of your current financial situation. This involves taking a comprehensive look at your income, expenses, assets, and liabilities to create a detailed financial picture. Start by examining your income from all sources, including your primary job, any side hustles, and investment returns. Next, list out all your expenses, including housing, food, transportation, health care, insurance, entertainment, and any debt. Don't forget to account for irregular expenses, such as annual insurance premiums or vacation costs.

Once you have a clear picture of your income and expenses, you can determine how much disposable income you have available to invest in house flipping. It's also essential to consider your assets and liabilities when assessing your financial situation. Your assets include any savings, investments, or property you own, while your liabilities encompass all your debts, such as student loans, credit card balances, or mortgages. This will help you make informed decisions about the level of risk you can comfortably take on and the types of projects that align with your financial goals. Understanding your net worth (assets minus liabilities) can give you a clearer idea of your overall financial health and the resources you have available to invest.

With a comprehensive understanding of your financial situation, you can set realistic goals for your house-flipping venture. These goals should be specific, measurable, and aligned with your broader financial objectives. For example, your goal might be to supplement your full-time income, retire early, or achieve financial freedom, which often means having enough passive income or investment returns to cover your living expenses without relying on a traditional job. To set effective goals, be clear about what you're trying to accomplish and why.

For instance, if you're aiming to leave your W-2 job and help your spouse retire, you'll need to determine the specific income required to make this transition. Consider factors such as the cost of self-employed health insurance compared to your current W-2 insurance, as well as any anticipated life changes that may impact your expenses, such as having children or relocating. By crunching the numbers and setting clear financial targets, you can create a road map for your house-flipping journey that aligns with your personal and financial goals. This might involve starting with smaller, lower-risk projects and gradually scaling up as you build experience and capital, or partnering with other investors to take on larger projects with potentially higher returns.

Knowing your starting point and understanding your net worth can help you determine how much you need to invest and what returns you need to generate to reach that goal. House flipping, when done successfully, can be a powerful tool for building wealth and achieving financial freedom, but it requires careful planning, budgeting, and risk management based on your unique financial situation.

SET HEALTHY GOALS

Setting clear financial goals is an essential component of a successful real estate investing strategy. Before embarking on your journey to financial freedom through property flipping, take a step back and assess your personal objectives. What does financial freedom look like for you? How many properties do you need to flip each year to achieve your desired level of income and wealth? What returns are necessary to reach your goals, and are these numbers realistic in your target market?

Additionally, consider any potential limitations or obstacles that could hinder your progress, such as market conditions, competition, or resource constraints. Finally, evaluate whether you have the right team in place to support your efforts and ensure that you can effectively execute your strategy.

One effective approach to goal setting is to begin with your long-term objectives and then reverse engineer your plan to determine the steps needed to get there. This method allows you to create a clear road map to financial freedom, built on the foundation of high returns and healthy profit margins. In the world of real estate investing, flipping properties has emerged as a popular means to rapidly grow capital, thanks to the potential for significant returns in a relatively short time frame. By knowing exactly what you're looking for in a property, you can make informed decisions, execute your strategy more efficiently, and ultimately maximize your returns.

When I first started flipping homes, my goal was to create additional income to complement my wholesaling business. My goal was to make an additional six figures a year, so I could spend less time working with clients and more time working for myself. I wanted to flip two or three properties a year at an average of $50,000 in profit per house. Today, my goal is to create over $1 million in profit annually and to reinvest 20 percent of the profit into rental properties so that I can live a passive lifestyle.

HOW TO CREATE YOUR BUY BOX

In order to get started in real estate, you have to establish your buy box. A **buy box** is a set of criteria that real estate investors use to guide their property selection process. It outlines the specific characteristics of the properties they are willing to purchase, based on their investment goals, risk tolerance, and available resources. Defining a clear and focused buy box is crucial for success in real estate investing, as it helps investors make swift, informed decisions and avoid wasting time on properties that don't align with their strategy.

A carefully crafted buy box serves as a powerful tool for guiding your investment decisions and ensuring that you don't overlook promising opportunities. The goal is to create an efficient filtering system that allows you to focus on the most relevant opportunities without being overwhelmed by the sheer volume of available properties in your market.

Your buy box should encompass a range of factors, including:

- **Price range:** What price range are you comfortable with for your buy box?
- **Budget:** What's your realistic budget for the deal?

- **Asset type:** What type of properties do you want to flip? Single-family? Condos? Mobile homes? Multifamily?
- **Location:** Where do you want to focus your deals?
- **Scope of work:** What level of renovation are you willing to take on? Remember, these include light rehabs to more extensive, studs-down renovations
- **Expected returns:** What returns are you aiming to make on the deal? (I will cover how to calculate your expected returns in Chapter 5.) I adjust the expected return based on market trends and forecasting.
- **Skill set/resources:** What is your current skill level in flipping properties? Are you a solo flipper? Do you have a team in place that can execute these projects?
- **Deal-breakers:** What problem properties will you absolutely not buy?
- **Short- and long-term goals:** What are your goals for the short and long term?

Price range. When considering the price range for your first deals as a new investor, it's essential to focus on what you can comfortably afford. As you gain more experience and build your capital, you may naturally gravitate toward higher-priced properties. However, it's crucial not to get ahead of yourself, especially when you're just starting out.

Budget. I'll discuss the specifics of what's included in your budget in Chapter 5, but the first step in creating a narrow buy box is to allocate your funds. What is the amount of liquidity you have decided you will use to buy properties? You need to have a certain amount of money set aside to flip properties (I discussed how to do evaluate your flipping funds at the beginning of this chapter). The more capital you allocate to your flip business, the more access to leverage you will have. Most investors need to bring 10–20 percent into the project to obtain financing for the rest of the deal. The more cash you allocate for your flipping projects, the more a lender can leverage you.

The next part of this scenario is to ask yourself how long you can lock that money up in a deal. It's one thing to have some extra money for a deal, but it's something else to have it locked in a property for six months or several years. If I have $100,000 allocated for a fix-and-flip, how long can I let that money sit? When do you need this return to come back to you? In the beginning, this is basically your best guess. Either way, this will dictate what kind of product you can buy. Timelines on flip properties vary based on numerous factors, such as age of the property, location, and the building department the property is located in. When you start to think of locations, it's easy to pick an area you're most familiar with. This can be a great strategy for new flippers. However, it's important to go where the deals are. Where will you get the most bang for your buck?

Additionally, you need to ask yourself where it is that your resources are going to be most efficient. Once you complete your skill set and resources evaluation, you can better define this target location.

Asset type. You'll need to get clear on what type of property you want to invest in. You can flip anything. It could be single-family properties, condos, multifamily, land, trailers on a property—literally anything. Real estate is vast. There are asset classes to consider, such as property condition, price point, location, and investment strategy.

Then there's types of properties, such as single-family, condos, multifamily, land, mobile homes, commercial, and everything in between. A clear understanding of what you want to flip will help you narrow your focus and tell you what kinds of teams to create. Identify what you want to flip, then identify what type of properties inside that asset class, based on the following:

- **Size:** Can your construction teams do large projects or are they better at doing cosmetic turns?
- **Style:** Is there a type of home that you want to target most? Are bedroom and bathroom count important to your market? Are some properties too big or too small?
- **Age range:** The older the home, the more renovation budget it will need. When I was a newer investor, I wanted to remodel homes that were 1970s or newer because they had better mechanical systems and layouts, thus they required smaller rehab plans.

Location, location, location. In real estate flipping, locations are often categorized into A, B, C, and D classifications based on their desirability, market stability, and potential for appreciation. My return expectations are a minimal of 60 percent annualized returns for A and B locations. Then, for C and D locations, I will shift to an 80 percent annualized return. If I'm going to take on a negative-impact property, like a house on a busy road, I'm going to need to see 100 percent annualized return. These classifications help investors determine their return expectations and adjust their investment strategies accordingly.

Here's a breakdown of each location type and how it impacts my return expectations:

A locations are the most desirable and sought-after areas. They are typically characterized by high property values, strong job markets, excellent school districts, and low crime rates. These areas tend to have stable housing markets and are less susceptible to economic downturns. In A locations, I aim for a minimum annualized return of 60 percent, as these properties often have lower-risk profiles and more predictable resale values.

B locations are still considered desirable but may not have all the premium features of A locations. They generally have solid job markets, good school districts, and relatively low crime rates. Property values in B locations are typically more affordable than in A locations, but they still offer strong potential for appreciation. Like A locations, I target a minimum annualized return of 60 percent in B locations, as they offer a balance of stability and profitability.

C locations are less desirable than A and B locations and may have some challenges that impact their market appeal. These areas may have weaker job markets, lower-quality school districts, or higher crime rates. Property values in C locations are generally lower, and the housing markets may be more volatile. To compensate for the increased risk and uncertainty in C locations, I adjust my return expectations to a minimum annualized return of 80 percent. This higher return threshold helps to ensure that the potential rewards justify the added challenges of investing in these areas.

D locations are the least desirable and often present the greatest challenges for real estate investors. These areas may have high crime rates, struggling job markets, and underperforming school districts. Property values in D locations are typically the lowest, and the housing markets can be highly unpredictable. Given the significant risks associated with investing in D locations, I require a minimum annualized return of 80 percent, just like in C locations. This higher return expectation helps to mitigate the potential downsides and ensure that the investment is worthwhile.

Scope of work. What level of renovation are you willing to take on? If you are new to the flipping business, you may want to consider light condo rehabs before taking on larger projects. Light rehabs, such as cosmetic updates to condos or single-family homes, provide an excellent opportunity to learn the fundamentals of project management, budgeting, and working with contractors. These projects typically involve tasks such as painting, flooring, and minor kitchen or bathroom updates, which can be completed relatively quickly and with fewer variables to manage. Starting with these more straightforward projects enables you to build a strong foundation of skills and knowledge that will serve you well as you progress to more complex flips.

If you're past the newbie phase of flipping, you'll be able to take on larger, more involved flips. These can include projects like changing the layout of a property, removing walls, adding or expanding closet space, etc. These larger-scale projects often come with a bigger scope of work and require a higher level of expertise and management skills. Knowing this level of work will help you know what to search for when looking for deals.

Expected returns. Begin your search with the end in mind. What return do you hope to reap from your flip? Usually, the bigger the renovation project, the larger the potential profit margin. However, taking on more extensive projects also comes with increased complexity, risk, and capital requirements. If you're a new investor, it's essential to grow into these larger-scale renovations as you gain experience and confidence. The decision to take on bigger projects should be based on your experience, skills, and resources; the decision shouldn't be made on the expected return. There's no point taking on a scope of work you're not comfortable with because the potential for profit is there. If you're stressed, overworked, and unskilled to execute the work, the success of the project won't reap the financial rewards anyway.

Carefully evaluate the potential rewards of your desired scope of work and weigh them against the associated risks and challenges.

Based on my experience and market, when I do a fix-and-flip property, I target a 30–40 percent cash-on-cash return in a six-month window. Knowing that, I can run the numbers in my flip calculator and figure out the anticipated return. I don't expect a certain profit on specific properties. Instead, I want to know how much cash I have to put in the deal and what my return is—then I start to further investigate the deal.

Skill set/resources. As a new real estate investor, it's crucial to have a realistic understanding of your capabilities and limitations. Consider the resources at your disposal, such as capital, time, and expertise. Determine which neighborhoods align with your budget and investment strategy. Be honest with yourself about the types of projects you can successfully execute based on your current skills and experience.

Not all investors may have the resources or desire to take on extensive, full renovations, especially when starting out. In such cases, you're buy box might include properties that require lighter updates or cosmetic improvements. Look for listings with older or outdated photos, which could signal opportunities for smaller flips or value-add projects. Another option is to search for properties listed as "fixer-uppers" or those described as needing minor repairs or updates. These could be ideal for investors seeking projects that require less extensive work and potentially lower initial investment.

When I first started in real estate investing, I focused on smaller, more manageable projects in specific areas due to limited resources and experience. As I gained more knowledge, built a reliable network of professionals, and increased my capital, I gradually took on larger and more complex projects across a wider geographic area. Today, with well-established teams and years of experience, my company can handle a variety of major real estate projects throughout Seattle. However, this growth was the result of starting small, learning from each project, and consistently building upon my experience over time.

For example, just forty minutes down the road in Tacoma, Washington, there's a great real estate market. However, my teams are primarily based in Seattle and not well equipped to handle projects in Tacoma. The contractors, subcontractors, and other professionals I work with are familiar with the Seattle area and have established relationships with local suppliers and permitting offices. Asking them to travel to Tacoma on a regular basis would be inconvenient and could lead to logistic challenges, increased costs, and potential delays.

My expertise and efficiency in executing projects in Seattle don't necessarily translate to Tacoma. If I do decide to invest in Tacoma, which I do occasionally, I focus on properties that require relatively simple cosmetic updates rather than extensive renovations. This approach allows me to minimize the need for my Seattle-based teams to travel and helps me avoid the logistic complexities that can arise from managing major projects in a different city. By recognizing the geographical limitations of my teams and adjusting my investment strategy accordingly, I can still take advantage of opportunities in Tacoma without overextending my resources or compromising the quality of my projects.

Deal-breakers. What's *not* in your buy box is just as important as what *is*. It's important to understand what your deal-breakers are for a project and incorporate this into your buy box. Certain issues can be property red flags for you. Personally, I avoid environmental issue properties that have issues like oil spills, water tables, or polluted sites. There's simply too much red tape to deal with, which means delays. I don't buy ECAs (environmentally critical areas), such as slide zones, high water tables, or floodplains. I don't like big negative impacts or any other type of project that has unknown timelines and unknown added costs.

If you're just starting out, you may not know what your hard no's will be when it comes to your buy box. That's why it's important to revisit your buy box and make adjustments as you gain experience, knowledge, and adjust to the market conditions.

Consider the utilities. When considering a house flip, assess the availability and condition of utilities, such as water, electricity, and sewer. If a property lacks these essential utilities, it can significantly impact the budget and timeline of the flip. If there's a nice house but it's out in the woods so far that there's no on-site water or electricity, and those utilities will have to be brought in, those expenses are hard to put a number on.

This can involve running new water lines or drilling a well, installing a septic system or connecting to the municipal sewer, and running new electrical lines and upgrading the electrical panel. These costs can be substantial and are often difficult to estimate accurately. Investors may need to consult with local utility companies, contractors, and engineers to determine the feasibility and cost of bringing utilities to the property. For properties without municipal water and sewer connections, they can consult with well-drilling companies and septic system installers. Additionally, working with experienced contractors and engineers who can provide detailed estimates based on the specific property and local regulations can be invaluable.

Given the complexity and potential for hidden costs, many experienced investors choose to avoid flips that lack essential utilities. The uncertainty surrounding these costs makes it challenging to create an accurate budget and increases the overall risk of the project. If you can't create a detailed budget because of too many unknowns, it's a much riskier deal, to say the least.

Unresolved boundary disputes or anything in open litigation. Boundary disputes can arise when there is a disagreement over the exact property lines between two adjacent parcels of land. This can happen due to inaccurate surveys, fences or structures being built in the wrong location, or simple misunderstandings between neighbors over the years. When purchasing a property, make sure there are no outstanding boundary issues, as these can lead to costly legal battles down the road. I've had a lot of problems with neighbors on previous deals because the seller we bought the home from had put a fence in the wrong place or parked vehicles in an area that turned out to belong to the neighbor.

When that happens, the new neighbor then wants to resolve that boundary violation issue with me as the new owner. Inheriting these types of bad neighbor situations is incredibly frustrating. The neighbors may demand that you move the fence or structures at your own expense, or they could take legal action to try to claim part of the land you thought you owned. Handling boundary disputes requires hiring surveyors, real estate attorneys, and potentially even going to court. It creates significant headaches, costs, and drama.

This business of flipping houses is hard enough with all the renovation work, budgeting, and selling process involved. Adding boundary conflicts and legal battles with neighbors on top of that just compounds the stress and risk. That's why I refuse to purchase any properties that have preexisting, unresolved boundary disputes or open litigation related to the land. It's simply not worth the potential nightmares that could ensue. Clear property lines and good relationships with neighbors are essential for a smooth house flip.

Short- and long-term goals. Your buy box all falls back on your short- and long-term goals. What exactly are you trying to accomplish and why? Start with your long-term goals and work backward to set those short-term goals. Take some time to write out your ideal future (whether that's retire by X age, achieve financial freedom, establish generational wealth, etc.). Don't buy deals without a plan. Know why you're buying each property for your short- and long-term goals. Flipping is a business, and no good business functions without a plan in place.

So, what's in my buy box? In the beginning, my buy box was light condo rehabs, which included updating the carpet, paint, and maybe appliances. These days, my buy box is bigger than most other investors because I've learned how to deal with lots and lots of problems over time (I'm also an admitted deal junkie!). That said, what I currently look for is any size project in any condition—aside from those environmental impacts in my key areas of focus in Washington, California, and Arizona.

When considering the condition of a property for flipping, I am comfortable with both cosmetic flips and heavy fixers. Additionally, I am willing to purchase properties at any price point, thanks to the leverage and partnerships I have established, which allow me to bridge any financial gaps. However, there are two types of properties that I consistently avoid: those with unknown timelines and those that are tenant occupied.

Properties with unknown timelines can be particularly problematic for house flippers. These are situations where there may be unresolved legal issues, such as liens or ownership disputes, which can significantly delay the acquisition and renovation process. Without a clear understanding of when these issues will be resolved, it becomes incredibly challenging to create an accurate budget and timeline for the flip. The longer these delays persist, the more holding costs, such as mortgage payments and property taxes, will accumulate, eating into potential profits.

Similarly, tenant-occupied properties can present significant challenges and risks. If a tenant is residing in the property at the time of purchase and refuses to vacate, the investor may face a lengthy and costly eviction process. Depending on local laws and regulations, this process can take several months, during which time the investor is unable to begin renovations and is still responsible for holding costs. A six-month delay in taking possession of the property can easily consume all anticipated profits from the flip, making it a highly unattractive proposition.

To mitigate these risks, my personal policy is to pursue only those properties where I can obtain full possession at the time of closing. This allows me to begin the renovation process immediately, without the risk of unexpected delays or legal complications. While this approach may limit the pool of available properties to some extent, it helps to ensure that each flip has the greatest possible chance of success and profitability. By avoiding the headaches and uncertainties associated with unknown timeline and tenant-occupied properties, I can focus my efforts on those opportunities that offer the most promising returns.

Otherwise, I'll buy most anything as long as it's not falling down. The same is true for price point. That said, I also don't buy properties that need an addition. I'd honestly rather just build a property from scratch. I don't buy properties with title issues unless I've done my research and know it won't get tied up in legal issues.

Then, I make sure to buy based on my resources, not my capital. You can leverage various assets and capabilities beyond mere financial capital when making an investment decision. This approach recognizes that success in real estate investing depends on a wide range of factors, and that focusing solely on the amount of money available for investment can be limiting. What I've learned is that even when you seemingly have a good deal in place, if you don't have a team ready to go, that good deal might not actually be all that good in the end. The simple fact is you'll have added time to execute the flip, and that is going to lead to a series of extra costs, missed deadlines, and overage costs. This makes your good deal just an average deal, and the return is not worth the risk.

Having a clearly defined buy box allows you to curate your search criteria to find deals that work for you. Dave Meyer has some great resources for creating your buy box in his book *Start with Strategy: Craft Your Personal Real Estate Portfolio for Lasing Financial Freedom,* which you can find at www.BiggerPockets.com/ReadSWS. Every step in your buy box is a way to filter out deals that aren't right for you just as much as they are to find the right deals. The buy box will change as you grow as a fix-and-flipper and as you make new connections and build new resources in the industry. My buy box changes every quarter. The right buy box that is customized for you will help you secure deals, scale your team, and reach your goals of financial freedom faster.

If you know someone in the business who runs a successful flipping business, have them take a look at your buy box. This is also something we do in my online community. I encourage you to show your work, share with others, and make sure you're going in the right direction by speaking with other pros in the industry.

A narrow buy box means you can narrow your focus on the properties you can best execute on. It helps you focus on approachable and achievable projects, which will help you get more deals in the long run. It also defines your product, defines your business plan, and teaches you when to say yes or no. When you see hundreds or thousands of deals available, narrowing your buy box makes it much easier to say yes or no. Your decision becomes binary: Does it fit my buy box or not? Yes—you take action. No—you pass on the deal.

Time is a killer in this business, so if you find a good deal, you need to be able to assess and confirm that deal as quickly as possible. When you focus on what you do best, you can then better articulate what you want to buy to deal-finders, so they know what types of products to bring your way.

Take some time to reflect on the following questions:

- What are your long-term goals for the next 1, 3, 5, and 10 years?
- What capital do you currently have, and what can you borrow?
- Where will you focus your investments in terms of location and property type?
- What skills do you bring to the table, and what level of renovation are you comfortable with?
- What level of return are you aiming for, and how will you calculate it?

 **You can find examples of investor buy boxes at www.BiggerPockets.com/FrameworkBonus.**

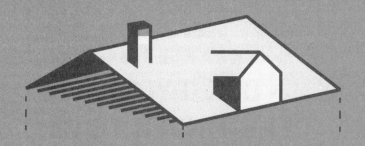

PART 2

FINDING &
FUNDING
FLIPPING
DEALS

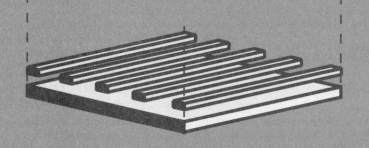

CHAPTER 3
BUILD YOUR DEAL-FINDER TEAM

There's no panic in this team...We stick together, believe in each other, believe in the plan and stay the course.
—AARON RODGERS, NEW YORK JETS

ONCE YOU'VE ESTABLISHED your buy box, what should you do with it? Whether you're a new or seasoned investor, you need to have a solid team of deal-finders to benefit your flipping business. Networking is vital for finding deal sources, which can significantly impact the success of your real estate investing business. To build a consistent pipeline of profitable deals, you need to cultivate relationships with a variety of sources, including:

- **Investment-minded brokers:** Real estate brokers can be valuable sources of deals, as they often have access to a wide range of properties and can help you identify those that align with your investment criteria.
- **Wholesalers:** These are individuals or companies that specialize in finding distressed properties and selling them to investors at a discounted price. They act as middlemen, connecting sellers with investors and facilitating the transaction.
- **Self-generated deals:** This involves proactively searching for potential deals by going directly to a seller. You'll use methods such as direct-mail campaigns, online listings, or driving for dollars (i.e., physically scouting neighborhoods for distressed properties).
- **Auctions:** Property auctions, such as foreclosure or tax lien auctions, can be excellent sources of deeply discounted properties. However, these opportunities often require careful due diligence and a solid understanding of the auction process.

- **Other investors:** Networking with other real estate investors can lead to deal-sharing opportunities and off-market transactions that may not be available through traditional channels.

By diversifying your deal sources, you can ensure a steady flow of potential investments and avoid relying on a single channel that may offer limited or mediocre options. Cast a wide net and evaluate multiple deals to find those that offer the greatest potential for returns.

HOW TO FIND BROKERS

Building relationships with the right real estate brokers can open doors to a wide range of investment opportunities, both on and off the market. Brokers not only identify properties actively listed for sale but also have access to **pocket listings**, which are off-market opportunities where a seller may prefer a quiet, discreet sale. When working with brokers, it's essential to target those who specialize in investor properties and have a deep understanding of the unique needs and goals of real estate investors. You can find an investor-friendly broker or agent through the BiggerPockets Agent Finder, www.BiggerPockets.com/BookAgent. Look for brokers who are well versed in buy and hold strategies, have experience working with investors, and possess the knowledge to structure deals that benefit all parties involved.

These brokers should be able to analyze the mathematics behind a potential investment, including factors such as cash flow, return on investment, and potential appreciation. They should also have a keen eye for identifying properties that align with your specific investment criteria and be able to provide valuable insights into local market trends and conditions. Building strong relationships with the right brokers can lead to a consistent stream of quality investment opportunities that may not be available to the public. Remember, though, that not all brokers are created equal.

When expanding your network, reach out to real estate brokers who currently list properties for other investors. They can be a valuable source of potential deals, including full renovations and smaller projects. Additionally, utilize online real estate platforms like Zillow or the MLS (if you have access) to search for listings in your local market. To find full renovation projects, start by filtering for properties in your target price range. For example, in a market like California, you might initially search for homes sold around $900,000 or higher. Then, narrow your search further by looking for listings with staged photos, which often indicate that the property has been fully renovated and is ready for resale.

One effective way to identify brokers who specialize in investment properties is to focus on estate sales or properties listed as "fixers." These brokers often have a concentration of similar listings because their marketing efforts are geared toward attracting sellers of properties that require extensive repairs or renovations. By targeting estate sales and fixer properties, you increase your chances of connecting with brokers who have the type of inventory that aligns with your investment goals. These brokers can become valuable sources of deals, as they are likely to have a pipeline of properties suitable for flipping or renovating.

When you encounter a broker who consistently lists fixer properties or handles estate sales, take the initiative to build a relationship with them. Inquire about their current and upcoming inventory, expressing your interest in potential investment opportunities. Explore ways to collaborate and structure deals that are mutually beneficial. Remember, these brokers are likely working with sellers who are motivated to off-load properties that require significant work, which could present opportunities for negotiating favorable terms or purchasing at a discount. By actively seeking out and cultivating relationships with brokers who specialize in fixer properties and estate sales, you can gain access to a steady stream of potential investment opportunities that align with your investment strategy.

Another cheat code is to look for brokers who rep LLCs on sales. These are going to be investors, rather than individuals, in most cases. For example, if you pull up my sales over the past fifteen years, you will see over 1,500 homes sold with LLCs as sellers. Our company helps investors find deals, provides contractor referrals, and assists designs, so it's possible you can find companies in your area who do the same.

Then, it's time to interview these brokers and make them earn your business. We want to be valuable to them, but we also want them to be valuable to us, right? So find out if they can enhance your business. Take the time to research and interview potential brokers, asking about their experience with investor clients, their knowledge of the local market, and their track record of successful transactions. By partnering with the right real estate brokers, you can gain a competitive edge in identifying and securing profitable investment properties that align with your long-term goals. Brokers who work with flippers need to be able to assist in underwriting future market values of potential deals. They also need to send you deals that fit your buy box, with enough information for you to make a quick decision. This saves time and therefore makes money for everyone involved.

When brokers send me deals, they send me the property, details, pictures, and a link to the comps that sold after being fixed up. I can then streamline my underwriting by reviewing pictures, creating a budget, and inputting into my pro forma (which allows me to see the true net profit of the property by calculating the hard and soft costs of the purchase, rehab, and sale of the property), so I can get them an offer price quickly. Remember, time kills all deals. The broker's assistance helps get a decision quicker, so the opportunity doesn't slip away.

And finally, interview the broker to find out what additional skills they might have. Investment brokers should have investment contacts to help your business. Whether it's contractor referrals, title rep referrals, lawyer referrals, and even lender referrals that their clients are already using, they can help you streamline your business.

Most of these brokers have been around construction, so they can often assist with design. They could help with staging and other ways that help you reduce overall costs to make more money and be worth their fee. If they bring me a deal and tell me it's worth X, then I can ask them what they think needs to happen to hit that ARV. Oftentimes, they can do this analysis for you. We often tell people something like "I see the $500,000 evaluation, but you're going to need to add another bed and bath to hit that goal." Or, in that same scenario, they tell you it's only worth $450,000 or $550,000 ARV, so have them explain how they got this result. Give them the full commission, but make them earn your business.

WHOLESALERS

One important source of deals is wholesalers, who are typically unlicensed companies or investors that have secured properties under contract and earn a fee by selling the rights to purchase those properties to other investors. To effectively work with wholesalers, it's essential to have a well-defined buy box, which outlines your specific investment criteria, such as property type, location, price range, and desired condition. By sharing your buy box with wholesalers, you can help them identify properties that align with your investment goals, increasing the likelihood of finding suitable deals.

The wholesaler's role is to secure a contract on a property at a price below market value. Once the contract is in place, the wholesaler sells the rights to purchase the property to another investor for a fee.

The total purchase price for the end investor consists of the original contract amount plus the wholesaler's fee. This arrangement allows the wholesaler to profit from their ability to identify and secure discounted properties, while the end investor benefits from access to deals that may not be available through traditional channels. However, investors need to conduct their own due diligence on the property and ensure that the numbers align with their investment strategy, even when working with wholesalers. Building strong relationships with reputable wholesalers can provide a consistent source of off-market deals and help investors grow their portfolios more efficiently.

WHOLESALER FEE VS. BROKER PERCENTAGES

Let me clarify the key differences between how wholesalers and brokers structure their fees in a real estate transaction:

BROKERS	WHOLESALERS
• Brokers typically charge a commission fee, which is a percentage of the sale price of the property. • The standard commission fee ranges from 3 to 6 percent, depending on the market and the specific agreement between the broker and their client. • In most cases, the seller is responsible for paying the commission fees to both the listing broker and the buyer's broker. • These fees are generally paid out of the proceeds of the sale at closing.	• Wholesalers earn money through assignment fees, which operate differently from broker commissions. • An assignment fee is essentially the price a wholesaler charges to sell or "assign" their rights to purchase a property under a specific contract to another buyer, typically a house flipper or investor. • The wholesaler first secures the property under contract with the seller, often at a significantly discounted price. • They then market the property to potential buyers, such as house flippers, and sell the rights to purchase the property under the terms of the original contract. • The assignment fee is the difference between the wholesaler's contracted price with the seller and the price at which they sell the contract to the end buyer. • The assignment fee is considered a buyer's closing cost and is paid by the end buyer (the house flipper or investor), not the seller. • The specific amount of the assignment fee and the terms of the transaction are outlined in a separate assignment contract between the wholesaler and the end buyer.

While brokers earn commissions as a percentage of the sales price, which are typically paid by the seller, wholesalers earn assignment fees by selling their rights to purchase a property under contract to another buyer. These assignment fees are paid by the end buyer as part of their closing costs and are specified in a separate assignment contract. Understanding these differences is essential for investors who are looking to work with both brokers and wholesalers in their house-flipping business.

The size of the assignment fee can vary significantly depending on the quality of the deal that the wholesaler has secured. As an investor, understand that the assignment fee is a reflection of the wholesaler's efforts and the value they bring to the table by providing you with a potentially profitable investment opportunity. One of the most counter-productive things you can do when working with a wholesaler is attempt to negotiate or haggle over the size of their assignment fee. This approach can damage your relationship with the wholesaler and may ultimately lead to fewer deals being brought to your attention.

Instead, focus on evaluating the deal based on your own investment criteria and buy box. If the numbers work for your specific goals and target returns, then the wholesaler's fee should not be a primary concern. Adopt the mindset that as long as you can achieve your desired outcomes, it's less important what the other parties in the transaction are earning. This pragmatic approach to wholesaler relationships can set you apart from other investors who may get hung up on trying to squeeze every last dollar out of a deal.

By being an "easy buyer," who is more concerned with the overall viability of the investment than the specific assignment fee, you can position yourself as a preferred buyer for wholesalers. They will be more likely to bring you deals consistently, knowing that you are a reliable and efficient partner who can close quickly when presented with a good opportunity. That being said, there are certainly scenarios where the size of the assignment fee may warrant additional scrutiny. For example, if a wholesaler is charging an unusually high fee, such as $100,000 (which, while rare, does happen), it's reasonable to expect that the deal itself offers a significant upside potential. In these cases, you should still aim to achieve the upper end of your desired return percentage to justify the higher assignment fee.

Understanding Wholesaler Fees

When working with wholesalers, it's important to understand how assignment fees are structured and paid. Assignment fees are the compensation that wholesalers receive for locating and securing a property under contract, which they then assign to you, the investor, for a fee. Typically, assignment fees are paid either prior to or at closing. However, it's generally safer to pay the fee at closing to ensure that the transaction proceeds smoothly and all parties fulfill their obligations. Paying the fee up front can be risky, as there have been instances of fraudulent wholesalers collecting fees without delivering on the deal. In one cautionary tale, a wholesaler required an investor to wire money before closing, only to be revealed as a scam artist. The investor had to take legal action to recover their funds.

To avoid such situations, it's best to hold the assignment fee until closing. When it comes to the payment structure, deposits are often made to secure the deal, with the balance paid at closing. The size of the assignment fee can vary based on the estimated profit of the deal. As a general rule, larger deals tend to command higher assignment fees. Regardless of the fee size, it's crucial to thoroughly review all assignment disclosures and contracts well before the day of signing. The assignment fee will typically be listed as a Buyer's Closing Cost on the HUD settlement statement.

If you are working with a new wholesaler or one who is new to working with you, it's prudent to suggest depositing the assignment fee into escrow, to be released upon the successful closing of the deal. This arrangement provides security for all parties involved. To illustrate how assignment fees work in practice, let's consider a real-life example. Suppose you are a wholesaler who has locked up a house at $220,000. If you can market that deal to a house flipper for $225,000, you would earn a $5,000 assignment fee for locating and securing the deal. As the wholesaler, you would send the full contract to the investor for review, and the investor would then sign a separate assignment contract confirming that you will receive your fee at closing.

The fee is added to the buyer's closing costs. It's worth noting that wholesalers may go by various names, such as "property scouts," "investment finders," "lead generators," "deal scouts," "property hunters," or even "bird dogs." When working with wholesalers, it's essential to carefully read the paperwork or, better yet, have them use your own vetted contracts. Be cautious of any arrangements where the wholesaler gets paid regardless of whether the seller backs out of the deal, as this could leave you, the investor, out of pocket, without any control over the outcome. Ensure that the contract terms create a win-win scenario for all parties involved.

Last, it's important to discuss with your lender whether they will finance the wholesaler's fee as part of the deal. Lender policies vary, and some may only consider standard closing costs, requiring you to source the assignment fee funds separately. By understanding the intricacies of assignment fees and taking proactive steps to protect your interests, you can build successful, mutually beneficial relationships with wholesalers and expand your deal pipeline in the house-flipping business.

DISCOUNTS DO NOT EQUAL PROFITS

Once you have the right deal-finders in place, make sure you take care of these people. Not only do you want to do deals together, but it might make sense to take them out for coffee or lunch or host events, if you feel comfortable with them. This business is about relationships, so the better relationships you have, the more deals you can all do together. There's a lot of people out there who are grinders, and you want to be their favorite client. Get to know them.

The more you know your network, the more you are going to grow together. Some of the brokers I work with now I've bought probably hundreds of homes from over the last two decades. So you want to treat them like a person, not just a resource. And, more than likely, they'll return the favor. Whenever I meet someone, I make sure to introduce myself, qualify myself as an investor, and communicate my buy box. What I don't do too early in the relationship is ask about their fees or even get their number too soon. I want to make sure it feels like a fit and that we can help each other before we move forward on any deal.

A major mistake many new investors make is assuming that discounts equal profits. Discounts on properties are one thing (although you should build a budget and evaluate your returns whenever there's a deal that seems too good to be true), but expecting brokerage and agent commission discounts can be tricky.

Some investors think that just because they're a real estate investor and will likely complete multiple deals with their broker/agent, they should get a discount on the commission rate. If you decide to nickel-and-dime them and negotiate their established commission rate down rather than pay their full rate, why on earth would they want to work with you? Especially when they have other clients who pay their full commission rate.

When it comes to maximizing your time and profitability as a real estate investor, it's often more beneficial to pay the full fee for a brokerage that offers comprehensive support. By investing in a brokerage that provides a wide range of services, you can free up your time to focus on other aspects of your business, ultimately leading to increased earnings. Your broker is an asset to you, and they will put in work in a way that doesn't call for a discount

---

CHAPTER 4
SOURCING DEALS

The harder you work, the harder it is to surrender.
—VINCE LOMBARDI, FORMER HEAD COACH,
GREEN BAY PACKERS

FINDING THE RIGHT deals is the foundation of a successful house-flipping business. The saying goes "The money is made on the buy," which emphasizes the importance of acquiring properties at the right price. This means that your ability to generate a profit is largely determined by the price you pay for a property rather than the price you sell it for. When you purchase a property at a significantly discounted price, you create a buffer that allows for unexpected expenses and market fluctuations while still maintaining a healthy profit margin. This is why it's essential to focus on finding deals that offer the greatest potential for returns based on your investment criteria and return expectations (a.k.a. your buy box).

When searching for real estate inventory, consider both on-market and off-market deals. **On-market deals** are properties publicly listed for sale on the MLS or other real estate websites. One of the biggest white lies you hear in real estate is that there aren't any flipping deals on market. Honestly, I buy about 70 percent of my deals from the MLS. The BiggerPockets Deal Finder (www.BiggerPockets.com/BookDeals) is also a great tool to find on-market deals. Alternatively, **off-market deals** are properties that are not publicly listed but may be available for purchase through various channels.

TO LOOK FOR ON-MARKET DEALS	TO FIND OFF-MARKET DEALS
• **Utilize the MLS:** Work with a real estate agent who can access the MLS and set up automated searches for properties that meet your criteria, such as location, price range, and property condition. • **Browse real estate websites:** Explore popular sites like Zillow, Redfin, and Realtor.com to find listed properties in your target area. • **Analyze the listings:** Pay attention to key details such as the property's age, condition, days on market, and price history. Look for properties that have been on the market for an extended period or have undergone recent price reductions, as these may indicate motivated sellers.	• **Drive for dollars:** Drive through your target neighborhoods looking for properties that show signs of distress or neglect. These may include overgrown lawns, boarded-up windows, or accumulated mail. Keep track of these properties, and research ownership information through public records. • **Utilize public records:** Search for properties with delinquent taxes, code violations, or other public record indicators that suggest the owner may be motivated to sell. • **Network with wholesalers:** Connect with local real estate wholesalers who specialize in finding off-market deals. They often have access to motivated sellers and can provide a steady stream of potential investment opportunities. • **Attend local real estate events:** Participate in real estate investor meetings, seminars, and networking events to meet other investors, wholesalers, and industry professionals who may have access to off-market deals. • **Advertise your services:** Create a website or use social media to advertise your interest in purchasing properties in specific areas. This can attract potential sellers who may not have considered listing their property on the open market.

Finding the right investment property takes time, effort, and patience. Consistently applying various strategies to search for both on-market and off-market deals will increase your chances of finding suitable investment opportunities that align with your business goals and target market conditions.

OTHER WAYS TO SOURCE DEAL FLOW

There are lots of other ways to source deals in your flipping business. Networking can be one of the key ways to find opportunities to additional deal-finders.

Title officers. If you can find title officers in your deal-finder network, they can provide data for direct-to-seller campaigns, referrals to other resources, and discounts on closing. They can pull you a list of brokers who sell LLC properties and estate sales. They are your deal-finder data providers. Title reps are constantly out building new relationships to increase their title business. They are doing the hard work for you. Find the rep who works with builders and investors in your market. They are typically well connected to the people you need to find. A great way to find this person is to look when brokers are selling a flip property. What title company is their transaction opened with?

Title officers are professionals who work for title companies and are responsible for conducting thorough title searches, identifying any encumbrances or defects in the property's title, and ensuring that the transfer of ownership is properly documented and recorded. Their expertise is invaluable, especially when dealing with complex situations such as trustees, foreclosures, or other specialized circumstances. When it comes to finding the right title officers, many investors look to larger, established title companies. These companies often have extensive networks of experienced professionals who are well versed in handling various types of transactions, including those involving trustees, foreclosures, and other intricate scenarios.

One advantage of working with larger title companies is the breadth of their resources and expertise. These companies typically employ a diverse team of title officers, with specialized knowledge in different areas of real estate law and title work. This allows you to tap into the appropriate expertise for your specific needs, whether it's navigating the intricacies of a foreclosure sale or dealing with complex trust arrangements. To find suitable title officers, you can start by researching reputable title companies in your local area. Reach out to other investors, real estate professionals, or industry associations for recommendations on companies or specific title officers who have a track record of excellence in handling investment transactions.

Additionally, consider attending industry events or networking gatherings where you can connect with title officers directly and gauge their knowledge and experience. Don't hesitate to ask specific questions about their expertise in handling the types of transactions you typically encounter as an investor. Remember, title officers are compensated for their services through fees associated with each transaction. As such, it is in their best interest to work efficiently and effectively to facilitate successful closings. Building strong relationships with reliable and knowledgeable title officers can streamline your investment process and provide valuable legal protection throughout the life cycle of your real estate deals.

Social media. So many investors are simply documenting their journeys and finding deals this way. In today's world, the more people who follow you, the more deals you can possibly get. This probably won't be your first stack of deals, but by documenting your journey, teaching others what you've learned, and sharing deals online, you will find other buyers, deal-makers, and investors to partner with. It'll start with referrals from friends, family, and followers and grow from there. You'll be able to build up your resources and simply let people know what you're doing. When it comes to social media, the louder the better.

Feel free to document everything at first, see what works to increase engagement, and then lean into the aspects that work best. For flipping, as one example, people love transformation photos—those classic before and after photos. This is why there's so many of those shows on television. It's immediate payoff for your followers, so showcase your journey and grow online to grow your wallet. Honestly, this is a little painful for me to say because I was against social media for years, but some of the best deals I get today come from connections made on social media. Don't stress about this; just document what you're doing. We also regularly have plumbers, framers, and electricians reach out to us because they know we do fix-and-flips. And, because they know we do flips, they give us better rates than individual homeowners.

Direct-to-seller. As I said in the beginning of the book, I got into this business by wholesaling and knocking doors rather than working with brokers and agents. So marketing direct-to-sellers is a way to find deals without using a broker or wholesaling channel (it's actually what wholesalers do to find deals in the first place). It's a way to source your own investment opportunities, and you can negotiate directly with the seller rather than paying additional fees. We did a lot of these deals before we became flippers, which was especially handy the last few years when there were too many buyers in our market. So we created a direct-to-seller arm for additional deal flow. This way, instead of getting a 30 percent deal, you might get a 50 percent deal in one of your A/B locations.

The direct-to-seller approach is a powerful method for finding investment properties without relying on brokers, agents, or wholesaling channels. It involves directly marketing to and negotiating with property owners, allowing you to source your own investment opportunities and potentially secure better deals by eliminating middleman fees.

Here's how to pursue this approach.

1. **Identify your target market:** Start by defining your ideal investment criteria, such as preferred neighborhoods, property types,

price ranges, and desired profit margins. This will help you narrow down your search and focus your efforts on sellers who are more likely to have properties that fit your investment goals.

2. **Locate motivated sellers:** Look for sellers who may be more open to negotiating favorable deals, such as those facing foreclosure, divorce, relocation, inheritance, or other life circumstances that could motivate them to sell quickly or at a discount. These sellers may be more receptive to your direct approach.

3. **Utilize data sources:** Leverage various data sources to build a list of potential sellers. Public records, county assessor's offices, and online real estate databases can provide valuable information on property ownership, tax records, and other details that can help you identify potential targets.

4. **Implement targeted marketing:** Once you have a list of potential sellers, employ targeted marketing strategies to reach out to them directly. This can include direct mail campaigns, door-knocking, online advertising, or leveraging social media platforms to connect with homeowners in your target areas.

5. **Develop a compelling value proposition:** Craft a clear and compelling message that highlights the benefits of working with you directly. Emphasize your ability to provide a hassle-free sales process, flexible closing timelines, and the potential for a fair cash offer without the need for extensive repairs or renovations.

6. **Build relationships and negotiate:** When connecting with potential sellers, focus on building relationships and understanding their unique situations and motivations. Be prepared to negotiate terms that are mutually beneficial, such as offering a fair cash price, flexible closing dates, or even the option to rent back the property for a period after the sale.

By implementing a strategic direct-to-seller approach, you can effectively source investment opportunities without relying solely on traditional channels. This method allows you to negotiate directly with sellers, potentially securing better deals and increasing your profit margins on successful transactions.

Wholesaling your own deals can be advantageous, as you can make money on deals that do not fit your buy box. But there is a risk of becoming emotionally attached to a property and compromising your investment criteria, leading to a suboptimal deal. Maintain an objective mindset, and evaluate the opportunity as if it were brought to you by someone else, avoiding the trap of ego or pride that could blind you to potential issues or cause you to stray from your established buy box.

On the other hand, wholesaling your own deals offers several advantages. You can avoid costly assignment fees, negotiate terms that align with your specific investment goals, and target properties that may not be readily available through traditional channels. Additionally, it provides an additional income stream and allows you to create a long-term pipeline of steady deal flow. By understanding and mitigating the potential drawbacks while capitalizing on the benefits, investors can effectively leverage their ability to source and wholesale their own deals, diversifying their investment strategies and maximizing potential returns.

The direct-to-seller method is not suitable for everyone, but it can be as simple as placing a "We Buy Houses" sign in your yard, with proper permits. These signs work well in strategic locations, like busy intersections. If you choose to purchase internet leads, remember to "speed the lead"—contact the seller immediately. Set up an appointment quickly, as motivated sellers are likely filling out multiple forms. Being the first to respond can secure the deal. For direct-to-seller methods, you need to be available most of the day to answer calls and make contacts. Expect to handle around one hundred calls per day to get a warm lead.

Skiptracing services can help obtain potential sellers' contact information and filter out warm leads, saving time but costing money. Consider setting up a call room with a team dedicated to cold-calling potential leads and a closer to handle warm leads. This approach can significantly reduce the cost per warm lead compared to internet leads but requires consistency and a dedicated budget to ensure success. Maximize your time by wholesaling deals that don't fit your investment criteria, earning assignment fees while focusing on your primary flip projects. Consistency is key—turning marketing channels on and off can cause you to miss opportunities and lose momentum. To build a sustainable business, continually work on expanding your skill set, maximizing leads, and nurturing seller contacts, even when they're not immediately ready to sell.

All in all, the more contacts you have, the more contracts you're going to get. When it comes to direct-to-seller methods, we consider routes such as door-knocking, mailers, bandit signs, and then phone contacts like cold-calling, texting, or AirDrop messages.

Door-knocking in real estate is a proactive approach where agents physically visit homes within a targeted area to engage with homeowners directly. The purpose is to establish personal connections, provide information about the local real estate market, and potentially generate leads for buying or selling properties. It involves engaging in conversations, handing out flyers or business cards, and often involves follow-up activities to nurture relationships and convert leads into clients.

Whether or not you knock doors, if you see a dilapidated house, you should consider writing the address down. There's a chance you could leave a note or find the phone number and buy the property. Give yourself a few notes or take a picture if it feels appropriate (you can also find an image on Google Maps). From ages 22 to 25, I knocked thirty to forty doors per day. People are so scared to do this, but I never had anything bad happen to me. Do people occasionally slam the door in your face or reject you? Yes, but the benefit of finding a deal this way—financial freedom—far outweighs the fear and small likelihood of being rejected.

Mailers in real estate refer to marketing materials, such as postcards, brochures, or letters, that are sent out via traditional mail to targeted audiences. These materials typically contain information about available properties, recent sales, market updates, or personalized messages from real estate agents or agencies. The goal of mailers is to generate leads, stay top of mind with potential clients, and promote the services of the real estate professionals sending them.

Effective mailers are designed to capture attention, provide valuable information, and encourage recipients to take action, such as contacting the agent or visiting their website. This is a great way to target people without the fear that comes along with practices like knocking on doors or cold-calling. This way, they contact you, but it costs more money than knocking on doors. So direct-to-seller is more about the question of time or money. If you have more time, knock on doors. If you have more money, use mailers. There are companies you can use for preferred pricing, which I share in my online communities and on my social channels, so follow me for up-to-date resources. These keep our costs down and you can name-drop me for better pricing.

We've actually had people contact us several years after we mailed to ask if we were still buying properties in the area. Door-knocking is perhaps the most cost-effective but also the most time-consuming method. It's essentially free (except for car maintenance and gas) when you compare something like using ads on the internet (anywhere from $100 to $1,000 per month for pay-per-click; we pay around $500 per lead in the Seattle market) or mailers, where leads can cost $50–$1,000 per lead, depending on the area.

Bandit signs in real estate are small, typically homemade signs placed strategically in public spaces to attract attention from potential buyers or sellers. Like mailers, you flip the script to have interested parties call you as opposed to you calling potentially interested (or uninterested) parties. These signs often contain simple messages such as "We Buy Houses" or "For Sale By Owner," along with contact information.

While they can be effective for generating leads quickly and at a relatively low cost, bandit signs may also be subject to local regulations and restrictions, as they can be seen as visual clutter or illegal advertising in some areas. Therefore, real estate professionals must carefully consider the legality and potential consequences of using bandit signs as part of their marketing strategy. Ironically, the less personal, less professional method actually works best, so you're going to want to handwrite these signs or leave-behind notes when door-knocking as opposed to professional, printed signs. The easiest, low-risk advertising is to post your company's contact outside of your jobsites.

Cold-calling in real estate involves contacting potential clients, such as homeowners or property investors, via telephone without any prior relationship or introduction. Real estate agents typically use cold-calling to prospect for leads, offering their services to those who may be interested in buying or selling a property. This method requires agents to have a persuasive pitch, good communication skills, and the ability to handle rejection. While effective for reaching a large number of prospects quickly, cold-calling can also be intrusive and may yield mixed results depending on the agent's approach and the receptiveness of the individuals contacted. When you do things like text or AirDrop messages, where legislation is changing constantly, you want to make sure you're not breaking any laws. There are various companies and software and even virtual assistant services that can help you with these methods.

CONDUCT MARKET RESEARCH

As you begin or build your flipping business, complete market research. On-market deals will give you more access to market data as you evaluate properties. You can use the MLS, Zillow, and Redfin to find market-specific data to evaluate. New flippers who are trying to learn or conduct their own market research often face challenges, as flipping can feel like learning a new language—there's a lot of information to process and factors to consider. To effectively conduct market research in the real estate business, beginners should start by familiarizing themselves with key concepts and terminology, such as comparable properties (comps), median home prices, days on market, and local market trends.

The first thing you'll be able to notice about your local market is the available inventory. This is simply the number of available homes in your desired market. When assessing the inventory in a particular area, pay attention to the number and type of available properties. If you're interested in a city or county but can't find any fixer-upper properties, it may indicate that your business plan might face challenges. While it's possible to work on a single deal in an area with limited flip activity, it can be difficult to scale your business and take on multiple projects if there are no clear signs of progress or demand for renovated properties. A lack of inventory in your desired area may require you to be creative in finding good deals. This could lead you to finding off-market deals. Additionally, expanding your search to neighboring areas or adjusting your criteria may help you identify more potential deals.

Another crucial aspect of market research is analyzing **comps**, which are recently sold properties similar to the one being considered for flipping. Beginners should learn how to identify relevant comps based on factors like location, property type, size, age, and condition. In addition to comps, new flippers should study local market trends, including population growth, economic indicators, employment rates, and upcoming developments that could impact property values. This information can be gathered from sources such as local government websites, chambers of commerce, and real estate industry reports.

Once you have gathered your initial data, an essential metric to analyze is the **days on market** (DOM), which represents the average time it takes to sell a property in your target area. Understanding the DOM helps flippers because each additional month a property remains unsold increases holding costs and reduces the annualized return on investment. To assess the market's absorption rate, pay close attention to the DOM. Flippers must think in terms of time because, as the saying goes, "time is money." This expression holds especially true when flipping a property, particularly if you encounter issues during the renovation process or struggle to find a buyer. The longer a property sits on the market, the more holding costs you'll incur, such as mortgage payments, property taxes, insurance, and utilities.

When researching the DOM, consider the following steps: Analyze recent sales data by looking at comparable properties that have sold in the last six to twelve months, and calculate the average DOM for those properties; assess current market conditions by examining the current inventory of available properties, and note the DOM for those that are most similar to your potential flip; and consult with local real estate professionals by reaching out to experienced agents, brokers, and other investors in your target area to gain insights into the current market conditions and expected DOM for your specific property type and price range. By thoroughly understanding the DOM and absorption rate in your target market, you'll be better equipped to make informed decisions when underwriting potential flips, setting realistic timelines, and maximizing your annualized returns.

Gathering data specific to the local market is crucial. Relying on generic information from other markets can lead to the development of investment formulas that are incompatible with your area's unique circumstances. Comparing different markets without considering their specific contexts is like comparing apples to oranges. Basing your strategies on irrelevant data can result in one of two unfavorable outcomes: missed opportunities due to a reluctance to invest or overpaying for properties due to inaccurate assumptions. When conducting market research, it's essential to organize and analyze this data effectively. Beginners should create spreadsheets or use specialized software to track comps, calculate potential ARVs, and monitor market trends. This data-driven approach will help new flippers make informed decisions and minimize risk.

Networking with local real estate professionals, including real estate agents, appraisers, and experienced investors, can also provide invaluable insights into the local market. Attending real estate meetups, workshops, and seminars can help beginners expand their knowledge and make valuable connections.

EXPLORING NEW MARKETS

Different real estate markets exhibit unique trends and characteristics that investors must consider when setting their return expectations. For instance, my friends in Arizona and Miami experience different returns compared to what we achieve in Washington. An acquaintance in Arizona aims for a 30 percent cash-on-cash return on their fix-and-flip projects. In contrast, we can target 40–50 percent returns in Washington, but this often involves investing in older properties that require more work but also yield higher profits. This doesn't necessarily mean one market is superior to the other; it simply highlights the distinct dynamics of each location.

When I'm looking at a new market or potentially partnering with an out-of-state flipper, there are several things I like to look at to run these new numbers, such as the sales price and the purchase price. Based on my experience and past flips, I subtract 15 percent for sales costs and lending costs (this isn't a hard-and-fast number, so your true number may change as you begin to flip homes, but this is a good place to start). That gives me an idea of the profit. Then I try to confirm these numbers with other investors and brokers in the area. A great way to meet investors is to attend local real estate meetup groups, social media forums, or conferences like BPCON (BiggerPockets Conference, which you can learn more about at www.BiggerPockets.com/BookBPCON). The more you build your network, the more informed you will be.

When researching a new location, utilizing websites like Zillow can be a valuable tool for working a deal backward and understanding the local market. To start, search the website for recently sold properties in the area you're interested in. Flipped properties are often easily identifiable due to their staged photographs and renovated appearance, which typically follows a somewhat standardized template.

Once you've found a potential flip property, gather information about its sales price from the website or public records. This sales price represents the purchase price for the investor who completed the flip. To dig deeper, examine the property's history on Zillow, paying attention to when it was last sold prior to the flip. This information can help you estimate the original purchase price of the property before renovations.

Next, analyze the property's features, square footage, and the extent of the renovations to estimate the potential renovation costs. Compare the property to similar homes in the area that have not been recently renovated to get a sense of the average price per square foot. This will help you gauge the potential after-repair value (ARV) of the property.

To further refine your analysis, consider the following steps:

1. Study the property's photographs to identify the types of renovations completed, such as kitchen and bathroom upgrades, flooring, or landscaping.
2. Research the average costs of these renovations in the local market by contacting contractors or using online resources like HomeAdvisor or *Remodeling Magazine*'s "Cost vs. Value" report.

3. Estimate the holding costs, including property taxes, insurance, utilities, and financing costs, based on the typical timeline for flips in the area.
4. Calculate the potential profit by subtracting the estimated purchase price, renovation costs, holding costs, and selling expenses from the ARV.

While this method can provide valuable insights, it's essential to validate your findings by connecting with local real estate professionals, such as agents, contractors, and other investors. They can offer firsthand knowledge of the market and help you refine your assumptions and projections. As you gain more experience and data, you'll be able to create more accurate deal analyses and make informed decisions when investing in a new location.

For example, let's say an investor purchases a property for $200,000, spends $50,000 on renovations, incurs $10,000 in holding costs, and estimates $25,000 in selling costs. After researching comparable sales, they determine the ARV to be $350,000.

Total Cost of the Flip
$200,000 + $50,000 + $10,000 + $25,000 = $285,000

Net Sales Proceeds = $350,000 - $25,000 = $325,000

Profit = $325,000 - $285,000 = $40,000

In this example, the investor would stand to make a profit of $40,000 from the flip. Once you have these numbers, you can take a guess at the anticipated profit. It's not exact, because you don't know exactly what they spent on the deal or any problems they might have run into, but it's a place to start. In addition, it shows you average timelines to purchase, flip, and resell a property. I like to do this four to five times in a new market so that I have an idea of what type of return I might get in this area.

When exploring new markets, investors should start by identifying specific locations or zip codes that show promise for real estate investment. The BiggerPockets Market Finder (www.BiggerPockets.com/Book Markets) is a great place to start if you're unsure what your target market is. This process involves analyzing several key conditions. In the context of real estate, **conditions** refer to the various factors and characteristics that influence the viability and profitability of investing in a specific market. These conditions can vary significantly from one location to another, making it crucial for investors to thoroughly research and understand the unique dynamics of each market they are considering.

These conditions include:

ECONOMIC FACTORS	Consider the local job market, major employers, industries, and economic growth prospects. A strong and diverse economy often indicates a stable housing market and potential for appreciation.
DEMOGRAPHIC TRENDS	Examine population growth, age distribution, income levels, and education attainment. These factors can influence housing demand, rental rates, and overall market stability.
HOUSING MARKET INDICATORS	Analyze median home prices, price-to-rent ratios, vacancy rates, days on market, and appreciation rates. These metrics provide insight into the current state of the market and its potential for growth.
NEIGHBORHOOD CHARACTERISTICS	Evaluate the quality of local schools, crime rates, access to amenities, and transportation infrastructure. These factors can significantly impact property values and desirability to potential buyers or renters.
LOCAL LAWS AND REGULATIONS	Research zoning laws, landlord–tenant regulations, property taxes, and any other legal considerations that may affect your investment strategy.
RENTAL MARKET CONDITIONS	If you plan to invest in rental properties, assess the demand for rental housing, average rent prices, and the potential for cash flow generation.

Even within a single city, conditions can vary greatly from one neighborhood or zip code to another. For example, a city might have strict zoning laws in one area, limiting the potential for certain types of investments, while another area may offer more flexibility. Similarly, school districts can vary significantly within a city, affecting property values and rental demand. To account for these variations, investors should break down their research into smaller subgroups, such as counties, neighborhoods, or even specific streets. The more granular the analysis, the better equipped investors will be to make informed decisions and accurately project potential returns.

Conducting thorough research on these conditions may involve a combination of strategies, such as analyzing online real estate data and market reports; networking with local real estate professionals, including agents, property managers, and other investors; attending local real estate events and workshops; and visiting the location in person to get a firsthand understanding of the market and neighborhoods. By dedicating time and effort to understanding the unique conditions of each market, investors can optimize their deals, minimize risk, and maximize returns. This research process is ongoing, as market conditions can change over time, requiring investors to stay informed and adapt their strategies accordingly.

Market research is an ongoing process. Real estate markets are dynamic and can change quickly, so make sure to stay updated on the latest trends and adapt strategies accordingly. By continually learning, networking, and analyzing data, beginners can gradually master the art of market research and make well-informed decisions in their real estate investments.

SIGNS OF PROGRESS AND NOVELTY FEATURES

When researching a specific neighborhood or area, I actively look for signs of ongoing development or revitalization efforts. Are there new construction projects underway, such as residential or commercial developments? Are there renovations or home improvement activities happening in the vicinity? These activities can be positive indicators of an area experiencing growth and increased desirability.

To gather this information, I conduct thorough research on the area. This may involve searching online for news articles or reports on "new development" or "new infrastructure" specific to that location. Local news outlets and community forums can be valuable sources of information regarding upcoming projects, zoning changes, or planned improvements that could positively impact the area's appeal and property values. Identifying areas that are in the "path of progress" can be a strategic investment approach. When a neighborhood or region is undergoing revitalization efforts, such as infrastructure upgrades, the introduction of new amenities, or the development of desirable commercial or residential projects, it can drive increased demand and potentially lead to property value appreciation. By positioning your investment in an area that is experiencing positive growth and development, you can potentially benefit from the ripple effects of these improvements.

As the area becomes more desirable, property values may rise, allowing you to capitalize on the increased demand and potentially generate higher returns upon resale or through increased rental income. But exercise caution and conduct thorough due diligence when evaluating signs of progress. Not all development plans may come to fruition, and it's crucial to assess the credibility of the sources and the likelihood of the proposed improvements materializing within your investment timeline. By combining a strategic focus on areas experiencing positive growth and development with a comprehensive understanding of the local real estate market dynamics, you can increase your chances of identifying lucrative investment opportunities that align with your goals and risk tolerance.

If I know the property's on the upswing, there's a good chance that my values could increase over the life of the project. Path of progress, where infrastructure and neighborhoods are being improved, can lead to big jumps in your resale values. If buyers know there are stores, shopping, and amenities that make a location more convenient, they'll pay a lot more when you go to sell. If I'm looking at a property and things in the area are shutting down, the opposite is perhaps true. Path to progress can make a big difference on whether your property's going to go up or down in value during its lifetime.

I'm also looking for novelty features. Is there something that will help sell this property for more? Does the property have nice sidewalks out front? Does it have a park on the side? Does it have view potential? Is there private access to something because it's in a certain community? These things can drastically change the value. When I'm looking at establishing novelty items, I'm also looking for negative things that will drop the value of it. Common things that will affect the pricing on your property are:

- Busy roads
- High crime
- Bad neighbors
- Noise pollution from trains or planes
- Overhead power lines
- House positioning

If the house isn't facing the street, but it's facing sideways, that's actually worth less, because people are not willing to pay as much for this problem. Is there a nightclub or other noise disturbance at night? Things that will cause people annoyances will reduce the value. People want to avoid non-livable places or, at the very least, don't want to pay a premium for these nuisances. In these scenarios, I'm going to factor it

in for my whole cost, like areas that have bad schools, bad neighbors, or bad crime. It takes longer to sell them, so we've got to find that person who's okay with those issues.

EXCLUSIVE MARKETS

In Seattle, there are numerous neighborhoods that offer waterfront access, but their desirability extends far beyond the mere presence of a waterfront. These areas thrive due to a strong sense of community and the lifestyle experiences they provide. Residents in these waterfront communities actively engage in creating a vibrant atmosphere through events and activities. They organize neighborhood gatherings, such as Fourth of July celebrations, quarterly meetups, and various other social events. These experiences foster a sense of belonging and contribute to the overall appeal of living in these areas. The marketing appeal of these neighborhoods is not solely about the waterfront access itself but rather the entire lifestyle package that comes with it.

Prospective buyers are attracted not only by the ability to "dip their toes in the water" but also the opportunity to be part of a close-knit, vibrant community that offers a unique living experience. Conversely, it's equally important to recognize that this lifestyle may not appeal to everyone. Some buyers may prefer a more tranquil and quiet environment, without the social activities and community engagement that these waterfront neighborhoods offer.

When promoting the advantages of a waterfront community lifestyle, it's equally important to acknowledge that this may not align with the preferences of buyers seeking a more private or secluded living experience. By thoroughly evaluating and marketing the community aspects, amenities, and lifestyle factors associated with a particular neighborhood, you can more effectively match properties with the right buyers. This approach not only increases the likelihood of successful transactions but also ensures that buyers are fully informed about the living experience they can expect, setting realistic expectations and fostering long-term satisfaction with their investment.

Be on the lookout for exclusive schools. When evaluating a neighborhood or specific property, be aware of the presence of exclusive or highly sought-after schools in the area. Certain properties may be designated within the boundaries of desirable school districts or catchment areas, which can significantly influence their value and desirability. For example, in the Wallingford neighborhood of Seattle, there is a small

radius of houses that falls within the catchment area of the prestigious International School. This school is renowned for its exceptional quality and has a substantial wait-list, with families willing to relocate just to gain access to it. The properties within this small radius command a premium price because they offer the coveted benefit of enrollment eligibility for the International School.

Families are willing to pay a premium to secure a home within this specific area, as it guarantees their children access to one of the best elementary schools in the city. Similarly, other neighborhoods or communities may have their own exclusive or highly rated schools that drive up property values within their respective catchment areas. Prospective buyers, particularly those with school-age children, are often willing to pay a premium to live in areas that provide access to these sought-after educational institutions.

As a real estate professional, be aware of these localized factors and their impact on property values. During the underwriting process (which I will explain in detail in Chapter 6), identifying properties within the boundaries of exclusive or high-performing school districts can help you accurately assess their potential value and market demand. By factoring in the presence of desirable schools and their associated catchment areas, you can better advise clients, set appropriate pricing strategies, and effectively market properties to buyers who prioritize access to exceptional educational opportunities for their children.

WHERE I WOULD LOOK FOR DEALS

From my perspective, wholesalers are going to be some of your best friends. Remember, a **wholesaler** is a company or individual who contracts a property below market value. The wholesaler sells their option on the contract, so you pay them a fee. This fee is usually 5–10 percent margin on the deal. When a wholesaler knows my buy box, they know to look for my exact criteria—and they know *where* to look for those deals.

To build a strong network of wholesalers, actively seek out opportunities to connect with these valuable deal sources. One of the most effective ways to meet wholesalers is by attending local real estate networking groups, such as real estate investor associations (REIAs) or meetups specifically designed for wholesalers and investors. These events provide a platform to introduce yourself, share your "buy box," and establish relationships with potential partners. In addition to networking events, you can leverage your existing connections in the real estate industry to find wholesalers. Ask

other investors in your area if they can recommend reliable wholesalers they've worked with in the past. These personal referrals can be invaluable, as they often come with a built-in level of trust and credibility.

Social media platforms, particularly Facebook, have become increasingly popular for connecting with wholesalers. Join local real estate investment groups on Facebook and engage with the community by introducing yourself and sharing your investment goals. Many wholesalers use these groups to promote their deals and connect with potential buyers. Another way to find wholesalers is through sales calls and referrals from professionals in the real estate industry. Reach out to brokers, hard-money lenders, title companies, and escrow officers, and let them know that you're actively seeking investment opportunities. These professionals often work with wholesalers and can provide valuable introductions and referrals.

One unique method of finding wholesalers is by keeping an eye out for "bandit signs" in your target investment areas. These signs are typically handwritten on plain, white, corrugated-plastic boards and feature messages like "We Buy Houses" or "Cash for Your House" along with a phone number. While these signs are primarily intended to attract distressed homeowners looking to sell quickly, they can also serve as a direct line to local wholesalers. When you come across a bandit sign, take a moment to write down the phone number. Call the number and explain that you're an investor looking for off-market deals that fit your specific buy box. By proactively reaching out and expressing your interest, you can turn these signs into valuable connections with wholesalers who are actively sourcing deals in your target markets. Building a robust network of wholesalers takes time and consistent effort.

Finding deals is a key component of flipping houses. If you don't have a deal to flip, then you aren't a flipper! Be proactive in your outreach, attend networking events regularly, and always be ready to share your investment criteria and explain how you can add value as a buyer. By cultivating these relationships and maintaining open lines of communication, you can create a steady stream of high-quality deals that will help grow and sustain your house-flipping business.

However you find these connections, online or otherwise, understand that there are lots of new people in this business all the time and the information is not always correct, so you always want to run your own numbers. In the end, however you get the deal, it's your responsibility to take care of yourself and your team. Don't rely on someone else's numbers. Verify all the information. At local meetings, don't just go to

the meeting and sit there—shake hands with people, introduce yourself, talk about your business, ask them about their business, and let people know your haves and wants.

Don't be nervous to go up to the front. Everyone wants to hear what you want to buy. If you're a newer investor, walk up to the front and tell them who you are and what you want. As I meet people from Facebook groups or on BiggerPockets forums or local meetups, I make sure to check in with them often. I want to be first in front of people, so they think of me when they do have deals. Make calls. Send texts. Attend the groups. Stay in touch. As you build these resources, utilize a CRM (client relationship management) program to keep track of all your deal-finders, rate them, and remind you to reach out to check in with them.

CHAPTER 5
UNDERSTANDING COSTS AND BUILDING A BUDGET

The man who complains about the way the ball bounces is
likely the one who dropped it.
—LOU HOLTZ, FORMER PROFESSIONAL FOOTBALL COACH

MASTERING THE ART of cost estimation can make or break your house-flipping venture, especially for newcomers to the real estate investment game. As a new investor, it's essential to understand the various expenses involved in the process, including purchase price, renovation expenses, holding costs, and other associated fees.

First, consider the purchase price of the property. This is the initial cost of acquiring the house you intend to flip. To determine a fair purchase price, research the local real estate market, analyze comparable properties, and consult with experienced real estate agents. Keep in mind that you'll want to buy the property at a price that allows room for renovation expenses and profit.

When considering the purchase price of a property for flipping, it's essential to conduct thorough research and analysis to ensure you're making a sound investment decision. Start by studying the local housing market to understand current trends, demand, and price points. Look at factors such as population growth, economic conditions, and neighborhood developments that could impact property values. This information will help you gauge whether the market is favorable for flipping and what price range you should target.

A key principle in the house-flipping business is encapsulated in the saying "You make the money on the buy." This adage underscores the critical importance of acquiring properties at the right price to maximize your profit potential. When you purchase a property at a favorable price point, you create a buffer that allows for unexpected expenses and market fluctuations while still maintaining a healthy margin. Conversely, overpaying for a property can severely limit your profitability and increase your exposure to risk. By focusing on acquiring properties at a significant discount, you effectively build in a profit before any work has even begun, setting the stage for a successful flip. It's worth noting that the decision not to buy a property can be just as important as the decision to move forward with a purchase. If a deal fails to meet your predetermined criteria or does not offer the necessary profit margins, it's often prudent to pass on the opportunity.

Next, analyze recently sold properties similar to the one you're considering in terms of size, age, condition, and location. These **comparable properties** or **comps** will give you an idea of the current market value and help you determine a fair purchase price. Pay attention to the sales prices, days on market, and any unique features that may have influenced the final price.

Another crucial factor to consider is the property's expected value after renovations are complete, known as the **after-repair value** or ARV. Estimate the ARV by looking at comps of recently sold properties similar to what your property will be like post-renovation. This will help you determine how much you can afford to spend on the purchase and renovations while still making a profit. Many experienced investors use the 70 percent rule as a guideline for determining a property's maximum purchase price: Pay no more than 70 percent of the property's ARV minus the estimated renovation costs.

For example, if a property's ARV is $200,000 and you estimate $40,000 in renovation costs, your maximum purchase price should be $100,000 (70% × $200,000 − $40,000 = $100,000). The goal is to purchase the property at a price that allows for sufficient renovation budgets and a profitable resale. Be cautious of overestimating the ARV or underestimating renovation costs, as this can eat into your potential profits.

Next, estimate the renovation expenses. Estimating renovation expenses is a critical step in the house-flipping process, as it directly impacts your budget and potential profitability. To begin, create a detailed list of all the updates and repairs needed for the property. This may include items such as flooring, painting, kitchen and bathroom remodels, landscaping, electrical and plumbing work, and any structural repairs. Be thorough in your assessment and consider the property's current condition, as well as any necessary upgrades to meet local building codes or make the property more attractive to potential buyers.

Once you have a comprehensive list of renovations, start researching the costs of materials and labor. Obtain quotes from multiple contractors and suppliers to get a realistic picture of the expenses involved. When comparing quotes, make sure to consider factors such as the contractor's experience, reputation, and timeline for completion. Keep in mind that the lowest quote may not always be the best choice if it compromises quality or reliability.

In addition to materials and labor, don't forget to factor in the costs of any necessary permits. Depending on the scope of your renovations and local regulations, you may need to obtain permits for electrical work, plumbing, structural changes, or other significant alterations. These permits can add to your overall expenses and should be accounted for in your budget. To find out the actual costs of these permits, you can visit your local building department.

As you estimate your renovation costs, it's essential to be realistic and avoid underestimating expenses. Many inexperienced investors make the mistake of assuming they can complete renovations for less than the actual costs, which can lead to budget overruns and decreased profitability. To mitigate this risk, include a contingency fund in your budget to cover unexpected expenses that may arise during the renovation process. A contingency fund of 10–20 percent of your total renovation budget is typically recommended to provide a buffer for unforeseen issues, such as hidden damage, material price increases, or delays in construction.

Another factor to consider when estimating renovation costs is the timeline for completion. The longer the renovations take, the more you'll spend on holding costs such as mortgage payments, insurance, and property taxes. Be sure to factor these ongoing expenses into your overall budget and work with your contractors to establish a realistic timeline for the completion of the renovations.

Finally, it's important to prioritize your renovations based on their potential impact on the property's value and appeal to buyers. Focus on key areas such as kitchens, bathrooms, and curb appeal, as these tend to have the highest return on investment. Consider the preferences and expectations of buyers in your target market, and make renovations that align with their needs and desires.

By carefully estimating your renovation expenses, including materials, labor, permits, and a contingency fund, you can create a realistic budget for your house flip.

Holding costs are another important consideration. Holding costs represent the ongoing expenses you'll incur while you own the property. These costs can quickly add up and eat into your potential profits, so it's crucial to have a clear understanding of what they entail and how to factor them into your overall budget. To accurately estimate your holding costs, create a detailed budget that includes all the expenses you'll incur while you own the property. Be sure to factor in a buffer for unexpected expenses or delays, and regularly review and adjust your budget as needed throughout the flipping process. By carefully managing your holding costs and sticking to a realistic timeline, you can minimize your expenses and maximize your potential profits on the flip.

One of the most significant holding costs is the mortgage payment. Unless you're able to purchase the property with cash, you'll likely need to obtain financing to acquire the property. Mortgage payments include both principal and interest, and the amount depends on factors such as the purchase price, down payment, interest rate, and loan term. Be sure to shop around for the best financing options, and consider the impact of the mortgage payment on your overall budget and timeline for the flip.

Property taxes are another holding cost to consider. These taxes are assessed by local governments and can vary widely depending on the location and value of the property. You'll need to research the property tax rates in the area where you're investing and factor these costs into your budget. Keep in mind that property taxes may increase over time, so it's important to have a buffer in your budget to account for any potential increases.

Insurance is another essential holding cost. As the property owner, you'll need to maintain insurance coverage to protect against potential risks such as fire, theft, or damage. The cost of insurance will depend on factors such as the property's location, age, and condition, as well as the level of coverage you choose. Be sure to shop around for the best insurance rates, and consider the impact of these costs on your overall budget.

Utilities are another holding cost to factor into your budget. Even if the property is vacant during the renovation process, you'll still need to maintain basic utilities such as electricity, water, and gas. These costs can add up quickly, especially if the renovation process takes longer than expected. Be sure to estimate the utility costs based on the property's size and location, and consider any potential savings from energy-efficient upgrades or utility programs.

Maintenance costs are also an important consideration. As the property owner, you'll be responsible for maintaining the property and addressing any issues that arise during the holding period. This may include tasks such as lawn care, snow removal, or minor repairs. Be sure to factor these costs into your budget and consider hiring a property management company to handle these tasks if you're unable to do so yourself.

Finally, create a realistic timeline for the flip when estimating your holding costs. The longer you hold the property, the more these expenses will add up, so have a clear plan for completing the renovations and selling the property as quickly as possible. However, be cautious of rushing the renovation process or cutting corners to save time, as this can ultimately hurt the quality of the finished product and reduce your potential profits.

What are some ways to narrow down how long projects will take?
- Talk to your contractors and find out how long it typically takes them to complete the scope of work.
- Talk to the city's building department in any area you are looking to flip. What is the permit process? How long will it take to get permit approval?
- Research the market times. How long do similar properties sit on the market before they sell? Researching these timelines will help you identify how long it will take you to make a return and what kind of holding costs to factor for.

Other costs to consider include closing costs, real estate agent commissions, and marketing expenses, all of which can significantly impact your overall budget and profitability. **Closing costs** are fees associated with finalizing the purchase and sale of the property. These costs can add up quickly and include items such as title insurance, escrow fees, and transfer taxes. Title insurance protects you and your lender against any potential issues with the property's title, such as liens or ownership disputes.

Escrow fees cover the costs of the escrow company's services, which include holding and distributing funds during the transaction. Transfer taxes are fees charged by local governments for the transfer of property ownership. The amount of these fees can vary widely depending on your location, so it's important to research the specific closing costs in your area and factor them into your budget.

Real estate agent commissions are another significant cost to consider. When you sell the property, you'll typically need to pay a commission to both your listing agent and the buyer's agent. These commissions are usually a percentage of the sales price and can vary depending on your location and the agent's experience. In some cases, you may be able to negotiate a lower commission rate, but keep in mind that experienced agents can often help you sell the property more quickly and at a higher price, which can offset the cost of their commission. **Marketing expenses** are also an important consideration when flipping a house. To attract potential buyers and sell the property quickly, you'll need to invest in marketing efforts such as professional photography, staging, and advertising.

Professional photography can help showcase the property's best features and make it stand out online, while staging can help buyers envision themselves living in the space. Advertising expenses may include online listings, social media ads, or print materials such as flyers or brochures. While these expenses can add up, they're often essential for generating interest in the property and securing a quick sale. As a new investor, it's crucial to do your due diligence and thoroughly research all the costs involved in flipping a house. This includes not only obvious expenses like purchase price and renovation costs but also less visible costs, like closing fees, commissions, and marketing expenses.

One of the best ways to gain a comprehensive understanding of these costs is to consult with experienced investors, real estate agents, and contractors. These professionals can provide valuable insights and advice based on their own experiences and help you avoid common pitfalls and mistakes. When consulting with experienced professionals, be sure to ask detailed questions about their own experiences with flipping houses and the specific costs they've encountered. Ask about any unexpected expenses they've faced and how they've managed to stay within budget. Inquire about their strategies for minimizing costs and maximizing profitability, and seek their advice on how to navigate the local real estate market and regulations.

EVALUATE EXPECTED RETURNS

Once you establish and understand these costs, you can use them to determine your potential profit and your potential return on investment (ROI). ROI is a metric used to measure the profitability of an investment, expressed as a percentage of the original cost. If an investor purchases a property for $100,000 and sells it for $140,000 after all expenses, their ROI would be 40 percent. Most of the time, we are targeting 100 percent annual return on our properties. That allows for us to grow quickly, build liquidity, and buy more. This is the type of skill set that not only builds financial freedom in the present but optimizes your path for the future.

Let's look at another example.

The purchase price of a property you're wanting to flip is $200,000. Assume that the renovation costs are $50,000. The holding costs are $10,000. Next, we'll factor in the closing costs, real estate commission, and staging expenses, which adds up to $25,000.

To determine the potential profit and ROI, use the following formulas:

$$\text{Potential Profit} = \text{ARV} - \left(\begin{array}{c} \text{Purchase Price + Renovation Costs} \\ \text{+ Holding Costs + Selling Costs} \end{array} \right)$$

Example:
$$\$350{,}000 - (\$200{,}000 + \$50{,}000 + \$10{,}000 + \$25{,}000) = \$65{,}000$$

$$\text{ROI} = \left(\frac{\text{Potential Profit} \div}{\text{(Purchase Price + Renovation Costs + Holding Costs)}} \right) \times 100\%$$

Example:
$$(\$65{,}000 \div (\$200{,}000 + \$50{,}000 + \$10{,}000)) \times 100\% = 25\%$$

Another useful concept to understand when evaluating potential returns is annualized return. **Annualized return** is a formula that allows you to compare the profitability of investments with different holding periods on a consistent, annual basis. This metric is particularly relevant for house flipping, as the duration of each project can vary significantly. The formula for annualized return works like this:

$$\begin{array}{c} \text{Annualized} \\ \text{Return} \end{array} = \left(\frac{\text{Profit} \div}{\text{Cash Invested}} \right) \times \left(\frac{12 \div}{\text{Months to Completion}} \right)$$

Many investors overlook the importance of calculating annualized return when evaluating the success of their house-flipping business. Failing to consider this metric can lead to confusion and frustration, as investors may struggle to balance their flipping activities with their primary job. To set realistic goals and ensure that your house-flipping venture is a profitable one, it's essential to determine your target annualized return based on concrete data and insights from experienced investors.

VALUE ADJUSTMENTS

When should you make value adjustments? When evaluating a potential real estate flip, it's crucial to make value adjustments based on various factors that can impact the property's desirability and potential resale value. These adjustments help investors account for the increased risk and potential challenges associated with certain properties, ensuring that their return expectations align with the level of risk involved.

One common example of a value adjustment is properties located on busy roads. Houses situated on high-traffic streets can be less appealing to potential buyers due to noise pollution, safety concerns, and reduced privacy. As a result, investors may need to adjust their expected resale value lower to account for this negative factor. A general rule of thumb is to reduce the expected resale value by approximately 10 percent for properties on busy roads. However, the exact adjustment may vary depending on the specific location, type of road, and local market conditions.

Other negative impacts that may warrant value adjustments include:

- Poor school districts.
- High crime rates in the area.
- Proximity to industrial zones or other undesirable locations.
- Unusual or unconventional floor plans.
- Structural issues or significant repair needs.

In these cases, investors should carefully assess the potential impact on resale value and adjust their expectations accordingly. The magnitude of the adjustment will depend on the severity of the issue and the local market's tolerance for such factors.

Permit issues are another critical consideration when making value adjustments.

Permit Problems

A seemingly minor oversight in permit acquisition can lead to significant project delays and potential legal issues, as illustrated by a recent renovation experience of mine. In this case, the contract explicitly assigned responsibility for obtaining all necessary permits, including building and mechanical permits, to the contractor. Despite this clear stipulation, the project encountered a major setback five weeks into the renovation when the project manager made a startling discovery: The city had issued a red tag on the property.

A **red tag**, or stop work order, is a serious enforcement action taken by municipal authorities when construction or renovation work is being conducted without proper permits. This order halts all work on the site until the required permits are secured and any potential code violations are addressed. The situation not only caused unexpected delays but also raised concerns about the contractor's adherence to contractual obligations and local regulations.

The city and electrical inspector were furious, as a red tag can be a major headache, slowing everything down and often resulting in fines. However, because we had taken the proper steps and had a signed contract, the city expedited the process and fined the contractor instead. We ended up firing the contractor, and the city actually provided our permits faster because they sympathized with our situation.

When faced with these scenarios, which are bound to happen at some point in your flipping career, it's essential to meet with the city in person. I explained my hardship, the costs incurred due to the contractor's negligence, and my desire to complete the project correctly. Building a personal connection can help navigate these difficult situations and potentially avoid fines. Having a clear contract that specifies who is responsible for permits is crucial.

It's important to have a thorough due diligence process when evaluating potential flips. Investors should carefully review the property's history, including any modifications or improvements made by previous owners. If unpermitted work is discovered, investors must factor in the potential time and cost required to rectify the situation and obtain the necessary permits.

In some cases, the value adjustment for permit issues may need to be more significant than the standard 10 percent for busy roads (from the example above). The adjustment should account for the potential delays in completing the flip, additional holding costs, and the risk of not being able to obtain the required permits at all.

How can investors mitigate some of these risks?
- Include contingencies in their purchase offers that allow for a thorough inspection and due diligence period
- Work with experienced real estate attorneys and contractors who can help identify and resolve permit issues
- Build a buffer into project timelines and budgets to account for potential delays and additional costs

By making appropriate value adjustments and thoroughly evaluating each property's unique risks and challenges, real estate investors can make more informed decisions and set realistic return expectations for their flips. This approach helps to minimize surprises and ensures that investors are adequately compensated for the level of risk they are taking on with each project.

STARTING A BUDGET

Building a budget and pricing for your local market takes time, but getting a grasp of costs is essential for a fix-and-flipper. In the world of real estate investing, obtaining accurate bids from contractors is essential for creating a realistic budget and ensuring the profitability of a flip. I will discuss bids in more detail in Chapter 11. Eventually, you'll have created a budget for flipping houses that you can use to evaluate whether or not you can afford to make an offer on the property.

How do you actually build your budget? To build your budget, you will need the market install rates for the surfaces you will be updating/renovating. These will be the price per hour or the price per project that installers charge to work on your project. You can determine what the market install rates are by talking to contractors. Next, get professional inspections and contractor quotes to accurately budget all repair and rehabilitation costs down to each line item. Calculate the all-in acquisition costs, including the purchase price, closing costs, carrying costs, loan fees, and a contingency reserve.

The next thing you need to know is your vendor pricing. Understanding vendor pricing is a critical step in home building or renovation. The process of obtaining this information is straightforward—simply ask stores or suppliers for average price ranges and use this data to establish your allowances. Having these predetermined price points helps in setting realistic allowances for different projects. By applying this method to flooring and other building materials, you'll create comprehensive specifications sheets ("spec sheets") that streamline your budgeting process and maintain consistency across various projects. I'll explain spec sheets in detail in Chapter 11.

Market-specific permit costs are very important. Permit costs can vary significantly from one city to another, and these differences can have a substantial impact on your project budget. Research and understand permit costs for each city where you plan to work. When building your budgets, investigate not only permit fees but also connection and utility costs. These expenses can quickly add up to thousands of dollars.

If you're uncertain about exact costs in a particular area, it's wise to budget for the higher end of permit costs across all your projects.

This approach provides a buffer in cities with lower fees. During your research, inquire about submittal times as well. Understanding how long the permitting process takes in each jurisdiction is vital for project planning and scheduling. Services from permit-related professionals, such as architects, engineers, and surveyors, often have varying fees based on project size. Engage with these teams to understand their costs and timelines. This information allows you to budget accurately and plan for when these professionals need to start their work.

You will also want to model different scenarios, like if it takes longer to renovate or if you have to sell for less than projected. Scrutinize every number and assumption to identify all possible risks and pitfalls. Only once you have stress tested the deal through comprehensive underwriting (which I will cover in the next chapter) should you move forward, and then only if the projected returns outweigh the estimated risks based on your investment criteria.

By taking the time to thoroughly research and understand all the costs involved in flipping a house, you can create a detailed and accurate budget that accounts for all of your expenses. This budget should include a buffer for unexpected costs and contingencies, as well as a realistic timeline for completing the renovations and selling the property. By staying organized and disciplined throughout the process, you can minimize your financial risks and increase your chances of a successful and profitable house flip. Flipping houses is not a get rich quick scheme but rather a serious investment strategy that requires careful planning, hard work, and a willingness to learn from others.

CHAPTER 6
CORE UNDERWRITING TECHNIQUES

It's not the will to win that matters—everyone has that.
It's the will to prepare to win that matters.
—PAUL "BEAR" BRYANT, FORMER HEAD COACH,
UNIVERSITY OF ALABAMA FOOTBALL TEAM

UNDERWRITING IS ONE of the single most important skills to have as a real estate investor. It's how you evaluate risk and protect yourself while conducting business. If you are off on your underwriting or your numbers are a little skewed, it can lead to detrimental consequences: loss of profit, buying the wrong deal, or having to leave too much cash in a deal, which is going to really affect your metrics down the road.

Underwriting is the process of rigorously analyzing a potential real estate investment deal to assess its risks and profit potential. Underwriting is different for every type of asset class, whether it's a fix-and-flip property, a BRRRR deal, or apartment building development. You have to look at each one differently. But it all really comes down to the same core mechanics. **Flip underwriting, specifically, is the process of evaluating a home's potential future market value, while creating the renovation plan and budget to get it to that new established value.** Then, you calculate the potential profit after all costs, which would include soft costs and hard costs. **Soft costs** are typically going to be your development costs, utility costs, debt service, and other general expenses to carry the investment. **Hard costs** are the fixed, direct expenses related to the physical construction or renovation of a property. They include acquisition costs like the purchase price, closing costs, and transfer taxes. Site work expenses such as demolition, grading, and landscaping are also hard costs.

A major hard cost is construction materials—everything from lumber and drywall to flooring, cabinets, countertops, and finishes. Labor is another key hard cost, covering general contractors, subcontractors, electricians, plumbers, and other skilled tradespeople. Don't forget permits, inspection fees, and other regulatory costs. Permanent fixtures like appliances, lighting, and plumbing fixtures are hard costs, as are architectural and engineering fees for designs and structural work. Budget for equipment, tool rentals, and insurances too. Finally, be sure to include a contingency reserve to cover any unexpected overruns. Accurately capturing all these hard costs during underwriting is essential to properly assess a potential flip's profitability and avoid eroded margins that could derail the entire project. Underwriting is key to any successful flipping business.

Underwriting in real estate helps establish the "as is" value of a property. The **"as is" value** refers to the current market value of the property in its existing condition, without any repairs or improvements. This is important because it serves as the baseline for determining the potential profitability of the investment. The purpose of underwriting is not only to assess risk and ensure a safe investment but also to identify opportunities to maximize value. By understanding the "as is" value, investors can determine if there is potential to add value through renovations, improvements, or by capitalizing on the property's highest and best use. In addition to evaluating risk, underwriting involves analyzing various factors that influence a property's value, such as location, condition, zoning, and market trends.

The "as is" value will be very important when it comes to financing your flip. This can significantly impact the terms of your financing and the amount of capital you'll need to contribute. The "as is" value will be a key factor in determining your **loan-to-value (LTV) ratio**, which is the ratio of the loan amount to the property's appraised value. The LTV is crucial because it affects how much of a down payment the lender will require and how much they are willing to finance for the construction or renovation costs. A lower "as is" value could result in a higher LTV, which may require a larger down payment from you or limit the amount the lender is willing to finance for the project.

Additionally, if you're seeking financing from more traditional lenders or banks, they may place greater emphasis on your personal credentials, credit history, and overall financial strength, in addition to evaluating the specific deal itself. Regardless of the lender's specific requirements, understanding the "as is" value represents the true starting point of your investment. It allows you to accurately assess the potential return on investment and ensure that you're not overpaying for the property's current condition relative to its potential future value after renovations.

ESTABLISHING YOUR "AS IS" VALUE

If you're concerned about the risks associated with flipping properties, one of the best strategies is to aim to purchase the property below its "as is" value. This creates what is known as a "walk-in margin," or instant equity from the moment you acquire the property. Let's say a property's current market value or "as is" value is $450,000. If you can negotiate and purchase that property for $400,000, you immediately have a $50,000 walk-in margin, or equity cushion, on the day you close the deal. This walk-in margin acts as a built-in safety net, reducing your overall investment risk. The deeper you can acquire a property below its "as is" value, the safer the investment becomes, because you've already secured equity from the start.

If you solely focus on the potential forced equity or value-add position after completing renovations, you could end up paying above market value for the property initially. This can be problematic, because if the market conditions suddenly shift or cool down, you may find yourself in a position where you've overpaid, and it becomes challenging to recoup that loss or generate the desired profit margins. Carefully analyze these metrics and strategically pursue walk-in margins whenever possible.

During cooler market conditions, it may be prudent to adjust your requirements and aim for deeper walk-in margins to mitigate risks further. Conversely, in hotter markets, you may be more flexible and willing to pay closer to the "as is" value, as long as the potential post-renovation profits align with your goals. Regardless of market conditions, it's essential not to skip these steps in the underwriting process. Continuously learning and refining your underwriting skills, especially if you're new to the field, will help you make more informed decisions and increase your chances of success in real estate investing.

THE HIGHEST AND BEST USE VALUE

After establishing the "as is" value, the next step in the underwriting process is to determine the property's highest and best use, also known as the **future market value (FMV)** or **after-repair value (ARV)**. This involves evaluating how the property can be optimized or improved to achieve its maximum potential value. For example, let's consider a property with a 1,000-square-foot, two-bedroom, one-bathroom house upstairs and an additional 1,000 square feet of unfinished basement space. In this scenario, the highest and best use analysis would explore ways to maximize the property's value, such as:

- **Finishing the basement:** Converting the unfinished basement into livable space or potentially adding another bathroom or additional bedrooms can significantly increase the overall square footage and, consequently, the property's value.
- **Calculating square footage value:** Properties are typically valued based on price per square foot, so increasing the livable square footage can directly impact the property's overall value.

The goal is to determine how the property can be renovated or improved to maximize its value based on the highest price per square foot achievable in that market. This may involve finishing previously unfinished spaces, adding square footage through additions or expansions, or reconfiguring the layout to create more desirable living spaces. Once the highest-and-best-use scenario is identified, the next step is to calculate the associated costs required to execute the planned improvements or renovations. This cost analysis will help determine the feasibility of the project and whether the potential increase in value justifies the investment. The highest-and-best-use analysis should consider not only physical improvements but also factors such as zoning regulations, neighborhood characteristics, and market demand for different property types or configurations. By evaluating the highest and best use, investors can make informed decisions about the most profitable way to utilize a property, maximizing its potential value while carefully weighing the costs and potential return on investment.

While aiming for the highest and best use by maximizing the finished square footage can be desirable, it's not always the smartest approach. It's crucial to consider the potential return on investment and ensure that the planned improvements or renovations don't exceed the property's maximum value potential in that particular area or market. For example, let's say you purchase a property for $450,000 and invest $150,000 in renovations to maximize the square footage and achieve the highest and best use.

If the highest comparable property in that area is only valued at $800,000, you may have "topped out," or exceeded the maximum value potential for that property, regardless of the improvements made. In such a scenario, it would be more prudent to optimize the improvements and renovations to achieve a healthy profit margin while staying within the area's value limits. An alternative plan could be to purchase the same property for $450,000, invest only $50,000 in renovations, and sell it for $650,000, which may provide a better overall return on investment.

The concept of highest and best use is not solely about maximizing the sales price or obtaining the highest possible value; rather, it's about determining the optimal improvements or utilization that will generate the most profitable return while considering the area's value constraints. The goal should be to strike a balance between maximizing the property's potential and ensuring that the investment in improvements or renovations doesn't exceed the potential return or market value in that specific location. Ultimately, the highest-and-best-use analysis should focus on identifying the most profitable strategy for that particular property, taking into account the area's market dynamics and value limitations.

TIMELINE CONSIDERATIONS FOR HIGHEST AND BEST USE

During times of market uncertainty or economic concerns, such as recessions, the approach to evaluating the highest and best use for a flip project needs to be more cautious and risk averse. A key strategy to reduce risk in such conditions is to prioritize shorter project timelines over maximizing potential value through extensive renovations. When underwriting a property, I consider not only the potential profit margins but also the expected project duration. While a longer, more extensive renovation may dramatically increase the property's value, it also exposes the investment to greater market volatility and potential risks, especially in a questionable market. Instead, a safer approach is to aim for quicker projects with shorter timelines, even if it means sacrificing some potential profit margin.

For example, rather than pursuing a twelve-month renovation plan, I may opt for a more modest scope of work, focusing on essential updates or renovations that can be completed within a shorter time frame, such as six months or less. By minimizing the project duration, I limit my exposure to adverse market shifts or corrections that could occur over a longer period. Shorter timelines reduce the risk of being caught in a rapidly declining market, which could potentially erode or eliminate any anticipated profits. Furthermore, expediting projects often involves streamlining processes, such as obtaining permits more efficiently or coordinating contractors effectively. This not only accelerates the timeline but also minimizes carrying costs and potential holding expenses, further reducing risk exposure.

In a stable or appreciating market, longer renovation timelines may be more viable, as the potential value increase could outweigh the additional market risk. Conversely, in volatile or declining markets, prioritizing shorter flips with tighter margins becomes a more prudent risk-management strategy. Ultimately, the goal is to strike a balance between maximizing potential profits and managing risk exposure based on current market conditions. By considering project timelines and adapting the highest-and-best-use approach accordingly, experienced flippers can navigate varying market cycles while minimizing risks and optimizing returns.

EXIT STRATEGY OPTIONS

When determining the highest and best use for a property, consider various exit strategies, as this will impact your overall approach and risk assessment. Having multiple viable exit strategies can significantly reduce the overall risk associated with a particular investment. When evaluating a property, I may be willing to offer a higher purchase price with a smaller profit margin if the deal presents multiple potential exit avenues, as this flexibility reduces the risk exposure. Some common exit strategies in real estate investing include:

- **Fix-and-flip:** This strategy involves purchasing a property, renovating or improving it, and then reselling it for a profit in a relatively short time frame. In this scenario, the focus is typically on the "as is" value and any potential forced appreciation that can be achieved through minor improvements or updates. The goal is to purchase the property below market value, complete any necessary cosmetic work, and then resell it quickly to realize a profit margin.
- **Buy and hold:** In this approach, the property is purchased and held as a long-term rental investment, generating passive income from rental payments over an extended period. To execute this strategy effectively, conduct a thorough analysis during the underwriting process, considering factors such as potential rental income, expenses, cash flow, and overall ROI. This analysis will

help determine if the property is suitable for a buy and hold exit strategy, should the need arise.

- **Wholesaling:** This strategy involves securing a property under contract and then assigning or selling the contract to another investor for a predetermined fee without ever taking ownership of the property.
- **Seller financing:** The investor acts as the lender, providing financing to the buyer in exchange for periodic payments and interest, effectively creating a passive income stream.
- **Rent-to-own:** The investor purchases the property and leases it to a tenant with an option to purchase the property after a specified period, potentially at a predetermined price.

By considering multiple exit strategies during the underwriting process, I can evaluate the potential risks and returns associated with each scenario. For instance, if market conditions become unfavorable for a quick resale (fix-and-flip), I may pivot to a buy and hold strategy, allowing me to generate rental income until conditions improve for a more profitable sale. Additionally, when underwriting a deal with a tighter profit margin, the presence of multiple exit strategies can justify a higher purchase price, as the flexibility reduces the overall risk exposure. However, it's essential to factor in the potential holding period for each exit strategy, as prolonged holding times can impact cash flow and overall returns. Ultimately, by considering various exit strategies during the underwriting process, investors can make more informed decisions, manage risk effectively, and maximize returns by capitalizing on the most favorable exit opportunity based on market conditions and individual investment goals.

GETTING STARTED UNDERWRITING

To begin the underwriting process, the first step is to obtain comprehensive property details. This includes specifications such as the lot size, buildable square footage, and other relevant information. You'll need to review the location to ensure it fits within your predetermined investment criteria (your buy box), identify any potential negative impacts, establish a future market value, create a detailed budget for renovations or improvements, and ultimately calculate the profitability using a tool like the flip calculator. The ARV is the estimated market value of the property after completing the planned renovations and improvements. This is the difference you often see in the "before" and "after" photos on social media and reality shows about flipping houses. Understanding the "as is" value allows you to assess how much you are paying for the property in its current state compared to its potential value after renovations (ARV).

The primary source for obtaining property details is the tax record. When an investment opportunity is presented to you, your first action should be pulling the tax record for that specific property. Tax records are public information and provide detailed specifications about the property. States and counties typically have an online public web search or interactive map where you can enter the property address and access the tax record information. In your local area, you may have a dedicated website that allows you to input an address and retrieve all the relevant property specifications from the tax records. If you're unable to locate this resource, reach out to a trusted real estate broker or professional within your network.

They should be able to assist you in obtaining the tax record information, either by accessing public records, the MLS, or specialized software that consolidates property data from various sources. Leveraging the expertise and resources of your real estate team, such as brokers or agents, is a valuable way for them to add value to your investment process. By delegating tasks like property data retrieval to the appropriate professionals, you can focus your efforts on the critical aspects of underwriting and deal analysis. It's essential to have accurate and up-to-date property details, as this information forms the foundation for your underwriting calculations and investment decisions. By starting with the tax record and leveraging the resources available to you, you can ensure that you have the necessary data to proceed with a comprehensive underwriting process and make informed investment choices.

When analyzing the property details, the lot size will help you identify similar properties in the area, which is essential for accurately assessing the potential value. The year the property was built is also a critical factor to consider. Not only does it indicate the age of the structure, but it also provides insights into potential renovation costs and the degree of modifications required. Older properties may necessitate more extensive renovations or updates to meet modern building codes and standards, which can impact the overall budget and timelines for the project. Additionally, the age of the property can dictate the architectural style and floor plan layout, which may influence the extent of renovations or reconfiguration required to optimize the property's highest and best use.

Properties built within a specific era often share similar construction methods and floor plan designs, making it easier to identify comparable properties for valuation purposes. When compiling a list of comps, it's advisable to stay within a ten-year range of the subject property's construction year. For instance, if the property in question was built in 1920, you would look for comps built between 1910 and 1930. This approach ensures that you're comparing properties with similar characteristics, construction methods, and architectural styles, which can help provide a more accurate valuation.

One of the key objectives in the underwriting process is to determine the potential for increasing the finished square footage, as this can directly impact the property's value. By analyzing the existing floor plans and exploring possibilities for additions, expansions, or reconfiguring the layout, you can identify opportunities to maximize the usable space and, consequently, the potential sales price or rental income. Consider not only the physical structure but also the local zoning regulations, building codes, and any potential restrictions that may impact your ability to modify or expand the property. Consulting with architects, contractors, and local authorities can help you navigate these considerations and develop a comprehensive plan to optimize the property's highest and best use while staying within the bounds of regulatory requirements.

If, for example, a property has 1,000 square feet of unfinished space in the basement, but I have to spend $100 per square foot to get that finished space, that's going to cost me $100,000. If it drastically increases the value, though, that's a win. Maybe it costs me $100 per square foot to finish that space, but the ARV is $400 per square foot, which is huge. There's my margin right there, so it's important to note those unfinished spaces.

The next thing you want to underwrite is your location. Location is a critical factor that can dramatically influence a property's resale value and potential returns. The real estate mantra "location, location, location" is repeated for a reason—it underscores the profound impact that a property's location can have on its marketability and overall value. In highly desirable or supply-constrained areas, location becomes even more paramount, as developable land is finite and in high demand. This scarcity can create significant variations in property values, even within a relatively small geographic area. For instance, in the central district of Seattle, a prime neighborhood, the difference in values between properties just a couple of blocks apart can be as high as 10 percent.

This means that a property valued at $800,000 on 28th Street could potentially have a comparable property valued at $1 million on 30th Street, just a stone's throw away. Such drastic variations in value within a localized area highlight the importance of thoroughly understanding the nuances and dynamics that shape a specific location's desirability. Factors such as proximity to amenities, school districts, crime rates, and accessibility can all contribute to these micro-level differences in property values. As an investor, a thorough understanding of the local real estate market is crucial, as is being able to recognize and analyze the factors that drive value from one street to the next. Failing to account for these location-specific variables can lead to inaccurate valuations, missed opportunities, or potentially overpaying for a property that may not yield the expected returns.

When evaluating properties in metropolitan areas, consider amenities that cater to the specific needs and preferences of urban buyers. One key factor is the availability of secure parking facilities, such as garages or dedicated parking spaces. In today's climate of heightened security concerns, particularly in densely populated areas, buyers prioritize privacy and the ability to protect their possessions, making secure parking a highly sought-after feature.

The growing adoption of electric vehicles (EVs) has created a demand for charging stations, which are often more accessible in properties with garages or dedicated parking areas. The absence of these amenities can be a deal-breaker for some buyers, potentially impacting the property's marketability and value. Basic needs, such as secure parking, combined with conveniences like EV charging stations, can significantly influence a property's perceived value, especially in metropolitan regions. In markets like Seattle, the lack of parking facilities can result in a substantial price drop, ranging from 10 to 20 percent, highlighting the importance of this amenity for urban buyers. By thoroughly evaluating the availability and condition of amenities like parking and EV charging stations, you can better understand the property's appeal to potential buyers and accurately assess its market value within the local context.

UNDERSTANDING NEGATIVE IMPACTS WHEN UNDERWRITING

It's important to pay attention to those negative impacts as you're underwriting. While you're underwriting to determine whether or not a deal has the potential to be successful, the bottom line is knowing you have to eventually sell this property once the renovations are complete. When you're looking at the path of progress on these flips, that is the secret sauce—not just for flips, but also for BRRRR properties. These paths to progress are like opportunity zones, meaning there's tax incentives for businesses and developers to put money into certain class areas. You can literally google "opportunity zone in your area" and it'll pull up a map of those areas. These companies are getting tax incentives and tax breaks to put money into the community. This means more stores are coming and therefore more infrastructure is coming.

Those are great places to do flips and buy and holds because the overall neighborhood is improving. When that starts up and moves forward, that creates buzz. Then more and more people move to these areas. If there was a lot of crime, for example, a path of progress also brings in more police so that crime will drop, and it becomes even more beneficial. Then there's more jobs, more schools, and so on.

In Seattle, we were actively involved in flipping single-family homes, where we would acquire properties, enhance the landscaping, and resell them at a higher value. However, during this time, the city implemented a massive upzoning initiative that eliminated single-family zoning restrictions. This zoning change had a significant impact on property values.

For homeowners and investors alike, the upzoning meant that their previously single-family-zoned properties now had the potential for higher-density development, effectively increasing their value. The underlying principle is that if buyers perceive a property to have greater potential or versatility, they are willing to pay a premium for it. In the case of upzoning, the perception of increased value stemmed from the newfound ability to develop the land more densely, potentially for multi-family or mixed-use purposes. However, progress and development can also have negative consequences on property values in certain scenarios. For instance, if a previously well-established, desirable single-family residential street undergoes upzoning, allowing for the construction of multifamily dwellings or high-density developments, it could potentially diminish the value of the existing single-family homes in that area.

The introduction of higher-density housing, increased traffic, and potential changes to the character of the neighborhood could adversely impact the desirability and perceived value of the remaining single-family properties. Therefore, when evaluating the potential impact of progress and development on property values, consider both the positive and negative implications. While upzoning and increased development potential can drive up values in some cases, it can also lead to a decrease in value for existing properties that may no longer align with the changing character and dynamics of the area. As real estate investors, it's essential to stay informed about zoning changes, development plans, and the potential impacts they may have on the specific areas and properties we invest in. By thoroughly understanding these factors during the underwriting process, we can make more informed decisions and better anticipate potential shifts in value, whether positive or negative.

TWO TYPES OF COMPS FOR UNDERWRITING

When underwriting a deal, we pull two types of comparable properties (comps). First, we look at comps that represent the property's highest and best use, considering the maximum buildable square footage. Then, we analyze like-for-like comps with similar finishes, square footage, bedrooms, and bathrooms, representing the property in its current condition.

For both sets of comps, we consider several key factors.

- **Year built:** We look at properties built within ten to fifteen years on either side of the subject property's construction year
- **Lot size:** We aim for comps with similar lot sizes, typically within a quarter-acre range
- **Usable land:** If a property has unusable land (heavily wooded or sloped), we compare it to comps with smaller but more usable lots
- **Total square footage:** We look at the overall livable square footage of the property
- **Bedroom and bathroom count:** Consider the number of bedrooms and bathrooms
- **Parking:** Type of parking (garage, carport, driveway) are factored in
- **Style code:** We consider the architectural style of the property (ranch, two story, split-level)
- **Comp radius:** In metro areas, we keep the comp radius very tight, often within a tenth of a mile, as property values can vary significantly between streets. In rural areas, we may expand the radius up to five miles, as longer commutes are more common

Once we have the property specs and comps, we run two different calculations to estimate renovation costs.

1. Price-per-square-foot model (simple):
   - Cosmetic updates: $50/sq. ft.
   - Full rehab (no layout changes): $75/sq. ft.
   - Studs-down renovation or finishing square footage: $100–$125/sq. ft.
2. Cosmetic-plus system (itemized):
   - Itemize costs based on individual components (roof, electrical, plumbing, HVAC)

For a quick estimate, we often use $50/sq. ft. for cosmetic updates and then add itemized costs for major systems or components as needed.

To find accurate local costs, networking with other investors and contractors is essential.

After calculating the renovation costs and potential ARV, we input these numbers into a pro forma to determine the net profit, total cash required, and cash-on-cash return. This analysis helps us evaluate whether a deal aligns with our investment criteria and decide if it's worth pursuing further.

SYSTEMS AND TOOLS FOR UNDERWRITING

Efficient property analysis is crucial for successful real estate investing. Utilizing software that automatically pulls comps can significantly streamline your underwriting process. Having immediate access to comps when reviewing a property record allows for quick initial assessments of a property's potential, helping you determine whether further investigation is warranted. When setting up your underwriting process, the goal should be to reach a comprehensive analysis as swiftly as possible. This efficiency is vital to avoid wasting valuable time on properties that don't meet your investment criteria. Therefore, prioritize software with robust auto-comparable features.

Look for platforms that provide visual data on comparable properties and recent sales. The ability to view images of comps is invaluable for evaluating potential renovations and estimating costs. If your chosen software doesn't include this feature, ensure you have a systematic process in place to access this information through alternative means. Some applications offer rehab photos, allowing you to assess the property's condition and estimate the scope of work required. This feature can be particularly useful in determining the appropriate purchase price and potential profit margin. Companies like Property Radar, Privvy, and PropStream can provide you with the purchase price, the sold price, and the interior/exterior photos of the property—which can help you build your scope of work and budget.

Real estate investors use different calculators for various stages of the investment process to balance speed and accuracy. An underwriting calculator provides quick initial estimates with 90–95 percent accuracy, allowing for rapid decision-making when submitting offers. This tool is especially useful for assessing multiple properties efficiently. A more detailed construction calculator, while time consuming, offers precise cost estimates. This secondary tool is crucial for budgeting once a property is acquired and is typically used by project managers for estimating, scheduling, and budget management.

USING A FLIP CALCULATOR

Investment profitability is a crucial calculation that determines the potential profit margin of a flip project after accounting for all associated costs. To accurately assess profitability, you need a reliable flip calculator. This calculator helps you adjust various factors, such as rates, costs, and sales prices, to evaluate the viability of a deal and determine if it aligns with your investment criteria. You can find a flip calculator spreadsheet at www.BiggerPockets.com/FrameworkBonus.

The flip calculator considers the following key elements:

- **After-repair value (ARV) or future market value:** The estimated sales price of the property after completing all planned renovations and improvements
- **Sales costs:** Expenses related to selling the property, such as real estate commissions, closing costs, and transfer fees
- **Rehab costs:** The total cost of renovations, including materials, labor, and any contingency reserves
- **Acquisition costs:** The purchase price of the property, closing costs, and any other up-front expenses
- **Lending and debt costs:** Interest payments, origination fees, and any other costs associated with financing the project
- **Soft costs:** Variable expenses such as utilities, holding costs, staging, and miscellaneous costs incurred during the renovation process

After inputting these costs, the flip calculator will provide you with the total profitability figure, which is the estimated net profit you can expect to earn from the project. Additionally, the calculator should also calculate your cash-on-cash return, which is a crucial metric discussed in the "buy box" section. This metric evaluates the return on your actual cash investment, taking into account any financing or leverage used in the deal. There are various flip calculators online that work like spreadsheets, but a basic flip calculator works like this:

$$\frac{\text{Potential}}{\text{Profit}} = \text{ARV} - \frac{\text{Sales}}{\text{Costs}} - \frac{\text{Rehab}}{\text{Costs}} - \frac{\text{Acquisition}}{\text{Costs}} - \frac{\text{Lending/}}{\text{Debt Costs}} - \frac{\text{Soft}}{\text{Costs}}$$

To calculate the cash-on-cash return, the formula would be:

$$\text{Cash-on-Cash Return} = \text{Potential Profit} \div \text{Total Cash Invested}$$

$$\frac{\text{Where Total}}{\text{Cash Invested}} = \frac{\text{Acquisition}}{\text{Costs}} + \frac{\text{Rehab}}{\text{Costs}} + \frac{\text{Soft}}{\text{Costs}} - \frac{\text{Borrowed Funds}}{\text{(Any Financing)}}$$

The flip calculator's profitability figure and the cash-on-cash return should align with your predetermined investment criteria (a.k.a. your buy box). If the calculated profitability and return meet or exceed your target numbers, the deal may be worth pursuing. However, if the numbers fall short, you may need to adjust your offer price or reconsider the deal altogether. Ultimately, your buy box helps you run the numbers, and the flip calculator serves as a powerful tool for assessing the potential profitability of a flip project, allowing you to make informed decisions based on your investment goals and risk tolerance. By carefully evaluating all costs and projected returns, you can increase your chances of success and maximize your profits in the competitive world of real estate investing.

I can go into any market and start breaking these types of numbers down because I've underwritten so many different types of properties, so don't be overwhelmed in the beginning. Just take your time to learn these systems and double-check your math. I've also been through over 3,000 transactions, so I've seen how deals have worked out or not, but underwriting is a key step.

By accurately assessing the optimal improvements, renovations, or alternative uses that maximize a property's value, you can secure these overlooked properties at incredible margins. This level of expertise enables you to capitalize on opportunities that the majority of investors miss, allowing you to achieve superior returns on your investments.

While others may be deterred by the perceived risks or complexities, your mastery of underwriting equips you with the knowledge and confidence to navigate these scenarios successfully.

By thoroughly analyzing the numbers, identifying the highest and best use, and executing a well-crafted plan, you can transform undervalued properties into highly profitable investments. This ability to uncover hidden value and operate in a space where few others are willing to tread sets you apart from the competition and positions you for exceptional returns in the real estate market.

One example of this is when my company bought a property on the market for $2.6 million. We put $1.4 million in, and we sold it for $6 million, making $1 million on a deal that anyone could have bought, as it was publicly listed. But it was putting the right plan on it for highest and best use and then maximizing that and making sure the value was locked down that led to our success. The property had actually been listed for years, and everyone had passed on it. It wasn't a unicorn great buy or anything like that; in fact, we paid market value. But underwriting to highest and best use and putting the right plan together made the difference.

DON'T OVERLOOK CRITICAL FACTORS

In 2010, I learned a valuable lesson about the importance of thorough underwriting, when I purchased a property adjacent to a gun range. One of my brokers brought the deal to me, stating that I could acquire the split-level home for $250,000 and resell it for $450,000 after a cosmetic update. He assured me that a comprehensive inspection wasn't necessary, as our team had a well-established system for quick cosmetic flips.

Trusting his assessment, I proceeded with the deal without personally inspecting the property. The comparable properties in the area seemed to align, with similar square footage, bedroom count, and bathroom count. The listing even described the property as "quaint" and backing up to a park, which seemed like a desirable feature. However, after listing the property, I soon realized the critical oversight in my underwriting process. Prospective buyers started complaining about the noise levels, prompting me to investigate further. It turned out that within a mile of the property was an active gun range, creating a persistent and disruptive noise akin to a war zone. To salvage the deal, I had to adjust my marketing strategy and significantly reduce the listing price by approximately 20 percent, ultimately selling the property at a loss after factoring in the necessary price concession.

This experience taught me a valuable lesson: No matter how seemingly straightforward a deal may appear, thorough underwriting is essential. Overlooking critical factors can have severe consequences, eroding potential profits or even resulting in losses. Since then, I have become more diligent in my underwriting process, accounting for various factors that could impact a property's value and desirability. Elements such as traffic congestion from nearby stop signs, proximity to commercial spaces, or undesirable neighbors are all factored into my calculations. While these issues may not deter me from pursuing a deal entirely, they do warrant adjustments to my flip calculator and buy box parameters.

For instance, if a property has an undesirable neighbor, I may reduce the estimated value by 10 percent. Similarly, if the property is situated on a busy road, I might apply a 10 percent discount to account for the potential impact on marketability and resale value. These numerical adjustments help me define realistic metrics and set appropriate buy box criteria, ensuring that I accurately assess the true potential of a property and mitigate potential risks or surprises during the investment life cycle. Through this experience, I learned the hard way that comprehensive underwriting is not a luxury but a necessity in the world of real estate investing. By meticulously evaluating all factors that could influence a property's value and desirability, I can make informed decisions, manage risks effectively, and maximize my chances of achieving profitable outcomes.

CHAPTER 7
OFFER STRATEGIES

*Football isn't necessarily won by the best players.
It's won by the team with the best attitude.*

**—GEORGE ALLEN, COACH, LOS ANGELES RAMS AND
WASHINGTON COMMANDERS**

NOW THAT YOU'VE found a deal, completed your market research, and executed some serious underwriting, it's time to make an offer on the property. Making an offer can be a complex process, especially with fix-and-flip properties.

TYPES OF TRANSACTIONS

In our real estate community, the types of transactions we see most are purchase contracts, auctions, assignment/LLC transfers, and direct-to-seller.

Purchase contract. This is when you enter into purchase and sale contract terms directly with a seller or representative broker. It's used with direct-to-sellers and on-market transactions, and it's one of the best ways to negotiate your own terms for closing. Rather than working with a wholesaler who sets up the terms, you have a say in this scenario to set up your own terms. Basically, it's an A-to-B transaction. I prefer to be the one negotiating the terms. There's also not a wholesaler on the deal, so there's no assignment fee, and you can get right to the decision-makers and close the deal as efficiently as possible.

Public auction. A public auction is a process where properties are sold to the highest bidder through an open and transparent bidding process. In real estate, public auctions can take place for various reasons, such as foreclosures, bankruptcy proceedings, or estate sales.

There are typically two types of public auctions.

- **Trustee auctions:** In these auctions, a court-appointed trustee is responsible for overseeing the sale of the property. This often occurs when a property has gone through foreclosure, and the lender has taken possession. The trustee's role is to ensure a fair and impartial auction process to recover as much of the outstanding debt as possible.
- **Auction service companies:** These are third-party companies that specialize in conducting public auctions for real estate properties. Sellers (such as banks, asset management companies, or individual owners) hire these companies to facilitate the auction process. Examples of well-known auction service companies include auction.com, realtybid.com, and xome.com.

Public auctions can be conducted both on-site (physical location) and online. Online platforms have gained popularity, as they conveniently allow bidders from anywhere to participate in the auction process. The auction process typically involves registering as a bidder, submitting a refundable deposit or proof of funds, and participating in the live bidding. Properties are sold to the highest bidder, subject to meeting any reserve prices or minimum bids set by the seller or trustee.

Public auctions can present opportunities for investors to acquire properties at potentially discounted prices, but they also come with risks. Thorough due diligence, understanding the auction terms and conditions, and having the necessary funds readily available are crucial for successful participation in public auctions.

You can bid online or at the courthouse steps. In many cases, there's a 10 percent cash or check deposit required, and the auction winner has thirty days to close the sale. However, there are some "buyer beware" scenarios to think about: There's no title insurance; you may have to deal with a tenant-occupied property; there's no inspection and more often than not, you have to buy sight unseen; this could be a distress sale or bank foreclosure.

One difficult situation here might be a homeowner who got foreclosed on but didn't leave in their vacant window (where I live, a tenant has about twenty days to exit, but it's different in every state). Now you have to make them leave, perhaps with the aid of a sheriff. This could take months of your time (maybe four to five months for eviction) just to get full ownership of the property.

When participating in a public auction, use a third-party company, such as a title representative, who can conduct thorough research and pull information on any existing liens, foreclosure proceedings, or outstanding back taxes on the property. This due diligence helps ensure that you're aware of any potential encumbrances or financial obligations that may come with the property, safeguarding your investment. **Liens** are legal claims or rights against a property, often resulting from unpaid debts or obligations, such as mortgage loans, tax liabilities, or contractor fees.

You can learn more about bidding on foreclosed properties in *Bidding to Buy: A Step-by-Step Guide to Investing in Real Estate Foreclosures*, by Aaron Amuchastegui and David Osborn (www.BiggerPockets.com/ReadBidding).

Back taxes refer to unpaid property taxes that may have accumulated over time. Failing to address these issues could result in additional financial burdens or potential legal disputes after the purchase. Despite the risks, public auctions can present exceptional opportunities for investors to acquire properties at significantly discounted prices that others may have overlooked. Investing in land at auctions is also a viable strategy, as many bidders primarily focus on residential properties, leaving land parcels with potentially attractive pricing. To facilitate the bidding process, you can collaborate with a hard-money lender or investment company that can attend the auction on your behalf and provide immediate cash payment if you secure a winning bid.

This approach ensures that you have the necessary funds readily available to complete the transaction. However, it's important to note that bidding service companies or auction platforms typically charge additional fees, often ranging from 3 to 5 percent of the purchase price, to facilitate the bidding process and handle the associated paperwork and logistics. These fees should be factored into your overall investment calculations and projections. While public auctions present unique opportunities, it's crucial to thoroughly understand the process, conduct comprehensive due diligence, and be prepared to address any potential encumbrances or financial obligations associated with the property. Working with experienced professionals and having a solid plan in place can help mitigate risks and increase the chances of a successful acquisition.

Assignments. An assignment in real estate refers to the process of transferring one party's rights and obligations under an existing real estate contract to another party. It's a common practice used by real estate investors and wholesalers as an alternative to directly buying and selling properties. In an assignment transaction, the original party (often referred to as the "assignor") holds a contract to purchase a property, typically at a favorable price or terms. Instead of completing the purchase themselves, they transfer (or "assign") their contractual rights and obligations to a new party (the "assignee") for an agreed-upon fee, known as the "assignment fee."

It's important to note that an assignment does not involve the direct transfer or sale of the property itself. Instead, it deals with the transfer of the rights and obligations under the existing purchase contract between the original parties.

For investors or wholesalers buying assignment contracts, it's crucial to thoroughly review the terms and conditions of the original purchase contract before signing an agreement. Pay close attention to the assignment fee, which is the compensation you'll need to pay the assignor for taking over their contract.

Here are some key terms to understand in an assignment transaction:

- **Assignor:** The original party holding the purchase contract who assigns their rights and obligations to another party
- **Assignee:** The party receiving the assignment and taking over the rights and obligations of the original purchase contract
- **Assignment fee:** The fee paid by the assignee to the assignor for the transfer of the contract rights and obligations
- **Purchase contract:** The original legally binding agreement between the seller and the assignor, which outlines the terms and conditions of the property purchase

It's essential to read and understand the purchase contract thoroughly before entering into an assignment agreement. As the assignee, you are not in direct negotiation with the seller but rather agreeing to the terms and conditions set forth in the original purchase contract. Assignments can be a viable strategy for real estate investors and wholesalers, but they require careful due diligence and a clear understanding of the contractual obligations and potential risks involved.

As mentioned earlier, for me, the higher the assignment fee, the better the deal should be. However, as long as the deal fits my investment criteria and the numbers work in my favor, I don't haggle over a wholesaler's fees. There was one instance where I paid a friend and wholesaler an assignment fee of $175,000. While it was a substantial fee, he presented me with an exceptional deal that allowed me to achieve a 50 percent return on my investment, far exceeding the typical 30 percent return.

In the end, we both made a significant profit, and everyone involved was satisfied with the outcome. It's important to remember that real estate is not just a transactional business; it's a relationship-driven industry. Rather than solely focusing on nickel-and-diming fees, it's often more beneficial to prioritize building strong, mutually beneficial relationships with wholesalers and other industry professionals. When all parties can make money and find success, it creates a win-win scenario. By cultivating these relationships and maintaining a mindset of shared success, the potential for lucrative opportunities will naturally follow.

Purchasing under an LLC

It's common for investors to purchase properties using an LLC. An **LLC**, or limited liability company, is a legal business structure that provides a layer of protection for real estate investors by separating their personal assets from their business assets. This separation is important for mitigating risk and safeguarding personal wealth in the event of legal disputes, lawsuits, or financial difficulties related to the investment property. When you create an LLC for each property, you are essentially creating a separate legal entity that owns the property and assumes the associated risks and liabilities. If a lawsuit arises or the property encounters financial problems, only the assets held within that specific LLC are at risk. This means that your personal assets, such as your primary residence, personal bank accounts, and other investments, are shielded from potential legal claims or financial obligations related to the investment property.

Setting up an LLC for each property is a relatively simple process that involves filing the necessary paperwork with your state's Secretary of State office and paying the required fees. Once the LLC is established, you can transfer ownership of the property to the LLC, and all business transactions, including contracts and financial accounts, should be conducted under the LLC's name. In addition to asset protection, an LLC can offer potential tax benefits. By default, an LLC is treated as a pass-through entity, meaning that the business itself does not pay taxes. Instead, the profits and losses are passed through to the individual members of the LLC, who report them on their personal tax returns. This can provide flexibility in tax planning and may help avoid the double taxation that can occur with other business structures, such as corporations.

OFFER STRATEGIES

When pursuing off-market leads or newly discounted listings, you must act swiftly. We recommend employing a "six-hour blitz" strategy, which involves underwriting, driving to, and walking the property within six hours of its availability. The objective is to present an offer to the seller, wholesaler, or broker before other brokers have the opportunity to inform their clients about the property.

For experienced investors confident in their underwriting and with a built-in buffer, waiving contingencies can be a powerful tool. However, novice investors should exercise caution. Sellers gravitate toward committed buyers. Demonstrating seriousness by offering substantial earnest money, such as $50,000 or even $5,000, and waiving contingencies can be effective. Flexible terms also play a significant role in negotiations.

In real estate, "terms" refer to the various conditions and stipulations included in a purchase agreement beyond the price. These terms can significantly impact the attractiveness of an offer to the seller and the overall success of a real estate transaction. Here are some key terms to consider:

- **Contingencies:** Contingencies are conditions that must be met for the sale to proceed, such as a satisfactory home inspection, appraisal, or the buyer's ability to secure financing. Waiving contingencies can make an offer more appealing to sellers, as it reduces the likelihood of the deal falling through. However, buyers should be cautious when waiving contingencies, as it can expose them to additional risks.

- **Earnest money:** Earnest money is a deposit made by the buyer to demonstrate their commitment to purchasing the property. A substantial earnest money deposit, such as $5,000 or $50,000, can show the seller that the buyer is serious about the transaction. The earnest money is typically held in escrow and applied to the down payment or closing costs at closing.

- **Closing date:** The closing date is when the ownership of the property is transferred from the seller to the buyer. Offering a flexible closing date that accommodates the seller's timeline can make an offer more attractive, especially if the seller needs extra time to move out or find a new property.

- **"As is" condition:** When a buyer agrees to purchase a property "as is," they are accepting the property in its current condition without requiring the seller to make any repairs or improvements. This can be advantageous for sellers who want to avoid the hassle and expense of making repairs, and it can lead to more favorable deals for buyers willing to take on the necessary work. When buying a distressed property, purchasing it "as is" and hiring a demolition crew to handle the cleanup can be advantageous. This saves the seller from dealing with the hassle, especially in probate situations where they may be located far away and want to avoid further involvement. When writing offers, consider accommodating the seller's timeline. For example, propose a longer closing period for older sellers who aren't in a rush, but include a clause allowing them to close within sixty days with a five-day written notice. This approach gives sellers the flexibility to move at their own pace while still securing the deal.

- **Financing terms:** The type of financing a buyer uses can also impact the attractiveness of their offer (which I will discuss in more detail in the next chapter). Cash offers are often preferred by sellers, as they eliminate the risk of financing falling through. However, buyers can also make their offers more competitive by providing evidence of a strong financial position, such as a pre-approval letter from a lender.

By understanding and strategically leveraging these terms, experienced investors can create more compelling offers and negotiate more favorable deals. However, novice investors should carefully consider the risks associated with waiving contingencies or accepting properties "as is" and ensure they have a sufficient buffer to cover unexpected expenses.

THE SELLER'S NEEDS

When crafting offers, consider the seller's unique needs. For example, propose a longer close for sellers who are not pressed for time, but allow them the option to close within sixty days with a five-day written notice. This approach provides flexibility. When working with selling landlords, a flexible close date for a 1031 exchange can be advantageous.

Closing escalators can be another strategic tool. For instance, if a property is listed at $300,000 and you are willing to pay $350,000, structure your offer starting at $310,000 and escalate in $5,000 increments up to $350,000 until the deal closes. This strategy allows you to secure the property more quickly, although some sellers may prefer your best offer up front.

Releasing earnest money to the seller demonstrates your commitment to the transaction. Consider owner financing, as it may enable you to pay more due to potentially lower interest rates. The **feasibility period** is a negotiation term that provides time to verify facts and underwriting. It grants buyers the ability to terminate the contract within a specified number of days with written or verbal notice, depending on the contract's terms.

During the feasibility period, verify your construction plan by bringing contractors and project managers to assess costs. Ensure your financing is prepared for closing, particularly if working with soft-money lenders who may require an appraisal. Secure loan terms and commitment, and explore alternative lenders if necessary. Inspections also occur during this period. Refrain from waiving feasibility until you have full confidence in your funding and plans.

Then review your title. When reviewing a property's title, identify any potential issues or restrictions that could impact your investment. Here are some key points to consider:

- **Encroachments:** Check for any encroachments on the property, such as a neighbor's fence or structure crossing the property line. These issues need to be addressed to avoid future legal disputes.
- **Title issues:** Ensure there are no outstanding liens, judgments, or other title issues that could complicate the purchase or future sale of the property.
- **CC&Rs (covenants, conditions & restrictions):** Carefully review any CC&Rs associated with the property, especially if it is part of a homeowners association (HOA). These regulations can dictate various aspects of property maintenance and improvements.

If you are working with a broker, have them or their title representative (preferably an investment specialist) thoroughly review the title documents and provide guidance on any potential concerns. When flipping a house, even seemingly minor HOA restrictions can significantly impact your renovation budget. For example, the HOA may require specific window types, colors, or roofing materials, which could increase your costs by $20,000–$40,000. Familiarize yourself with these requirements and incorporate them into your underwriting budget to ensure your project remains profitable. While it's acceptable to invest in high-quality materials, like an expensive roof, it's essential to factor these costs into your overall budget to maintain a viable investment strategy.

CLOSING TIMELINES

Closing timelines are the contractual obligation when the property closes. Understanding the seller's preferences and circumstances is key to negotiating a favorable deal. A quick close, such as within forty-eight hours, can be a powerful negotiating tool when the seller is in a distressed situation or needs to sell rapidly. While this puts pressure on the buyer to arrange financing and complete due diligence quickly, the potential discount may make it worthwhile. Be prepared to cover any additional costs associated with an expedited closing. The standard closing timeline of thirty to forty-five days is the most common in traditional real estate transactions, allowing sufficient time for the buyer to secure financing, conduct inspections, and review property documents.

Most sellers are comfortable with this time frame, as it provides them with enough time to plan their move and finalize their own arrangements. In some cases, an extended close of forty-five to sixty days or longer can be advantageous for both the buyer and the seller. It may allow the buyer to secure more favorable financing terms or provide additional time for thorough due diligence, while the seller might prefer it if they need extra time to find a new property or relocate. Offering a longer closing period can be a useful negotiating tactic when the seller is requesting a higher price than the buyer's initial offer.

When negotiating closing timelines, it's essential to communicate with your broker or wholesaler to understand the seller's motivations and preferences. Be flexible and willing to adjust your closing timeline to accommodate the seller's needs, and use closing timelines as a bargaining chip to negotiate a better price or more favorable terms. Ensure that your financing aligns with the proposed closing timeline, and be prepared to cover any additional costs associated with expedited or extended closings. Remember, closing timelines can directly impact your profitability. By being adaptable and understanding the seller's perspective, you can structure a deal that maximizes your returns while meeting the seller's requirements. Always factor in the closing timeline when evaluating a potential investment opportunity, as it can be just as critical as the purchase price in determining your overall success.

Title reps and escrow officers are key members of your real estate team, and play important roles in the closing process of a property transaction. Understanding their functions and how they can support your business is essential for success in house flipping. **Title reps**, or title representatives, work for title insurance companies. Their primary responsibility is to ensure that the property title is clear and free of any liens, encumbrances, or other issues that could prevent a smooth transfer of ownership. They conduct thorough title searches, examining public records and legal documents to verify the seller's right to transfer the property and to identify any potential title defects that need to be addressed before closing. In addition to their core responsibilities, title reps can be valuable networking resources for real estate investors. Some title reps are particularly business minded and well connected within the local real estate community. By building strong relationships with these individuals, you can leverage their networks to expand your own.

If you're looking to connect with specific types of professionals, such as contractors or property managers, a well-connected title rep may be able to provide introductions and referrals. **Escrow officers** are neutral third parties who manage the escrow process during a real estate transaction. They are responsible for holding and disbursing funds, as well as managing the exchange of documents between the buyer, seller, and lender. Escrow officers ensure that all conditions of the sale contract are met before the funds are released and the property ownership is transferred.

Like title reps, escrow officers can be valuable sources of information and connections within the real estate industry. They work with a wide range of clients, including investors, and may be aware of upcoming opportunities or potential partners that could benefit your business. In addition to title reps and escrow officers, brokers and hard-money lenders can also play important roles in expanding your network and deal pipeline. While not all brokers are enthusiastic about working with wholesalers, many recognize the value of investors who can close deals quickly and reliably. By demonstrating your professionalism and track record, you can build relationships with brokers who may provide you with off-market deals or early access to new listings. Similarly, hard-money lenders are often eager to work with active investors, as the more deals you complete, the more business they generate. Hard-money lenders can be excellent sources of market intel and may be able to connect you with other investors, contractors, or professionals in the local real estate scene.

The key takeaway is that every relationship in the real estate industry has the potential to lead to new opportunities and valuable connections. While it's common for people to compartmentalize their professional relationships, savvy investors understand the power of leveraging one connection to build another. By cultivating strong, multifaceted relationships with title reps, escrow officers, brokers, lenders, and other industry professionals, you can create a robust network that will support the growth and success of your house-flipping business.

CHAPTER 8

FINANCING STRATEGIES

If you want to win, do the ordinary things better than
anyone else.

—CHUCK NOLL, FORMER COACH, PITTSBURGH STEELERS

CONSTRUCTION FINANCING IS a vital aspect of your fix-and-flip business, as access to the right financing options can significantly impact your success as an investor. As a flipper, your financing choices can make or break your deal. By understanding the intricacies of construction financing, down payment requirements, and prepayment penalties, you can make informed decisions that set you up for success. Every deal is unique, and the ideal financing solution will depend on your specific circumstances. By equipping yourself with the right questions and being willing to explore various options, you can find lenders and programs that align with your goals and help you grow your fix-and-flip business.

You will want to get prequalified with a loan provider. **Prequalification** is the process of providing a lender with your financial information and investment plans to determine how much they are willing to lend you and under what terms. Loan products and requirements can vary significantly between markets. This step gives you a clear picture of the capital available to you and the requirements you must meet to secure financing. Different types of lenders will loan at different loan-to-values (LTV). And the down payments for investors vary. Prequalifying will tell you what type of project you can afford, how much money it will require, and what the costs associated with the loan are and how they will affect the profit.

By understanding your access to capital and the terms of your financing, you can make more informed decisions about the projects you take on and the returns you can expect. This knowledge will also help you develop a realistic plan for your business, as you'll have a clearer picture of how much capital you can deploy and how quickly you can grow your portfolio.

CONVENTIONAL FINANCING

Conventional lenders and private banks can be viable financing options for fix-and-flip properties. Conventional lenders offer mortgage products tailored to real estate investors. These loans often have interest rates that are a few percentage points higher than owner-occupied residential mortgages but still significantly lower than the rates offered by other types of lenders. For example, current investor interest rates for conventional loans hover around 7.5 percent, which can be 3–6 percent lower than the rates charged by alternative financing sources. This interest rate difference can have a substantial impact on the profitability of a fix-and-flip project, particularly for larger or more expensive properties.

Obtaining conventional financing for a fix-and-flip property can be challenging. Banks and credit unions typically have strict underwriting criteria, including requirements for the property's condition, the borrower's credit score, and proof of income. Another challenge with private banks and business banks is the extensive paperwork required. Investors must go through a full prequalification process, providing tax returns, bank statements, and other financial documentation. The banks want to ensure that you're a dependable borrower, so they'll thoroughly check your credit and examine your financial picture from every angle.

Conventional lenders may also require a larger down payment, often in the range of 20–35 percent, and may have limits on the number of investment properties a borrower can finance at one time.

Private banks, which cater to high-net-worth individuals and offer more personalized service, can be another option for financing fix-and-flip deals. These banks may have more flexibility in their underwriting process and can often make lending decisions more quickly than conventional lenders. However, private banks may also require a preexisting relationship with the borrower and may have higher minimum loan amounts.

One of the primary drawbacks of conventional and private bank financing for fix-and-flip projects is the longer closing timeline. Conventional lenders may take thirty to sixty days or more to close a loan. This extended timeline can be problematic in competitive markets where sellers prefer quick closings and may not be willing to wait for a buyer to secure traditional financing. However, some deals benefit from a long closing window.

The construction draw process with private banks and business banks is far more complex than other financing options (such as soft- and hard-money lending, which I'll explain later in this chapter). Typically, investors fund the construction themselves and then seek reimbursement from the lender. However, it's not as simple as providing an invoice. You must show paid checks, a completed budget, and secure lien releases every time you request a draw. While this process involves more paperwork and extensive documentation, it can be worth it if you're saving three to four points on your interest rate.

When comparing big banks like Wells Fargo, Chase, and Bank of America to smaller, local banks, note that big banks often offer lower interest rates, origination fees, and overall costs. However, this afford-ability comes with some challenges, particularly for self-employed fix-and-flip operators. Big banks focus heavily on debt coverage, and as flippers, we don't always fit neatly into their standard underwriting box. These banks prefer to lend to W-2 employees with steady income and predictable expenses, as it's a more straightforward analysis for them.

To determine whether conventional financing is the right fit for your project, evaluate whether the longer timeline and the lender's requirements align with your specific deal. If the numbers work and the financing terms are favorable, pursuing a conventional loan can be a smart move, especially for higher-end projects with longer timelines.

When exploring conventional financing options, follow these steps:

1. **Assess your project:** Determine if the property's condition, your timeline, and the loan amount align with the requirements of conventional lenders or private banks

2. **Prepare your documentation:** Gather all necessary information, including your budget, property details, and personal financial statements, to present to potential lenders

3. **Shop around:** Compare rates, terms, and requirements from multiple conventional lenders and private banks to find the best fit for your project

4. **Negotiate with lenders:** Don't hesitate to negotiate rates, fees, and other terms to secure the most favorable financing for your flip

5. **Coordinate with the seller:** If you need a longer closing timeline to accommodate the conventional lending process, work with the seller to ensure they are willing to accept these terms

The key to success in fix-and-flip financing is finding the right solution for each specific deal. While conventional lenders and private banks may not be the best choice for every project, they can be powerful allies when the circumstances align. By leveraging the strengths of each lending option and being creative in your approach, you can maximize your profits and grow your flipping business.

Ultimately, success in fix-and-flip financing comes down to thorough due diligence and asking the right questions up front. Don't hesitate to negotiate with lenders and push for terms that best suit your business needs. A little extra effort in the beginning can save you significant hassles and expenses down the road.

Here are some interview questions to ask lenders:

- How quickly can you close?
- Are you funding the deal? Or are you brokering to another lender?
- What are your LTV (loan-to-value) requirements?
- What are your interest rates?
- What are your loan origination fees? What other closing document or fees do you have?
- How does your construction draw process work? Are there charges for inspections? Do you advance funds or need to be reimbursed? What is your draw schedule?
- How long are the terms of your loans?

Another critical factor to consider when evaluating lenders is whether they charge a prepayment penalty. As a house flipper, it's best to avoid lenders that impose prepayment penalties. If you're able to sell the house quickly, either because of a cash offer or a neighbor's interest in purchasing the property, you don't want to be liable for additional points and fees to your hard-money lender. Prepayment penalties can jeopardize your deal and limit your exit strategies, so it's essential to clarify this aspect up front.

To make the loan application process seamless, follow these steps:

1. Build a strong resume. The more established you are as a real estate investor, the smoother the loan process will be. Include the number of deals you have completed, along with their addresses. If you are new to real estate investing, don't worry; include your relevant professional experience instead.
2. Prepare your bank statements in advance, as lenders will want to verify your liquidity.
3. Create a comprehensive scope of work and budget for the property you intend to purchase.
4. Submit the ARV comparables to the lender to justify your projected property value.

WHAT IS HARD MONEY?

Hard money is a form of bridge financing that real estate investors commonly used for fix-and-flip projects. **Bridge financing**, also known as a bridge loan or swing loan, is a short-term financing option used to bridge the gap between the purchase of a new property and the sale of an existing one, or until long-term financing can be secured. It is commonly used in real estate transactions, particularly by investors and homeowners who are buying a new property before selling their current one.

Key characteristics of bridge financing include:

- **Short loan terms:** Bridge loans typically have terms ranging from a few months to a year, although some may extend up to three years. This compressed time frame can put pressure on borrowers to complete their projects and either refinance or sell the property before the loan comes due. Some hard-money lenders offer extension options, allowing borrowers to extend the loan term for an additional three to twelve months, but these extensions often come with additional fees and points.
- **Higher interest rates:** Due to the short-term nature and increased risk, bridge loans often carry higher interest rates compared to traditional mortgages. Interest rates for hard-money loans can range from 11 to 12 percent or even higher, depending on the lender and the specific deal.
- **Quick funding:** Bridge loans can be approved and funded more quickly than traditional mortgages, often within a few days to a few weeks.
- **Collateral:** The new property being purchased, the existing property being sold, or both can serve as collateral for the bridge loan.
- **Repayment:** Bridge loans are typically repaid in full when the existing property is sold or when long-term financing, such as a mortgage, is secured for the new property.

Hard-money lenders, who are often also construction lenders, generally require a down payment ranging from 10 to 20 percent of the purchase price, although this can vary depending on the specific lender and the loan-to-value ratio of the deal. In some cases, hard-money lenders may be willing to offer more favorable terms, such as a lower down payment, if the loan-to-value ratio is particularly low or if the investor has a proven track record of successful projects. While hard money can be more expensive than traditional financing, with higher interest rates and fees, it can ultimately increase an investor's overall cash-on-cash return by allowing them to leverage their capital and take on more projects simultaneously.

This type of financing is particularly useful when the property being purchased is not eligible for traditional financing due to its condition or the need for extensive renovations. Often, flips are not financeable due to being in bad shape—blown roofs, safety issues, fire, mold. Hard-money lenders don't care about these conditions, whereas a regular bank would.

Hard-money lenders focus primarily on the collateral (the property) and the investor's ability to execute the project rather than relying solely on the borrower's credit score. This means that investors with less-than-perfect credit may still be able to secure financing if they have a strong deal and sufficient liquidity. This flexibility can be particularly valuable for investors who may have experienced financial challenges in the past, such as during the 2008 market downturn.

One of the primary benefits of using hard money is the ability to close quickly and with fewer contingencies. When approaching a seller, an investor can offer to close in cash without the need for an inspection or appraisal, as these are not typically required by hard-money lenders. This can be a significant advantage in competitive markets or when dealing with motivated sellers who prioritize a fast and hassle-free transaction. Similarly, if I buy a property at auction, I want to be able to buy that deal on-site and will need cashier checks in hand. The fastest money in town is always going to be hard money.

While hard money can be a powerful tool for real estate investors, it is important to carefully consider the terms of the loan and ensure that the project's projected returns justify the higher costs of this type of financing. This higher cost is due to the convenience and flexibility offered by hard-money lenders, and borrowers essentially pay a premium for the speed and simplicity of the transaction. By leveraging hard money strategically and executing projects effectively, investors can improve their cash flow, grow their portfolios, and even enhance their credit scores over time.

I, personally, love hard money because I'm an aggressive buyer. When I go in on deals, I am offering a two-to-five-day close. I'm doing that because I want the seller to know I'm a serious buyer and that I can close quicker than anybody else in town. Putting cash in people's hands has a powerful influence on their decision-making.

While bridge financing can be a valuable tool for facilitating real estate transactions and investments, it is important to carefully consider the costs and risks associated with these short-term, high-interest loans. Borrowers should have a clear plan for repaying the loan and carefully evaluate the terms and fees associated with the financing before proceeding.

Borrowers should also carefully select their deals and negotiate loan terms up front. If a lender is offering a higher interest rate, a borrower might negotiate for an extra three months on the loan term to provide more flexibility in completing the project. Hard-money lenders are often open to negotiation, so borrowers should always ask about potential adjustments to the terms.

Building a strong, long-standing relationship with a hard-money lender can lead to more favorable terms over time. As a borrower establishes a track record of successful projects and timely payments, they may be able to secure better rates and more flexible terms from their lender. However, it's still a good idea to periodically shop around and compare rates from different lenders to ensure that you're getting the best deal possible.

WHAT IS SOFT MONEY?

Soft money is a form of lending from essentially traditional banks or Wall Street institutions that have ventured into the hard-money lending space, offering products that bridge the gap between conventional financing and true hard-money loans. Soft-money lenders typically offer interest rates ranging from 8.5 percent to 10.5 percent in the current market conditions. However, it's worth noting that these rates can fluctuate depending on the overall economic environment. For example, when interest rates were at historic lows, some soft-money lenders were offering rates as low as 7.5 percent.

One key difference between soft-money lenders and traditional hard-money lenders is that soft-money loans often have more conditions and requirements. For instance, soft-money lenders may require appraisals to assess the value of the property, whereas hard-money lenders may be more flexible in this regard. Appraisals for fix-and-flip properties can be tricky, as investors typically request a loan amount for the highest and best use of the property (which I discussed in detail in Chapter 6). Many appraisers don't understand this concept and are just looking at what you pay for the property and what it could potentially be worth as-is. As such, they have a hard time justifying a higher loan amount, which is based on your rehab plan. Because of this, the appraisal can come in low. If you're using financing on a really good deal and your appraisal comes in low, it's either going to make you bring more money to the table or it can jeopardize your whole deal.

Additionally, soft-money lenders may have more stringent construction draw processes, which can impact the timeline and cash flow of a project. Hard-money lenders typically handle inspections themselves, while soft-money lenders rely on third-party construction companies to inspect the progress of the project. These third-party inspections can be costly and time consuming, potentially slowing down the rehab process and delaying the release of funds. If the third-party inspector is not satisfied with the work completed, the lender may withhold funds, creating additional obstacles for the investor.

When it comes to construction draws, hard-money lenders often provide an advance draw at closing to help investors get the project started. In contrast, soft-money lenders typically operate on a reimbursement basis, requiring investors to complete the work first and then request reimbursement for their expenses. This approach requires more cash out of pocket and can dilute the investor's cash-on-cash return. In many cases, the interest rate and point savings offered by soft-money lenders may not justify the decrease in cash-on-cash return.

To maintain their risk profile and satisfy their internal requirements, soft-money lenders need to ensure that each deal fits within their predetermined criteria. While soft-money loans may offer slightly lower interest rates than traditional hard-money loans, they may also come with more stringent requirements and a more involved underwriting process. Soft-money lenders often sell the loan to a note buyer or institution, while hard-money lenders hold the paper themselves. This means that soft-money lenders are subject to their note buyer's underwriting requirements, which can be problematic if market conditions change or the loan-to-value ratio drops. If the note buyer decides to audit the loan or freeze construction draws, the soft-money lender may have little control over the situation, potentially leaving the investor in a difficult position.

Despite these additional conditions, soft-money lenders still aim to fund deals quickly and efficiently. They typically have lines of credit or other funding sources that allow them to deploy capital rapidly.

Soft-money financing can be an excellent option for cosmetic flips. These properties require mostly superficial improvements and updates rather than extensive structural repairs. These types of projects often have lower budgets and can be completed relatively quickly, making them well-suited for soft-money loans. One of the main advantages of using soft money for cosmetic flips is that the appraisal process is typically more straightforward. Since the property is generally in good condition and only requires cosmetic enhancements, the appraiser is more likely to assess the value accurately and without significant issues. This can help ensure a smooth financing process and reduce the risk of the deal falling through due to appraisal-related problems. In cosmetic flip scenarios, sellers are often less concerned about a quick close and more focused on securing the best possible price for their property. This aligns well with the slightly longer timelines associated with soft-money loans, as the additional time required for the appraisal and underwriting process is less likely to be a deal-breaker for the seller.

Investors should carefully evaluate their project needs, timelines, and risk tolerance when choosing between hard-money and soft-money financing options.

WHAT IS PRIVATE MONEY?

Private-money lending is a unique form of financing that differs significantly from traditional institutional or private bank lending. In this arrangement, real estate investors partner with private individuals or a small group of investors who provide the funds for the project. These private lenders have the flexibility to set their own lending criteria and terms, as they are not bound by the same strict regulations that govern banks and other financial institutions.

Private money allows investors to bypass traditional lending guidelines and secure financing based on personal relationships. The paperwork involved is often much simpler compared to that required by soft-money lenders, typically consisting of a deed of trust, warranty deed, promissory note, and a basic loan term sheet filed against the property. This streamlined process can save investors significant time and effort. Additionally, the length of time needed to make a decision on the loan is significantly expedited. There is no need for lengthy approval processes or bureaucratic red tape. This ability to move quickly can be invaluable in competitive real estate markets.

One of the key advantages of private-money lending is the potential for greater flexibility in the loan structure. Private lenders may be willing to work with investors on a case-by-case basis, tailoring the loan terms to suit the specific needs of the project. This can include anything from interest rates and loan-to-value ratios to repayment schedules and collateral requirements. However, this flexibility can also be a double-edged sword, as some private lenders may have very specific or unconventional preferences that can make the lending process more challenging.

Interest rates for private-money loans can vary widely depending on the relationship between the lender and the borrower, as well as the perceived risk of the project. Some private lenders may offer rates comparable to hard-money lenders, while others may charge significantly higher rates in exchange for the added flexibility and the opportunity to invest in real estate without directly owning and managing properties.

One of the most significant advantages of private financing is that it's more cost-effective than bringing on an equity partner (which I will explain in detail in Chapter 9). An equity partner will usually has a 30–50 percent split, which they will take in profits. This is usually much higher than the interest rate a private-money lender will offer. Although private money may come with higher interest rates compared to traditional financing, investors can retain a larger share of their profits.

Private money can also help investors minimize their personal capital investment in a deal. When I first started flipping, I had only $7,000 to my name. By structuring my first deal with an 80 percent hard-money loan and a 20 percent private-money second from a lender who believed in me and the deal, I was able to get started with minimal personal funds. Although I paid a higher interest rate and points, that deal significantly grew my initial investment and paved the way for more traditional flipping.

Finally, private money can assist with liquidity management, particularly when investors are managing multiple projects simultaneously. Many private lenders offer interest reserves, allowing investors to defer debt service payments until the project is complete. This feature can be a valuable tool for maintaining healthy cash flow throughout the project.

While there are many benefits to private-money lending, there are some downsides to factor in as well, primarily the limited liquidity of the lenders. Unlike hard-money lenders, who have access to bank lines, or soft-money lenders who can sell off notes, private-money investors typically use their own cash to fund deals. This flexibility, which allows them to make quick decisions and lend more money on a deal, also limits their lending capacity. Private investors usually have a finite amount of cash available to lend at any given time, which means borrowers can quickly tap out their resources. If a private lender is funding multiple loans for different borrowers, they may allocate a significant portion of their capital to a single investor, leaving others on the sidelines.

To mitigate this risk, it's essential for real estate investors to build relationships with multiple private lenders and use them as a complement to other financing options. By diversifying their private-lending network, investors can increase their chances of securing funding when needed, but they should avoid relying solely on private money due to the potential liquidity constraints.

Another potential drawback of private-money lending is that personal opinions can influence the lender's decision to fund a deal. Even if an investor presents a comprehensive investment package with a solid property, rehab plan, and value proposition, a private-money lender may still decline the deal based on their subjective assessment. For example, I recently turned down a loan that had good data and a reasonable budget because I felt that the property's lack of a garage—opting for a carport instead—would negatively impact its marketability in that specific area. In such cases, the lender's personal opinion can supersede appraisal-based or value-based considerations.

Geographic constraints can also limit the availability of private-money lending for investors operating across multiple states. Some private lenders may be unwilling to lend in certain states due to complex lending laws or the cost of hiring legal counsel to prepare the necessary paperwork. As a private lender myself, I finance deals across four different states but avoid lending in states where the legal requirements are too burdensome or expensive. To overcome this challenge, investors should seek to establish relationships with private lenders in each state where they plan to invest, ensuring they have access to funding options that align with their geographic focus.

Ultimately, the key to success with private-money lending lies in building strong relationships. By cultivating a network of private lenders who believe in you and your deals, you can unlock a world of opportunities for your real estate investing business. Building and maintaining relationships with private lenders requires a combination of strong interpersonal skills, a proven track record of successful projects, and a thorough understanding of the lender's investment goals and risk tolerance. By taking the time to cultivate these relationships and presenting compelling investment opportunities, real estate investors can tap into the vast potential of private-money lending to finance their projects and grow their businesses.

To find private-money investors, it's essential to expand your network and actively promote your real estate investing activities. Attend local meetup groups, collaborate with other investors, and make it known that you're seeking private capital. Leverage social media and online real estate investing communities to connect with potential private lenders and learn about their investment preferences. Work with real estate attorneys, accountants, and financial advisors who may have clients interested in investing in real estate projects. You can also attend industry conferences and seminars to meet private lenders and learn about the latest trends in real estate financing.

CONSTRUCTION-TO-PERMANENT LOANS

Construction-to-permanent loans can be a game changer for fix-and-flip investors, particularly in a market with fluctuating interest rates. **Construction-to-permanent loans**, also known as "single-close" or "all-in-one" loans, are a type of financing that combines the construction loan and the permanent mortgage into a single loan. This means that borrowers only have to go through the loan application and closing process once, simplifying the financing process for new construction or substantial renovation projects.

Here's how construction-to-permanent loans work: The borrower applies for the loan, providing detailed information about the project, including plans, budgets, and timelines. The lender reviews the borrower's creditworthiness and financial stability and the feasibility of the project before approving the loan. Once the loan is approved and closed, the borrower can begin drawing funds to pay for construction costs. During the construction phase, the borrower typically makes interest-only payments on the amount of money disbursed. After construction is complete and the property receives a certificate of occupancy, the loan automatically converts into a permanent mortgage. The interest rate may change at this point, depending on the terms of the loan. The borrower then begins making regular principal and interest payments according to the terms of the permanent mortgage.

Additionally, If your flip includes a development component, such as building an accessory dwelling unit (ADU) that you plan to keep as a rental, private banks can provide locked-in financing for both the construction phase and the long-term mortgage. During the construction phase, you'll pay a higher interest rate, but still lower than other types of financing. Once the project is complete, your take-out financing is already secured at a competitive rate, streamlining the process of transitioning from a flip to a long-term hold.

Construction-to-permanent loans offer several benefits, including a single application and closing process, which reduces paperwork, fees, and time spent on the financing process. Some lenders also allow borrowers to lock in the interest rate for the permanent mortgage at the time of closing, providing protection against rate fluctuations during the construction period. Additionally, with a single loan, borrowers can more easily plan and budget for their construction and long-term financing costs. However, there are some drawbacks to consider. Because these loans cover both the construction and permanent financing, lenders may have stricter qualification requirements, such as higher credit scores, larger down payments, and more substantial cash reserves.

If the borrower's circumstances or the project plans change during construction, it may be more difficult to modify the terms of the loan. Additionally, interest rates for construction-to-permanent loans may be higher than those for separate construction and permanent financing due to the increased risk and longer loan term for the lender. Construction-to-permanent loans can be a useful financing tool for borrowers who want to simplify the process of financing new construction or substantial renovations. However, it's essential to carefully consider the terms, costs, and potential drawbacks of these loans and compare them to alternative financing options before making a decision. By weighing the pros and cons and selecting the most appropriate financing solution for their specific project, borrowers can successfully navigate the construction and long-term financing process.

CREATIVE DEALS AND SUBJECT-TO

There are a variety of creative deals within real estate, such as **seller financing** or **subject-to**, or sub-to. This has been all the rage in the real estate game over the last two years, thanks to sky-high mortgage rates.

With owner-financing deals becoming increasingly rare, especially in the fix-and-flip space, subject-to has emerged as a popular alternative. In a subject-to deal, you're purchasing a property from a seller and assuming their existing debt. Instead of the seller issuing you a new note, you're taking over their payments. There are two common structures for sub-to deals: assumable loans and traditional subject-to.

Assumable Loans

When a loan is assumable, the loan provision allows a new debtor (the investor) to take over the existing loan from the seller. This means that the investor inherits the loan's original terms, including the interest rate, remaining balance, and repayment period.

While the seller may agree to allow the investor to assume their loan, the lender must still approve the transaction. The investor will need to be fully prequalified by the bank and go through escrow, as the lender is essentially transferring the loan to a new borrower. This process can be challenging for some investors, particularly those who are self-employed or have unconventional income sources. Lenders will typically review the investor's credit score, income, debt-to-income ratio, and assets to determine their eligibility for the loan assumption. If the investor does not meet the lender's criteria, the assumption may be denied, even if the seller has agreed to the deal.

For new investors, this can be advantageous in several ways.

- **Lower interest rates:** If the seller's existing loan has a lower interest rate than what the investor could secure on their own, assuming the loan can result in significant savings over the life of the loan
- **Reduced up-front costs:** By taking over the existing loan, the investor may be able to purchase the property with little to no money down, as they are not required to provide a new down payment to the lender
- **Easier qualification:** Since the original loan has already been approved and underwritten, the investor may face fewer hurdles in qualifying for the assumption, compared to applying for a new loan
- **Speed and simplicity:** Assuming an existing loan can be a faster and more straightforward process than securing a new mortgage, as there is less paperwork and fewer steps involved

To mitigate this risk, new investors should:

- Carefully review the terms of the assumable loan to ensure they are favorable and align with their investment strategy.
- Have their financial documents and proof of income prepared and ready to present to the lender.
- Consider partnering with a more experienced investor or co-borrower who can strengthen their application and increase their chances of approval.
- Have a backup plan in place, such as alternative financing options or a contingency clause in the purchase agreement, in case the assumption is not approved.

Despite these challenges, assumable loans remain an attractive financing tool for new real estate investors. By allowing them to take over existing loans with favorable terms and reduced up-front costs, subject-to financing can help new investors get started in the market and build their portfolios more quickly. As with any financing strategy, investors should thoroughly assess the risks and benefits and work closely with experienced professionals to ensure a smooth and successful transaction.

Traditional Subject-To

Traditional subject-to is where you assume the seller's mortgage and make payments directly to their lender. The debt remains in the seller's name, and the property is typically transferred into a trust or rental entity. The majority of mortgages in America have a clause that prohibits this type of transfer. If you take on a property and start making payments, but the title is transferred to your investor entity, the bank can invoke the due-on-sale clause. This is a violation of the loan terms, and the bank can call the entire note due, putting the property into foreclosure and killing your deal.

To get around this, some investors will put the property into a trust or rental entity where the seller retains a small percentage of the title. This typically won't trigger the due-on-sale clause, but it's crucial to have a lawyer structure the transaction to protect yourself from liability. If you're making payments on behalf of the homeowner and fail to do so, it can negatively impact their credit, and they could come after you for damages. It's essential to structure the deal correctly, ensure the seller understands the transaction, and never miss a payment. There was a lot of this happening in 2008, where people were paying off mortgages and then letting the properties go into foreclosure, which was a double whammy for the seller.

The biggest pro of subject-to is the ability to take advantage of cheaper debt from historically low interest rates. Over the last three years, we have seen the cheapest debt in U.S. history, with many sellers refinancing at 3–3.5 percent. As investors, we're now faced with rates that are double or triple that, and hard money is even more expensive.

Subject-to financing can be a beneficial strategy for real estate investors, particularly when dealing with thinner deals that may not have substantial built-in equity. By assuming the seller's existing mortgage, investors can avoid the added costs associated with obtaining new financing, such as origination fees, points, and higher interest rates. This can make a thin deal with low debt costs just as profitable as a larger deal with higher financing expenses, as the investor's monthly cash flow is not burdened by high mortgage payments.

One potential drawback of using subject-to financing for fix-and-flip properties is that it often requires a larger up-front cash investment from the investor. This is because the investor is typically taking over the seller's existing loan balance, which may be higher than what they would have borrowed with a new loan. Additionally, the investor may need to provide a cash down payment to the seller to compensate for any equity in the property. If you're getting a property with owner financing at a 3 percent interest rate, that can be incredibly advantageous; however, if the seller requires a 20 percent down payment and you have to fund the rehab out of pocket, your cash-on-cash return is going to drop by half or more.

The key is to negotiate terms that work for your specific situation. It's not just about the interest rate and the term length—you need to consider how much cash you'll have to put into the deal up front. This comes down to the down payment, which is entirely negotiable. If you're buying a property that needs a significant rehab, you may be able to negotiate a lower down payment. On the other hand, if you're getting a great deal on the purchase price, you may be willing to put more money down. It's all about finding the right balance and structuring a deal that works for both parties.

To successfully utilize subject-to financing, investors should target properties with favorable existing loan terms, such as low interest rates and monthly payments. They should seek out motivated sellers who are eager to get out of the property but may not have the equity to sell through traditional means. Investors should also be prepared to provide a cash down payment to the seller, if necessary, to compensate for any equity in the property. Structuring the transaction correctly ensures a smooth transfer of the loan and protects both parties' interests. Finally, investors should have a solid plan in place to either refinance the property or sell it before the assumed loan reaches maturity. By understanding the advantages and limitations of subject-to financing, real estate investors can make informed decisions about when and how to use this strategy to maximize their returns and build their portfolios.

MITIGATING RISK BY EVALUATING LOAN TIMELINES

It's important to evaluate the loan timelines for your financing before you begin your flip. There are lots of factors that can lengthen the timeline for completing your flipping project, and you want to make sure you build in time in anticipation of these setbacks.

Hard-money lenders typically offer short-term loans with fixed repayment periods, often ranging from six to twelve months. If your lender is only providing a six-month loan term, but your renovation plans indicate a longer project duration, you're introducing an additional layer of risk to the deal. The mismatch between the loan term and the projected timeline could potentially leave you in a precarious situation at the end of the six-month period. You may face the prospect of having to renegotiate the loan terms, bring in additional funds, or even risk defaulting on the loan if the project is not completed within the allotted time frame.

To mitigate this risk, it's essential to negotiate hard-money loan terms that provide ample breathing room for your anticipated project timelines. For example, if you anticipate a nine-month renovation, securing a twelve-month loan term would be more prudent, as it eliminates the risk of running into a loan maturity deadline before the project's completion. Longer loan terms may come with additional costs or fees from the lender, but these expenses should be factored into your overall underwriting calculations. The peace of mind and reduced risk associated with a longer loan term can often outweigh the additional costs, particularly for more extensive renovation projects. Furthermore, thoroughly evaluate your lender's policies and procedures for loan extensions or refinancing options. Some lenders may offer extensions at predetermined fees, while others may require a complete refinance process, potentially leading to higher costs or stricter underwriting criteria.

By aligning your hard-money loan terms with your projected project timelines and thoroughly understanding the lender's policies, you can better manage the associated risks and ensure that your financing does not become a bottleneck or a source of unnecessary stress during the renovation process. Ultimately, the goal is to create a seamless and risk-mitigated experience by harmonizing all aspects of the deal, including the financing, project timelines, and the highest-and-best-use strategy, to maximize your chances of a successful and profitable outcome.

Ultimately, finding the right lender for each specific deal is key. For real estate investors focusing on fix-and-flip projects, it's essential to cultivate relationships with a diverse range of lenders, including hard-money, soft-money, and private-money sources. Having access to multiple financing options allows investors to select the best fit for each project based on factors such as the project timeline, anticipated returns, and the level of risk involved. In some cases, a big bank with cheap debt may be the best option, while in others, a nimble hard-money lender who can close quickly might be more advantageous.

Understanding the strengths and weaknesses of each option and leveraging them accordingly is crucial to success. As with any financing decision, thorough due diligence is essential. Ask questions, read the fine print, and ensure you fully understand the terms before committing to a lender. With the right lender in your corner, you can take your fix-and-flip business to new heights.

CHAPTER 9
BORROWING WITH PARTNERSHIPS AND LLCS

Every time I step on the field, I'm going to give my whole heart regardless of the score.
—TIM TEBOW, FORMER NFL QUARTERBACK

AS FIX-AND-FLIP INVESTORS, we often run into limitations when it comes to starting, maintaining, and scaling our businesses. Cash reserves can quickly become depleted, and we may need to bring in equity partners to continue growing and taking on more projects. While equity partners typically cost more than traditional lenders, they can provide significant value and help you reach new heights in your flipping journey.

Access to capital is undeniably the most crucial aspect of running a successful fix-and-flip business. Without sufficient funding, and even when presented with the most promising opportunities, the most skilled investors will struggle to achieve their goals. That's why I'm dedicating a significant portion of this discussion to exploring various financing options and strategies. By understanding the landscape of available capital sources, you can make informed decisions about how to fund your projects and grow your business. One particularly powerful strategy for scaling your fix-and-flip operations is partnering with equity investors.

Equity partners are individuals or entities that provide capital in exchange for a share of the profits generated by your flips. By bringing in equity partners, you can access larger pools of capital and take on more ambitious projects that might otherwise be out of reach. The key to successful equity partnerships is finding investors whose goals and risk tolerances align with your own. Some equity partners may be looking for hands-off investments where they can passively deploy their capital, while others may want to take a more active role in the decision-making process.

One of the primary benefits of working with equity partners is that it allows you to optimize your skill set as a flipper. When you're not constrained by limited personal capital, you can focus on what you do best: identifying promising properties, executing value-add renovations, and selling the improved assets for a profit.

By leveraging your expertise and track record, you can attract equity partners who are eager to invest in your projects and share in the returns. For many investors who don't have the time, expertise, or desire to be actively involved in the day-to-day operations of flipping houses, partnering with a skilled flipper who has access to capital can be a mutually beneficial arrangement. The equity partner provides the funding needed to acquire and renovate properties, while the flipper handles the heavy lifting of managing the project from start to finish.

Operating agreements play a vital role in defining each partner's roles, responsibilities, and expectations. A well-defined operating agreement can prevent conflicts and potential lawsuits. Avoid using vague or boilerplate operating agreements, as they can lead to disputes. Instead, consult a lawyer to draft a comprehensive operating agreement that clearly outlines each party's duties and obligations.

You'll need to include financial obligations in the operating agreement. If the operating agreement says that the investor will contribute all the capital for the property, you'll want to spell out what happens if cost overruns occur, or the project runs out of funds. If cost overruns occur, the investor should be committed to covering the additional capital requirements. However, if the project runs out of funds, it becomes your responsibility to secure additional financing. These arrangements should be explicitly stated in the operating agreement to prevent misunderstandings and disputes.

Clarity is paramount in every partnership you establish. Walk through worst-case scenarios with a legal professional to ensure that both you and your investment partner are protected in the deal. Clearly define the terms of capital contributions, including how and when the invested capital will be repaid to the investor. This prevents any misunderstandings or unauthorized withdrawals from accounts. By paying attention to details in structuring partnerships and drafting operating agreements, you can mitigate potential conflicts and legal issues.

When structuring equity partnerships, joint venture agreements are the most commonly used approach. There are three main structures you can use within a joint venture.

SIMPLE JOINT VENTURE AGREEMENT

A simple joint venture agreement forms a partnership between a group of investors or individual investors who contribute to a specific project. Not all members of the agreement necessarily hold a formal title on the property. In many cases, the fix-and-flip operator purchases the property in their own name or entity, and a contract is recorded against the property stating the interest of the investor who is providing capital. This interest can be structured as an equity split or a profit share.

Recording the agreement against the title protects the investor's interest and ensures clarity for all parties involved. Joint venture agreements are my preferred method of partnering with other investors. They allow me to secure the title 100 percent in my own name or entity, without needing to qualify my partners with a bank. I maintain full control of the deal, and the document itself is simple in nature.

Joint venture agreements should always be structured by a lawyer to ensure all parties' interests are protected. The terms can be customized, with various responsibilities assigned to each partner. Clarity in these responsibilities helps avoid issues down the road.

Joint venture agreements can also help secure your hard-money loan and prevent issues with lender covenants that prohibit second-position loans. A **second-position loan**, also known as a junior lien or subordinate mortgage, is a loan secured by a property that ranks below the first mortgage in order of priority. These loans can provide additional capital for fix-and-flip projects, but many hard-money lenders prohibit them to protect their interests.

By structuring additional capital as an equity partnership through a joint venture agreement instead of a second-position loan, flippers can access the funds they need without violating their hard-money loan covenants. The equity partner provides capital in exchange for a share of the profits, but their investment is not secured by the property itself.

By understanding the interplay between second-position loans, hard-money lender covenants, and joint venture agreements, fix-and-flip investors can create effective capital-raising strategies that allow them to scale their businesses and take on larger projects while navigating the complex landscape of real estate finance.

LIMITED LIABILITY COMPANY (LLC) STRUCTURE

Another common approach is to create an LLC or business entity for a specific venture that can be used for future partnerships between a cash investor and an operator. In this scenario, the LLC would own the title to the property, and the cash investor and operator would be members of the LLC, with their roles and responsibilities outlined in an operating agreement.

The benefit of using an LLC agreement for your private lender or other people's money is that they may feel more secure because they're going on title with you and have an equity position. Being on title together can foster a stronger personal relationship between you and your investor. They provide the money, and you provide the services, creating a sense of partnership. But make sure to carefully consider all aspects of the agreement before moving forward with an LLC structure. Take the time to think through the long-term implications and ensure that the arrangement aligns with your goals and those of your investor.

The LLC agreement should include the percentage ownership for each party (I'll explain common equity splits later in this chapter). It should also include the division of profits and losses, the responsibilities of each member, the process for making decisions, the exit strategies and timelines for the project, and provisions for dispute resolution and potential buyout scenarios. To establish these terms, the cash investor and operator should have open discussions about their goals, expectations, and risk tolerances. It's essential to work with experienced legal and financial professionals to draft the operating agreement and ensure that it comprehensively addresses all relevant aspects of the partnership.

When specifying the roles and responsibilities of each partner, pay particular attention to distinguishing between the managing partner and the passive partner. In many of my agreements, the person providing the capital often takes the role of the passive partner. The operator, then, assumes the role of the managing partner and is responsible for writing checks and overseeing day-to-day operations.

The passive partner will expect a yield and a return, and is typically not involved in the project's operations. This should be clearly laid out in the operating agreement. You don't want to get into a situation where the passive investor starts making operational decisions. The managing partner, then, has the authority to secure debt, modify operational plans, make the sole decision to sell the property, hire and fire contractors, and obtain permits—essentially, everything an investor would do if they owned the property individually. The passive partner is expected to remain hands-off, allowing the managing partner to run the show.

Another critical aspect to spell out in the LLC agreement is who is responsible for the debt and who has the authority to sign for it. If not clearly stated, both partners may be required to sign loan documents, which can be inconvenient for private investors who don't want to be involved in the paperwork. In our LLC agreements, we explicitly state that the operator is taking on the debt and personally guaranteeing the loan, eliminating the need for additional signatures from the passive investors. Additionally, the operating agreement can specify that one partner or the majority ownership in the partnership has the full authority to sign on behalf of the LLC. This streamlines the process, making things faster and simpler from a paperwork perspective.

Additionally, if your investor is on title with you as the operator, they may be required to sign on the debt, which can make them nervous and reluctant because they are now personally liable. However, having a cash investor on the deal can work in your favor if you have lower capital, as their strong signature may help you qualify for better loan terms and give you access to more financing options.

Once the operating agreement is signed, the deal terms cannot be changed without the consent of all members, providing a level of protection and predictability for both the cash investor and the operator. The LLC agreement is more complex to change, and if you own a property at the time of the change, it can trigger transfer taxes for that portion of the deal. Additionally, updating the agreement requires modifying tax filings, bank accounts, and other administrative tasks (like LLC filings), which can be cumbersome. If the operator wants to renegotiate the terms of the partnership, it's often easier to scrap the existing LLC and create a new one rather than amending the current structure. This lack of versatility can be a downside.

By clearly defining the roles and responsibilities of each partner and outlining the managing partner's authority, you can create an LLC agreement that protects the interests of all parties involved while ensuring smooth operations and efficient decision-making throughout the project. It will create a framework for a successful partnership and provides a road map for navigating the fix-and-flip process together. This approach offers flexibility and protection for both parties, making it an attractive option for those looking to build long-term relationships in the real estate investing space.

FLEXIBLE EQUITY OFFERINGS

If you're looking for a more versatile alternative to the LLC structure, an equity lender agreement can be a great option. This approach involves creating a single document per property, where the cash contributors provide all the necessary funds for the deal. Instead of recording the agreement with specific rates, terms, and lenders, the investors receive a percentage of the deal's profits.

As the operator, you still take title to the property on your own, and your first-position hard-money lender typically won't be concerned about who else is on title. This allows you to run the project as needed while securing the investors' money with a portion of the equity.

Equity financing involves giving investors an ownership stake in exchange for their capital. This aligns interests but means sharing profits based on the investor's equity percentage. The choice between debt and equity depends on factors like risk appetite, desired control, and expected returns. Sometimes a combination of both is used to balance risk and rewards.

Ultimately, the choice between an LLC agreement and an equity lender agreement will depend on your specific situation and the preferences of your cash investors. By understanding the pros and cons of each approach and structuring the partnership thoughtfully, you can create a mutually beneficial arrangement that helps you grow your flipping business and achieve your investment goals.

COMMON EQUITY STRUCTURES FOR EQUITY PARTNERS

Straight equity split. With a straight equity split, the operator and private investor(s) negotiate an agreed percentage for splitting the profits from the project. Common splits are 50/50, 70/30, or 60/40, depending on factors like the operator's experience level and the investor's return expectations.

When establishing equity offerings, many investors default to a 50/50 model. The operator finds the deal, creates the rehab plan, and sells the property, earning 50 percent of the profits. The investor puts up all the required capital and takes the other 50 percent. Remember, you don't always need to give up 50 percent of the deal. Find out what your investors are looking to make on the project and offer equity accordingly.

For example, let's say you have a flip deal with a projected 50 percent return, and your investor wants to make at least 15 percent on their money. Instead of offering a 50/50 split, which would yield a 25 percent return for the investor, you could offer them a 35 percent equity position, targeting a 17.5 percent return. The investor is happy because it exceeds their expectations, and you're happy because you retain an additional 15 percent of the equity.

As a newer operator, you may need to give up a higher equity percentage initially, such as 70 percent to the investor and 30 percent for yourself, in order to build your track record. However, as you gain more experience, you can negotiate for a larger equity share. The appeal of this straightforward structure is its simplicity—the investor provides all the capital, and the operator manages the project, with each party's expected profit share being transparent. That said, operators will often keep certain fees separate from the equity split profits, like acquisition fees, real estate broker fees if they list the property themselves, and so on.

By retaining these additional fees, the operator's total compensation ends up being higher than the stated equity percentage split. On a 50/50 split, the operator could effectively earn 60 percent once fees are accounted for. Full transparency about any fees is crucial—the operator must disclose up front anything they'll be keeping to avoid misaligned expectations with the investor. Before presenting a deal, it's wise to use tools like profit calculators to ensure the fee structure and equity split create a fair, win-win scenario. Aligning expectations through clear communication from the start prevents conflicts from arising later on in these equity partnerships.

You'll want to make sure you speak the same language as your investors and understand the types of deals they've participated in previously. This may lead you to consider a fee-based structure instead of a straight equity split.

Fee-based model. A fee-based model equity split refers to a partnership structure where the operator (typically the real estate investor/

flipper) receives compensation through a combination of equity ownership in the deal and predetermined fees rather than just a straight equity split of the profits.

When considering the equity split, it's important for you to take into account the time commitment you, as an operator, make. You'll want to be compensated for that time, and there are ways to ensure this through the operating agreement.

As an operator, I'll typically charge the following fees:

- **Acquisition fee:** 1–3 percent of the purchase price (usually 3 percent in flipping, similar to a standard real estate commission)
- **Financing fee:** 1 percent of the loan amount (if the cash investor provides 20 percent and the operator secures a $200,000 hard-money loan, they'll take a 1 percent origination fee)
- **Construction management fee:** 10 percent of the construction costs to help pay for the operator's staff and oversight
- **Disposition fee:** 3 percent of the sales price or a percentage of the profit once the property is sold

By incorporating these fees, flippers can offer investors a larger share of the equity while still generating the income needed to operate their businesses and cover associated costs. This approach allows you to structure deals that appeal to investors' desire for ownership while ensuring you have the cash flow to sustain your operations.

Preferred returns—syndications. Another option is a blended approach, combining a preferred return with an equity offering. This allows you to get the best of both worlds by blending debt and equity. In real estate syndications, investors pool their capital together to invest in a larger property deal that they likely could not afford individually. The syndicator is the real estate professional who sources the deal, manages it, and brings in investor capital. Investors in these syndication deals often receive what's called a "preferred return." This is an annual percentage return, typically ranging from 6 to 8 percent, that is paid out from available cash flow before the syndicator receives any profits. Think of it as the minimum expected return for investors. Passive investors often like this model because they get a guaranteed return and the potential for upside if the deal outperforms.

There is usually a profit-split structure after the preferred return hurdle is cleared. A common split is 70/30, where investors receive 70 percent of the remaining profits, and the syndicator receives 30 percent.

Equity partnership structures have their merits, and the choice ultimately comes down to your investors' preferences for security and how much profit you're willing to share. The key is to find the right balance that works for your specific situation and aligns with your goals as a flipper.

By understanding the various equity partnership options available and structuring deals intelligently, you can scale your flipping business, take on bigger projects, and achieve the success you've been striving for. Access to capital is the lifeblood of any flipping business. By leveraging other people's money and partnering with the right equity investors, you can unlock new opportunities and optimize your skill set.

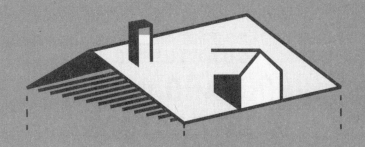

PART 3

MANAGING YOUR FLIP FROM START TO FINISH

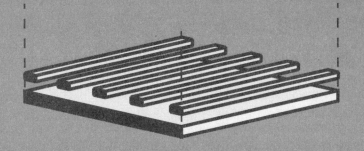

CHAPTER 10
HIRING AND VETTING CONTRACTORS

If you are afraid of confrontation,
you are not going to do very well.
—BILL PARCELLS, FORMER NFL COACH

THERE ARE SEVERAL factors to consider when deciding whether you will take on a flip yourself or hire a contractor. First, honestly assess your experience and skills in home renovation, including carpentry, plumbing, electrical work, and project management. If you lack the necessary expertise, it may be wise to hire a contractor to ensure the work is done correctly and efficiently. Additionally, evaluate the project's complexity and scope; if it involves extensive structural changes or specialized skills, it's generally better to engage a professional contractor. Time constraints and availability also play a crucial role in the decision-making process. If you have limited time to dedicate to the flip due to other commitments, hiring a contractor can help keep the renovation on schedule.

Plus, if you're using financing for the flip, some lenders may require the involvement of a licensed contractor to protect their investment and ensure the work meets quality standards. Another option to consider is a hybrid model, where you take on some aspects of the flip yourself and hire contractors for others. This approach allows you to be involved in the process, gain hands-on experience, and potentially save money on labor costs while still leveraging the expertise of professionals for more complex or specialized tasks. For example, you might choose to handle demolition, painting, and basic carpentry yourself while hiring contractors for electrical, plumbing, and HVAC work.

Ultimately, the decision to do a flip yourself, hire a contractor, or use a hybrid approach depends on your individual circumstances, skills, goals, and risk tolerance. Be honest about your capabilities and limitations, and carefully weigh the pros and cons of each approach before making a decision. If you do choose to hire a contractor or use a hybrid model, thoroughly vet the qualifications, experience, and references of the professionals you engage to ensure a successful partnership and a profitable flip.

YOU CORE TEAM TO EXECUTE THE FLIP

When it comes to building a successful real estate flipping business, having a strong construction team is essential. The foundation of this team is what I call the "core team"—a group of professionals who are always needed on hand to keep projects moving smoothly. At the top of this list is the permit team, which includes an architect, engineer, and surveyor.

It's important to understand that every community, city, and county has its own unique permitting process. For example, in Washington state, the permitting requirements in Seattle are completely different from those in Tacoma, even though they're only forty-five minutes apart. To navigate these differences efficiently, I aim to have at least two architects per county on my bench. Having local expertise can save significant time and money, as architects unfamiliar with a specific area's processes can take two to three times longer to submit permits, potentially adding 20 percent to debt costs.

In addition to architects, I always strive to have two structural engineers and two professionals for each role on the permit team. Relying on a single person can lead to costly delays if they become unavailable or booked out for an extended period. I recently experienced this issue firsthand when our only civil engineer went out of town, forcing us to wait an additional two weeks. Permit teams are often in high demand, so finding one after purchasing a property can result in months of waiting for plans and permits, eating into profits.

Permit Considerations as You Build Your Team

Researching the permit process for flipping a property in a new area is an important step when planning your flip. Start by visiting the website of the local building department or planning commission to find online resources, guides, and checklists outlining the permit requirements for residential renovations. If the information available online is insufficient, contact the building department directly to inquire about the specific permits needed for your planned work. Attending local real estate investor meetings and connecting with experienced investors can provide valuable insights into the permit process, potential challenges, and tips for navigating local requirements.

Engaging a local architect or contractor with experience in the area can help you understand the permit process, timeline, and associated costs. They may also have established relationships with the local building department, which can streamline the process. In addition to building permits, investigate zoning laws and historic district designations that may impact the scope of work allowed and require additional approvals or adherence to specific guidelines.

Reviewing recent permit records maintained by municipalities can give you a sense of typical permit requirements, processing times, and common issues or delays encountered for similar properties. As you gather information, budget for permit fees and factor in expected timelines for permit approvals to ensure a realistic and profitable flip. Remember that permit requirements vary significantly between municipalities, so thorough research and engagement with local experts helps to navigate the process effectively and minimize potential setbacks.

For new house flippers, I highly recommend hiring general contractors for the first few projects. These are professionals who oversee the jobsite on the day-to-day basis. This allows you to observe how they organize and manage the site, providing valuable insights into their systems and processes. Having a knowledgeable point person running the site can be invaluable, especially when you're just starting out. General contractors can also help you flip houses while still maintaining your nine-to-five job and working toward your financial freedom goals.

When working with general contractors, it's essential to understand how they break down construction costs into different categories. This knowledge will help you better grasp your direct costs for future projects. For example, if a contractor charges $10,000 for plumbing, it typically indicates a 10–20 percent profit margin, suggesting that the actual plumbing scope of work costs around $8,000–$9,000 when hired directly.

While general contractors manage your jobsite, remember that they still require oversight. Posting permit packets, quotes, spec sheets, and floor plans at all jobsites helps maintain clarity and accountability. Walking the site with the contractor once a week allows you to monitor issues and timelines, ensuring the project stays on track. Even with a general contractor, this level of involvement is minimal compared to directly subcontracting every aspect of the project.

To further reduce costs and speed up timelines, building a trade bench with direct relationships with subcontractors is important. The core trades that should be on your bench include:

- **Demo crews:** These teams can kick-start a jobsite and clean up the property while you finalize bids. Look for smaller, local dump truck operators rather than large commercial companies to keep costs down.
- **Electricians:** Always aim to have two electricians on your bench to avoid price gouging when one is too busy.
- **Plumbers:** Two plumbers are needed for all plumbing work, including rough-ins, demo, valves, and trim.
- **Roofers:** Have two roofers on your team.
- **Framers:** Two framing crews are essential.
- **HVAC specialists:** Two heating and cooling professionals for furnaces, air conditioning, mini-split systems, and venting.
- **Siders, drainage, and septic contractors:** Key specialists for exterior work and site preparation.

The more of these roughing contractors you have on your bench the better, as their costs can vary significantly based on the age of the home, floor plan adjustments, and specifications. Having multiple options for each trade allows you to control costs and avoid overpricing when a contractor is fully booked.

In addition to roughing contractors, finish contractors are needed to complete the project after rough-ins. These include drywallers, millwork teams, painters, finish carpenters, flooring specialists, cabinet installers, tile installers, handymen, and trim-out teams. Building a diverse bench of finish contractors enables you to execute projects at various price points, from lower-end cosmetic flips to high-end luxury renovations.

Not all contractors offer the same quality, though, and prices can vary accordingly. Good finish work can cost two to three times more than that done by a standard contractor. Tailor your team to the specific needs of each project, using more affordable options for lower-priced flips and reserving high-end professionals for luxury projects.

As you build your vendor list, aim to have at least two companies for every trade you need. This depth will give you greater control over costs and timelines. In metro areas like Seattle, LA, Chicago, or New York, contractors are often in high demand, and their pricing can fluctuate based on their workload. Focus on building a strong bench of roughing contractors to mitigate these challenges.

Sourcing contractors takes time and effort, but it's a worthwhile investment as you grow your flipping business. Start by working with general contractors on your first few projects, learning from their processes and gradually building your own network of subcontractors. By carefully curating your construction team and maintaining a diverse bench of professionals, you'll be well equipped to tackle any project that comes your way, maximizing your profits and ensuring long-term success in the dynamic world of real estate investing.

WORKSHEET: VENDOR LIST

ROUGH-INS: 2 OF THE FOLLOWING

| General contractors |
| Demo crews |
| Architects |
| Engineers |
| Surveyors |
| Siders |
| Window installers |
| Roofers |
| Framers |
| Electricians |
| Plumbers |
| HVAC teams |
| Drainage teams |
| Decks and fences |
| Landscapers |

INTERIOR: 2 OF THE FOLLOWING

| Insulation |
| Drywallers |
| Cabinet suppliers |
| Millwork |
| Flooring |
| Tile |
| Cabinets |
| Painter |
| Trim-out team |
| Handyman |

 You can find a printable version of this worksheet at www.BiggerPockets.com/FrameworkBonus.

When it comes to flipping properties, sometimes the biggest rewards come from the most challenging projects. I remember one particular deal that truly embodied this idea—a 7,000-square-foot house in an upscale neighborhood in Bellevue, Washington. This property's history included the defeat of three different developers, over a seven-to-eight-year period. It was a tough nut to crack, but I knew that with the right execution, it could be a home run.

The property was listed for $3.1 million, which was a bit above our usual price range of $1.5–$2 million. However, after the seller had been on the market for a year and a half, on and off, we finally reached an agreement. We ended up paying $2.85 million, about a 10 percent discount—a reasonable deal considering the property's history.

We invested around $1.3–$1.4 million into the project, completely redesigning the house from a Mediterranean style to a contemporary one that better suited the Washington market. It took careful planning and multiple rounds of bidding to bring the costs down to a level that would allow us to turn a profit. Our efforts paid off when we sold the property for $6.5 million, generating over $1 million in profit after all the hard-money costs, sales costs, and partner costs.

The key to success in this deal was having the resources and versatility to take on such a challenging project. It's always advantageous to buy a property when there's no competition, as it often leads to a better deal. While others may have been hesitant to take on such a massive undertaking, we approached it with a clear vision and a well-established plan.

This deal goes to show that in the world of real estate investing, the greatest opportunities often lie in the projects that others are afraid to touch. By being prepared, resourceful, and willing to take calculated risks, we were able to transform a property that had defeated multiple developers into a highly profitable venture. It's a testament to the power of perseverance, expertise, and a keen eye for potential in the face of adversity.

WORKING WITH CONTRACTORS

When you look for general contractors, you want to find ones who specialize with investors. The contractor is key—they're going to execute your construction plan, and they need experience in flipping properties. Contractors who work for investors have different pricing, skill sets, and are essential for creating profit in a flip property. Some contractors do custom home renovations, but they also cost more. It is essential you hire a contractor who can help you control your costs. The more experience the better. This is what makes projects easier (less expensive) or more difficult (more expensive). The more resources you have, the more you can execute and maximize deals.

Find contractors in every city you want to work in. Just because you've found a good contractor in one area doesn't mean they'll drive to another to do the deal. Or, if they do agree to a larger area or multiple areas, they may spike the price because of the travel. As an investor, we look for two trades for each profession.

Here's a list of the main subcontractors I try to keep on my bench:

- General contractors
- Electricians
- Plumbers
- HVAC
- Roofers
- Flooring company
- Tile installer
- Framers
- Siders
- Drywallers
- Painters
- Millwork installers
- Architect and permit teams

There are many other resources and trades to always be sourcing. The more resources you have, the more opportunity there is to reduce renovation costs.

SOURCING CONTRACTORS

Finding the right professionals can be challenging, as every subcontractor and general contractor is different. Some contractors prefer working with investors and builders, as they appreciate the volume of work and prompt payment without the hassle of dealing with homeowners who may change their minds or have strong opinions on every detail. These contractors often charge less than those who primarily work with homeowners on renovations.

To find and vet the right contractors, I recommend permit tracking. Most cities have public websites that allow you to search for permits issued on specific properties. To access this information, simply google the city's name along with "permit issuing" and "permit tracking." These websites will typically provide details on how permits are tracked, issued, and submitted.

Once you've located the appropriate website, you can search for properties that have been sold and renovated by other flippers or developers. This will give you insight into the quality of work and the timeline of the project. More importantly, you can access the permits pulled for each project, which will list the contact information for the roughing contractors, such as electricians, plumbers, and general contractors.

By data mining properties from the MLS, Realtor.com, or Zillow.com and pulling the addresses of recently sold and renovated homes, you can create a list of permits to track down. While this method may not provide information on finish carpenters, it's an excellent way to find the roughing contractors who work with flippers and developers.

This permit-tracking strategy is my secret for sourcing contractors. It allows you to cut through the noise and find professionals who are experienced in working with investors like yourself. While some people may not find this method as effective, I believe it's a perfect way to get what you need and build a reliable bench of contractors for your flipping business.

Driving for dollars. Another effective method for sourcing contractors is driving for dollars. As I'm always out looking for potential investment properties, I make it a point to investigate any homes that catch my eye. If I come across a promising property, I'll go the extra mile and knock on the door to see what's behind it. This approach not only helps me find new deals but also allows me to connect with contractors who might be working on the property.

When I come across a site that's under construction, I take a moment to assess whether it's a homeowner renovation or a flip. Homeowner renovations often have company signs prominently displayed, as the contractors are proud of their work and are actively marketing their services to attract more retail business. On the other hand, investment contractors tend to be more discreet with their signage. The way the jobsite is run can also provide clues about the nature of the project.

If I see a construction site that piques my interest, I make it a point to get out of my car, introduce myself, and strike up a conversation with the people working there. This allows me to gather valuable information about the project and the contractors involved. Once I have their contact details, I can begin the vetting process, which we'll cover in a moment.

Another scenario where driving for dollars can be particularly useful is when I've been outbid on a property by other flippers. Let's say I've written thirty offers and haven't managed to secure a single deal. Instead of getting discouraged, I view this as an opportunity. Those thirty properties that slipped through my fingers are now active projects that I can add to my drive list. By checking on their progress and seeing who's working on them, I might uncover some valuable resources.

If I'm in dire need of reliable contractors, it's worth investing the time to investigate these projects. The flippers who outbid me might have access to contractors with lower costs, which could be a game changer for my own business. By connecting with these contractors, I could potentially save a significant amount of money on my future projects.

While driving for dollars might seem a bit old-fashioned, it's a tried-and-true method that consistently delivers results. Alongside permit tracking, it's one of the best ways to find high-quality contractors who are experienced in working with investors.

Talk to your title rep. Another resource to tap into is your title rep. They can provide you with a list of properties recently purchased by LLCs, which you can then drive by to see if any work is being done. This targeted approach can help you focus your efforts on properties that are most likely to have active construction projects.

Some people might question whether spending eight hours driving around looking for contractors is a productive use of time. But when you consider the potential savings, it becomes clear that it's a worthwhile investment. For example, if you find a general contractor who can complete a project 10–20 percent cheaper than your current options, you could save $10,000–$20,000 on a $100,000 estimate. That translates to an impressive hourly rate for the time spent driving for dollars.

Investor networking is another valuable way to find contractors. A personal referral from an investor who has worked with a contractor on a rental or flip property is always a strong endorsement. They can speak to the contractor's quality of work and adherence to timelines. The only challenge is that when an investor finds a great contractor, they may be reluctant to share them if they're already keeping the contractor busy with their own projects.

That said, there are still ways to leverage investor networking to your advantage, particularly when connecting with newer flippers. One approach is to offer your services in exchange for contractor referrals.

For example, you could propose a light internship where you drive by their properties once a week to take progress photos. This allows the investor to stay updated on the project's progress without taking up their contractor's time. In return, you ask for referrals to some of their contractors. It's important to be clear that you won't steal the contractors away—you're simply looking to learn and build relationships.

This arrangement can be mutually beneficial: The newer flipper gets free assistance with monitoring their projects, while you gain invaluable learning opportunities and the chance to build long-term relationships with flippers in your market. Over my career, I've had numerous investors offer to help with my business growth, drive projects, or even handle social media tasks. In exchange, they get to see our processes for acquiring, borrowing, and selling projects, as well as how we design and budget them. Many of these individuals have turned into long-term clients.

Another tip is to **follow local investors on social media**, as they often plug their vendors in their posts.

Meetup groups are another excellent resource for finding contractors. Many general contractors and subcontractors attend investor meetups because they're often working on their own projects or seeking investor work. They're actively looking for clients like you. However, it's crucial to vet them carefully. I've had some less-than-ideal experiences with contractors who are constantly hustling for work at these events. If they seem to be begging for work, there's likely a reason they don't have a steady pipeline. We'll discuss how to vet contractors later in this chapter.

Supply stores can also be great places to find contractors. When I order tile or flooring for a house, the supplier is often eager to recommend installers to secure the job. These vendors and stores are typically geared toward investor pricing, offering affordable products and installation services. Always ask if they have any recommended installers. I recently changed my flooring provider to a different store because they agreed to find me a few good installers at a reasonable price in exchange for buying all my materials from them. The store prioritized finding the installers to secure my ongoing business. It's all about creating win-win partnerships.

Every big city has areas known for their concentration of building supply stores. In Orange County, for example, many people head to Anaheim for cabinets, tile, flooring, and other supplies. Research your local area to identify these hubs. Investor networking can be a great way to get referrals for these locations. You can also try googling "investor kitchen cabinets" plus your location to find relevant suppliers.

VETTING CONTRACTORS

As a flipper, our success depends on third-party companies, like contractors, performing and completing their job as agreed upon. If a company fails to deliver, it can jeopardize the entire project, causing delays and cost overruns that kill profit. In the worst-case scenario, they might take your money and disappear. Thoroughly vetting contractors before hiring them is essential.

When hiring contractors, always verify that they are licensed and bonded. Once you've obtained the contractor's licensing and bonding information, it's your responsibility to validate it. Most states have a Labor & Industries (L&I) website where you can check the status of their license and bond. Ask for addresses of past projects and look them up online to see the finished results. Find out the budget for each property and compare the investor's purchase and sale dates to gauge how quickly the contractor works.

Take note of how long they've been in business. If a contractor claims to have been in the industry for ten years, but their license has only been active for two years, it's a red flag. Investigate what company they had before and why it was shut down. If a contractor has opened and closed numerous construction companies, it's a giant red flag, and you should typically avoid hiring them.

Often, contractors have to restart their business due to claims or insolvency, and you don't want to be involved with a company that might dissolve within the next twelve months. Additionally, use the list of addresses the contractor provided to see if permits were pulled and if those permits are in their name or another tradesman's. I once had a contractor give me a list of addresses they claimed to have worked on, but upon further research, I discovered that different general contractors had completed all the projects. The contractor was trying to mislead me with impressive pictures. Always verify the information, just as you would when buying a deal. By thoroughly vetting contractors, assessing compatibility, and verifying their licensing, bonding, and project history, you can make informed decisions and avoid potential risks associated with hiring unreliable or unqualified contractors for your real estate projects.

Seek referrals from other investors and talk to them about their experiences with the contractor. Set up a preliminary call to ask the contractor if they primarily work with investors or homeowners, as these are two different types of contractors. Knowing their preferred client type can save you time in the long run. Inquire about their preferred work locations, as contractors often provide better pricing for projects closer to where they live to minimize travel time and expenses.

After obtaining addresses of past projects, ask about the client's total investment to get the property to its current state. Most contractors provide free up-front estimates with a general scope and pricing, which allows you to evaluate if you want to pursue that contractor further. Request a copy of the quote to evaluate their pricing and ensure they're the right fit for your project. Frame this as valuing their time and not wanting to waste it on projects that don't align with their pricing.

HIRING BUDGET VS. LUXURY CONTRACTORS

When selecting contractors, know who you're hiring, as trade quality and pricing can vary dramatically. Take painters, for example. They often bid competitively on the first few projects but then gradually increase their prices, forcing you to find a replacement. To avoid this, always track your costs and compare past bids to current charges.

Quality also plays a significant role in pricing. For a standard flip, our paint costs an average of $2 per square foot (PSF) for the exterior and $3 PSF for the interior, when using our more affordable painters. On the other hand, our high-end painters, who invest more time in surface preparation and perfection, charge an average of $3–$4 PSF for the exterior and $4–$6 PSF for the interior. Higher-priced properties often come with elevated buyer expectations, and these buyers tend to notice the finer details.

To ensure you have the right professionals for every job, maintain a bench of at least two flooring installers, landscapers, handymen, exterminators, and other finish contractors. Handymen, in particular, can be invaluable for trim-out work, potentially reducing costs significantly compared to a general contractor. For example, a general contracting bid might include $2,500–$3,000 for installing door handles, closet racks, doorstops, and other finishing items, covering both materials and installation. However, the actual material cost for these items might only be around $500, and the labor could be completed in a single day by someone earning $50 per hour, totaling $400. By handling these tasks directly, you can save a substantial amount on markup costs.

The reason I always recommend having two professionals for each trade on your bench is to provide flexibility when general contractors are bidding on projects. This allows you to plug in your own subcontractors as needed, potentially reducing costs and improving efficiency.

I personally pay more for general contractors, but it saves money in the long run—that way, I can work *on* my business and not so much *in* my business. As you become an entrepreneur, you want to think about what your time is worth, so you can be the most efficient. The same is true if you're a W-2 employee with a nine-to-five and don't have time to visit your site. A general contractor who you've properly vetted can run the jobsite for you. If you can't get there, you want someone who can.

THE BUNDLE METHOD

When general contractors are busy and quoting my projects high, it's my job to pivot and figure out how to reduce costs while keeping projects moving forward. When subcontracting myself, I use what I call the "bundle method." The **bundle method** is a strategic approach to managing renovation projects that can optimize costs and maintain quality control. This method involves directly subcontracting simpler, stand-alone tasks such as demolition, roofing, gutter installation, and garage door replacement. The process then focuses on two main phases: the rough-in phase and the finish phase.

The **rough-in phase**, also known as the "rough" phase, refers to the initial stage of construction or renovation where the basic framework and essential systems are installed but not yet completed or covered. This typically includes framing of walls, floors, and ceilings; installation of electrical wiring and boxes; plumbing pipe installation; HVAC ductwork and system placement; and rough carpentry for doors and windows.

By bundling these rough-in tasks together, you can often achieve better coordination and potentially reduce costs through economies of scale. The finish phase, which comes after the rough-in, involves all the visible, final elements that complete the renovation. This includes tasks like installing drywall, painting, laying flooring, hanging doors, installing trim, and placing fixtures. By subcontracting this phase separately, you maintain greater control over the final appearance and quality of the property.

This method allows for more direct management of costs in the finish phase by personally selecting materials and finishes. It also provides flexibility in scheduling, as finish trades are typically easier to coordinate. The result is often a higher-quality final product at a lower overall cost, potentially increasing the profit margin on the property flip without compromising resale value.

CHAPTER 11

BIDDING, CONTRACTS, AND YOUR SCOPE OF WORK

It's the little details that are vital.
Little things make big things happen.
—JOHN WOODEN, FORMER AMERICAN BASKETBALL COACH

NOW THAT YOU'VE found and vetted your ideal contractor, it's time to make sure you have the appropriate processes and paperwork in place for an effective renovation. Implementing an effective plan is key for success in real estate flipping. While it's often said that money is made on the purchase, the plan itself is equally important. Your success hinges on developing the right construction strategy and optimizing the design for each property. The key is to recognize and maximize the potential in properties that others might overlook.

When hiring contractors for your real estate projects, make sure to understand their bidding methodologies and clearly define responsibilities up front. There are generally two approaches contractors use for pricing their work: time-and-materials billing or fixed-price bids. I strongly prefer fixed bids, especially when hiring general contractors, as they provide the cost certainty required to make informed decisions when evaluating and purchasing potential flip properties. With a fixed bid, the contractor provides a flat, agreed-upon total price for the entire scope of work before commencing any tasks.

This allows for accurate budgeting and financial projections, as the contractor absorbs any costs exceeding their bid amount. In contrast, time-and-materials billing involves the contractor charging for labor hours worked plus material costs, with no firm total price established up front. Costs can escalate quickly under this approach if a project runs over schedule. Another important consideration is clarifying whether the contractor handles responsibilities like permitting and material sourcing or if those tasks fall on you as the property owner. Neglecting to define these roles can lead to confusion and project delays.

However, I recommend never paying a contractor for a comprehensive, fixed-price bid, as experienced contractors should provide detailed bids free of charge when they want the job. By understanding bid methodologies, defining responsibilities like permitting and material sourcing, and avoiding paid bids, you can engage contractors with confidence and accurately budget for your real estate projects from the start, ensuring a more seamless and successful process.

LUMP-SUM BIDS VS. ITEMIZED BIDS

A lump-sum bid is a contract pricing method in which a contractor proposes a single, all-encompassing price for the entire scope of work, without providing itemized costs for individual components. While this approach may seem straightforward, investors should exercise caution when considering lump-sum bids. In the event of a contract termination, the absence of a detailed cost breakdown can potentially lead to disputes. Without an itemized list of expenses, accurately assessing the value of completed work becomes challenging, which may result in disagreements over appropriate compensation for services rendered.

If you paid a contractor $50,000 and had to fire them after only demo and framing were completed, the contractor could claim that the demo work was over $20,000 and the framing was over $40,000, potentially coming after you for an additional $10,000. Itemized bids provide clarity, showing the percentage of work completed for each line item. If the contractor has done 50 percent of the $10,000 electrical work, you can allocate $5,000 to what they've completed.

I only accept construction estimates that are itemized, with each section of the renovation broken down financially per line item, such as electrical, plumbing, HVAC, millwork, doors, and trim. The contractor should provide a price for each line item, with the total, including taxes, at the end of the contract. This is also essential for obtaining construction loans, as lenders want to see which line items are being paid for when you request progress payment draws. Itemized bids give you safety and clarity to keep your project funded and moving forward.

When transitioning from vetting to hiring contractors, an itemized bid proves invaluable for budget management. If a contractor's quote exceeds your allocated funds, a detailed breakdown allows for targeted adjustments. For instance, if your budget is $90,000 and the submitted bid totals $100,000, you can analyze individual line items to identify potential savings. This approach enables strategic decision-making about which services to retain under the general contractor and which to potentially outsource.

For example, if roofing is quoted at $10,000 within the overall bid, but direct engagement with a specialized roofer could reduce this to $7,000, you might achieve a $3,000 saving. By carefully reviewing each category, you can optimize costs while maintaining project quality and staying within budget constraints.

CONSTRUCTION CONTRACTS

A construction contract is key for keeping your jobsite moving forward and protecting your investment. While a contractor's bid and estimate serve as an agreement to pay them for their scope of work, they often don't address important aspects like procedures, time frames, licensing, environmental hazards, and permits. A construction contract provides clarity on these issues, ensuring that everyone is on the same page and acknowledging their responsibilities. The purpose of the construction contract is to outline who is responsible for various aspects of the project. In our construction contract, it clearly states whether the owner or the contractor is responsible for obtaining permits. This has saved me from significant issues on several occasions.

My construction contract covers the total price, completion dates, penalties for late completion, bonuses for early completion, environmental considerations, permit responsibilities, and the contractor's obligation to maintain their licensing and bonding throughout the project. It also outlines quality of work expectations and the consequences if the contractor fails to perform. I like to be crystal clear about what needs to be done before final payment is released. I will include a punch list in my contract (which I will explain later in this chapter).

A penalty clause states that if the contractor finishes past the agreed-upon date, a daily rate will be deducted for any additional days. When determining the penalty amount, I usually use my daily interest rate payment, sometimes with a small buffer. I include a similar clause for bonuses, stating that the contractor will receive the same daily bonus if they finish early. The contract also outlines the process for extending the completion date due to factors beyond the contractor's control, such as permit delays, inspector issues, or neighbor problems. In these cases, the contractor has a contractual obligation to send an email documenting the delay and the proposed extension. Verbal agreements are not acceptable.

The construction contract should clearly delineate the change order process, a crucial aspect of real estate renovation projects. **Change orders** are modifications to the original scope of work and are common in construction and renovation. However, if not managed properly, they can significantly impact a property investor's profitability. A well-structured contract should stipulate that all change orders must be submitted in writing by the contractor. These written change orders should include a detailed description of the proposed changes, the reason for the change, the impact on the project timeline, and a breakdown of additional costs or savings.

The contract should explicitly state that no changes can be implemented without the property owner's written approval. This approval should include acknowledgment of any cost adjustments and timeline modifications. It's advisable to avoid verbal change orders entirely. Relying on verbal agreements can lead to misunderstandings and disputes when it comes time for final billing. Written documentation provides a clear record of what was agreed upon, protecting both parties and ensuring transparency throughout the project.

Other important elements to include in the contract are warranties and guarantees provided by the contractor, insurance and licensing requirements, termination clauses, and dispute resolution processes. In the event that a contractor fails to fulfill their obligations, such as abandoning the project halfway through or disappearing with a significant portion of the funds, a solid legal contract provides the framework for holding them accountable. With a well-drafted contract, you have the legal grounds to pursue the contractor for damages, demand their return to complete the work, or seek other remedies as outlined in the agreement. Having a clear and comprehensive contract in place can also serve as a deterrent for contractors considering abandoning a project or engaging in fraudulent behavior.

In addition to the construction contract, we tie in allowances and create a spec sheet or design sheet for the contractors to sign, acknowledging the materials, quality, and overall look we expect within their scope of work. A spec allowance is a predetermined budget for specific items or materials in a construction or renovation project that haven't been fully specified at the time of contract signing. It's commonly used for elements like appliances, lighting fixtures, or flooring. This allows flexibility in selection while maintaining budget control. If the final cost of an item is less than the allowance, the client gets a credit; if it's more, they pay the difference.

While it's good to have flexibility on the budget from your end as the investor, it's important to include language that specifies that the contractor's bid is fixed for the included scope of work. This is important language to include in your contract to prevent contractors from claiming that their bid was only an estimate and subject to change. I've had contractors attempt to increase costs by stating that their original quote was just an estimate. By clearly stating that the bid is a firm number, you can protect yourself from these tactics.

Spec allowances help projects move forward without finalizing every detail but require careful management to avoid budget overruns. Having spec allowances means you can go up to a certain price point. It's up to you to source materials within that allowance. Most material cost increases are the investor's fault, not the contractor's. You have to control your own desires for how you want the house to look. Put the allowances in the estimate and commit to staying below those prices.

When having the contractor sign the construction contract, include a draw schedule that references sections of the bid. The contractor will not receive additional money until those specific items are completed. This helps keep the contractor on track and prevents them from constantly asking for more money when the work hasn't been done. Payment benchmarks should also match your construction draw schedule to ensure a balance with your capital. It's a great way to keep the contractor motivated, as you can point out that your lender won't approve more funds until certain milestones are met.

When communicating with contractors, it's important to avoid coming across as brand new to the business. Contractors, like anyone else, are trying to make money, and while they're not necessarily out to rip you off, they will take advantage of an opportunity if they sense inexperience. It's similar to how you might approach a seller who seems unsure about their property's value and is open to a low offer.

CREATE A CLEAR SCOPE OF WORK

Creating a clear **scope of work** (SOW) is key for effectively managing a renovation project. The SOW is a comprehensive description of all tasks required in a remodel, serving as a guide for contractors to estimate costs and understand the project's breadth. It helps maintain budget control and provides a clear road map for all involved parties.

The development of your SOW should be based on comparable properties and the anticipated after-repair value (ARV) of the project. Pricing can vary significantly depending on factors such as finish quality, location, and the extent of work needed. As an investor, it's critical that you, not the contractor, create the SOW. This is a common mistake among investors who rely too heavily on contractors to make project decisions. Instead, use market data from comparable properties to inform your decisions about what needs to be done. The contractor's role is to execute the plan and provide feedback on potential issues or implementation challenges.

The finished scope of work details all elements needed to complete and upgrade the home's interior. It should also include mechanical upgrades. This is accompanied by an allowance sheet specifying budget allocations and a spec sheet providing detailed material specifications, which guide contractors in accurate cost estimation.

When creating your scope of work, incorporate insights from your property walk-through alongside comparable market data. These are your **walk-through notes.** During your initial inspection, take detailed notes on visible issues, necessary repairs, and potential improvements. These observations might include structural problems, outdated systems, cosmetic deficiencies, or areas requiring immediate attention.

Your walk-through notes serve as a practical complement to market-based decisions, ensuring that your renovation plan addresses both property-specific needs and market expectations. This thorough approach of combining on-site observations with market analysis helps create a comprehensive and accurate scope of work. Investing time in this detailed planning process up front can significantly reduce unexpected issues, minimize budget overruns, and streamline the overall renovation process, ultimately leading to a more successful and profitable project.

One thing I like to do after writing my scope of work is have my project manager walk the project with it too (this could also be your spouse or business partner if you're brand new to the business). This gives me a second pair of eyes when building out my notes and renovation plan. To create this scope efficiently, we use a standardized checklist during property walk-throughs, noting window counts and specific repair or upgrade needs. This systematic approach ensures we capture all necessary details during the initial inspection, resulting in a comprehensive and accurate finished scope of work that aligns with both the property's requirements and the project's budget constraints.

A comprehensive scope of work for a house flip should include a detailed list of all renovations, repairs, and improvements planned for the property. Here are key items that should typically be included:

Exterior work:
- Roofing repairs or replacement
- Siding repairs or replacement
- Window and door replacements
- Exterior painting
- Landscaping and yard work
- Driveway and walkway repairs

Interior renovations:
- Flooring installation or refinishing
- Wall repairs and painting
- Ceiling repairs or updates
- Trim work and moldings
- Interior door replacements

Kitchen updates:
- Cabinet replacement or refacing
- Countertop installation
- Appliance upgrades
- Sink and faucet replacement
- Lighting fixtures

Bathroom renovations:
- Tub/shower replacement or refinishing
- Toilet replacement
- Vanity and sink installation
- Tile work
- Lighting and mirror updates

Electrical work:
- Upgrading electrical panel
- Adding or relocating outlets and switches
- Installing new light fixtures
- Bringing wiring up to code

Plumbing:
- Pipe repairs or replacements
- Water heater installation
- Fixing leaks
- Updating fixtures

HVAC:
- Furnace/AC repair or replacement
- Ductwork cleaning or replacement
- Thermostat upgrades

Structural improvements:
- Foundation repairs
- Wall removals or additions
- Support beam installations

Energy efficiency upgrades:
- Insulation installation
- Weatherstripping
- Energy-efficient window installations

Miscellaneous:
- Pest control treatments
- Mold remediation
- Asbestos or lead paint removal

SAMPLE LIST OF ITEMS TO INCLUDE IN YOUR SCOPE OF WORK

1. Kitchen renovation:
   - New cabinets and countertops (mid-grade quartz, approximately $3,000–$5,000)
   - Appliance package (stainless steel, mid-range brand, $2,500–$4,000)
   - Flooring replacement (luxury vinyl plank, $3–$5 per square foot)
2. Bathroom updates:
   - New vanity and fixtures ($500–$1,000 per bathroom)
   - Tile work (ceramic tile, $5–$10 per square foot)

3. Painting:
   - Interior and exterior painting ($1.50–$3.50 per square foot)
4. Flooring:
   - Carpet replacement in bedrooms ($2–$4 per square foot)
   - Hardwood refinishing in living areas ($3–$5 per square foot)
5. Exterior work:
   - Landscaping improvements ($2,000–$5,000)
   - Roof repair or replacement if needed ($5,000–$10,000 for a moderate-sized home)

You can find a sample Scope of Work at www.BiggerPockets.com/FrameworkBonus.

SPEC SHEETS

Each aspect of the renovation should include a **spec sheet**, which includes specific details about materials, quality standards, and any particular requirements. The scope of work should also outline the sequence of tasks and estimated timelines for completion. This comprehensive list helps ensure all aspects of the renovation are accounted for, aiding in accurate budgeting and project management.

Our construction contract states that the contractor's bid is inclusive of the written scope of work and the specifications provided by the investor. This means that even if the contractor forgot to include something in their estimate, they're still obligated to do it as outlined in the scope of work. It prevents minor mistakes from becoming major issues. If it's a significant discrepancy, work it out with the contractor. Remember, these are your partners, and you want the agreement to be fair for everyone involved.

If you don't have a spec sheet that calls for specific types of flooring, tile, cabinets, and other trim finishes, make sure to have a signed allowance page. This document outlines the allowances and maximum prices the investor will pay for their selections. It prevents the contractor from using cheaper fixtures than agreed upon. All agreements must be in writing, as verbal agreements often lead to overages and conflicts.

END OF PROJECT: FINAL PAYMENT AND PUNCH LIST

There's often a constant battle at the end of a project where the contractor wants their final payment, but you need to make sure everything is truly complete. That's where a **punch list** comes in. "Punching out" your house means going through the property with a fine-tooth comb, marking any contractor mistakes or unfinished items with blue tape. Even the best contractors will miss things, and it can be tough to get them back to finish up if you've already handed over the final check.

I start my punch list process two weeks before the scheduled completion date. I walk the property, take pictures, and use apps like Google Photos to create a gallery of items that need to be addressed. Under each photo, I write a description of the issue. You can also use paid apps like Punch List, but Google Photos is a free alternative.

A week before completion, I do another round of punch lists. Then, on the final day, we do a comprehensive blue tape walk, marking every little detail that needs attention. We take photos of each item, noting what needs to be done, and create a report for the contractor to sign off on. The contractor must complete every item on that list before receiving final payment.

Once the contractor finishes the punch list, we walk the property together to verify everything is complete. We don't want any unfinished items jeopardizing the sale. After confirming all punch list items are resolved, all permits are closed out, and the site is clean of debris, we release the final payment.

Have the property pre-inspected during the punch list process. Anything that was part of the contractor's original scope of work must be completed before final payment. If there are new items identified outside the original scope, that's a change order, and you can't fairly withhold payment for those.

Additionally, I make sure to obtain lien releases from all trades and the general contractor upon completion of their work. This practice protects you from potential legal and financial complications. To further mitigate lien risks, consider having your title company open a preliminary title report about a week before the project's final completion date. This proactive step helps identify any potential issues early, ensuring a smoother transaction when you sell the property.

For house flips, it's advisable not to offer personal warranties. Unlike new construction projects, where builders often provide warranties, flipped homes have existing structures and systems that require ongoing maintenance. Since you didn't build the property from the ground up, offering a comprehensive warranty could expose you to significant liability.

Instead of personal warranties, consider offering a home warranty through a reputable title insurance company or third-party provider. These warranties typically cost between $350 and $450 and can be included as part of the sale. This approach often satisfies buyers' concerns about coverage without placing undue liability on you as the seller.

For specific items like appliances, roofs, or HVAC systems that come with manufacturer warranties, transfer these directly from the vendor to the buyer. This practice ensures the buyer has direct access to warranty services without involving you as an intermediary, which could lead to ongoing service requests and potential disputes.

LIEN RELEASES

Lien releases are critical legal documents in real estate construction and renovation projects that protect property owners from potential financial claims. A **lien release**, also known as a waiver of lien, is a formal statement from a contractor, subcontractor, or supplier affirming that they have received payment for their work or materials and relinquish their right to place a lien on the property. To effectively use lien releases, require one with every final payment to a contractor, ensuring it states that the contractor has been paid in full and that all associated bills, including those to subcontractors and suppliers, have been settled.

Make the signing of a lien release a condition for final payment in your contract. The importance of obtaining lien releases cannot be overstated. If liens are filed against your property without a signed release, you may find yourself in the difficult position of negotiating with both the contractor and the lien holders, potentially leading to delayed property closings, legal complications, and additional unexpected costs. However, with a properly executed lien release, you gain significant legal protection. If liens are filed despite the release, you have options: You can pursue action against the contractor's bond, work directly with subcontractors to resolve issues, or use the release as evidence in legal proceedings, if necessary. By consistently using lien releases, you effectively transfer liability to the contractor, safeguarding your investment and ensuring a smoother renovation or construction process. This practice is essential for risk management in real estate projects and can prevent many potential legal and financial complications.

I've been involved in thousands of transactions, and while this scenario is rare, it's crucial to be prepared. I once had a situation where an electrician wasn't paid, despite the contractor claiming they had been.

The electrician placed a lien on the property right before closing, hitting the HUD with a $16,000 bill. I didn't want to pay it, as getting the money back from the contractor would have been nearly impossible. We showed the title company the contract and the lien release, which allowed us to bond around the lien and close the deal. The contractor and the subcontractor then had to work it out between themselves. Bonding around a lien is when the title company holds back a portion of the proceeds and bonds around the lien to facilitate the closing.

When making the final payment to a contractor, have them sign the lien release and write "final payment, paid in full" in the memo of the check. By cashing that check, the contractor acknowledges that they have been paid in full and can't come back later with additional bills.

CHAPTER 12
RISK MITIGATION

I signed up for this. Whatever comes with it, I'll take it.
—TERRELL SUGGS, FORMER NFL FOOTBALL PLAYER

AS YOU GAIN experience with house flipping, you'll develop a deeper understanding of proper budgeting and jobsite management. To mitigate the learning curve and minimize trial and error, I can share insights that will help you reduce risk and create a flexible budget sheet. With each project, you'll have the opportunity to refine and systematize your processes, including planning for contingencies.

When confronted with unforeseen expenses, such as $2,000 to fix damages from unexpected rot, don't panic. Instead, review your allowances and make strategic adjustments. For example, you might reduce flooring costs by $.50 per square foot or trim the appliance budget by 20 percent by selecting a different specification. These small changes can often offset unexpected costs without significantly impacting the overall quality of the renovation. Communication with your contractor is key in these situations.

Explain the situation and your proposed adjustments to the allowances. Since they've already agreed to these allowances, they should either credit you for the cost difference or procure the newly specified items without charging for the change order. This approach gives you versatility as an investor and helps prevent projects from spiraling out of control financially. To streamline future projects, consider creating templates for various styles and budgets. For instance, if you're working on a mid-century house, develop design and specification sheets for different budget levels. This ensures you maintain the appropriate style while offering flexibility in material choices and pricing.

By preparing three different specification levels for each house style, you'll be better equipped to adapt to market conditions and unexpected issues. These templated specification sheets allow for quick initial planning and easy modifications later. As you analyze local inventory and comparable properties, note the features and finishes at different price points. Use this information to set appropriate allowances for each price range, ensuring your renovations meet market expectations while maintaining profitability. By implementing these strategies, you'll be better prepared to handle the challenges of house flipping, maintain budget control, and adapt to changing circumstances throughout your projects.

To reduce risk while you're learning, focus on properties that require like-for-like change-outs. Start with cosmetic renovations. These projects mainly involve updating finishes, which are simpler to plan and execute. Most variances in these projects will stem from your choices in specifications and materials, giving you more control over the budget. Look for homes that need minor floor plan adjustments or those that don't require adding bathrooms, finishing unfinished spaces, or rewiring the entire house. By sticking to straightforward upgrades and finish work, you'll have more efficient projects, learn the process better, and minimize the risk of going significantly over budget.

As you gain experience and move on to more complex flips, the key to reducing risk is creating a clear scope of work and a corresponding detailed budget. These documents should clearly show your contractor how you arrived at your numbers and why. Avoid the common mistake of new flippers who choose arbitrary budget figures, perhaps suggested by wholesalers or brokers. Instead, ensure your budget accurately reflects the necessary work and materials.

Remember, successful house flipping involves a balanced relationship between you and your contractor. Both parties are running businesses, and the arrangement needs to be mutually beneficial. If a contractor underbids, they may face financial difficulties. Conversely, if you accept an overbid, you could find yourself in financial trouble. The goal is to find a fair middle ground that works for both parties. By following these guidelines, you can gradually build your skills and confidence in managing house-flipping projects, starting with simpler renovations and progressing to more complex ones as you gain experience.

STEPS TO MANAGE YOUR PROJECT

Creating a comprehensive project plan before soliciting bids is crucial for successful real estate investment. As an investor, you should develop a detailed scope of work, finalize your design vision, clearly define project parameters (including what should and shouldn't be done), and establish design allowances. This preparation helps avoid a common pitfall: rushing to bring general contractors on-site without a clear plan. Such haste often leads to costly change orders and project overruns.

Once you have your detailed plan, proceed with obtaining and finalizing bids from contractors. It's essential to have all agreements in place before any work begins. This includes a signed construction contract, a clearly defined project timeline, and detailed specifications of the work to be performed. Never allow contractors to start work without these elements in place. This approach ensures all parties have a clear understanding of the project scope, timeline, and expectations, reducing the likelihood of disputes or unexpected costs. By investing time in thorough planning and contract preparation, you set the stage for a more efficient and cost-effective renovation process.

I've made the mistake of having workers start on a project without getting everything in writing. I wanted to keep my timelines moving! I was aware of my hard-money costs and my debt costs, and I didn't want to wait on paperwork to get started. I kept pushing forward. Well, not having everything in writing cost me about 10–20 percent more on my bid because I wasn't organized in my detailing of the project. The contractor hadn't put everything in writing, so there were a lot of things subject to change. Don't make that same mistake.

As you're going through your construction process, set those benchmarks. Here's how we typically break it down: Let's say it's a $100,000 project. We give them 10 percent down at the very beginning to get the demo going. We want to see that demo completely done, permits applied for, and the site totally cleaned up. Once that's all taken care of, we move into the next set of draws. From there, we usually go 25 percent on the first set, which covers all the rough-ins. Then, once they get sign-off on the rough-ins, we give them another 25 percent to cover insulation, drywall, and getting to the finishing level. When they're ready for finishes and everything's been signed off on, we'll give them another 25 percent as they start installing those finishes. Then, the final payment comes once everything is 100 percent completed.

We're typically breaking our projects up into four to five draw payments, every time. The key is knowing when you want those things completed, because the amount of each draw is clearly listed on your bid. Based on their draw schedule, you can total up what needs to be done and what doesn't, and that tells you whether you should be putting in for those draws. Again, on a $100,000 budget, break it up into four or five different draws, make totals on their itemized bid, and set your benchmarks. You can even write it right there on their contract, so they know exactly when they're getting paid.

Always make sure your jobsite is set up with the right paperwork and access. Put a lockbox on there with a code, so people can get in and out. We post all our floor plans, construction contracts, bids—everything—right there on every jobsite. We also post our specs throughout, so as you're walking through, everything you need is right there in a clear folder. It's really important to keep a clean jobsite, with clarity and easy access. The last thing you want is to send a contractor out there when they're really busy, and they can't get in. They might not come back for another week, and that can cost you a good amount of money (maybe even up to $1,000) just from not having that lockbox in place. So make sure it's all set up.

Then, document all your walk-throughs with weekly pictures, budget updates, and statuses. It's key as you're working with contractors and getting them their draws. You know exactly what's been done, what hasn't, and if you're behind schedule. That clarity tells you when to pay people, what's been completed, and how to get things back on track, if needed.

JOBSITE "MUSTS" TO CONSIDER

To ensure a smooth and efficient renovation project, it's crucial to have all important documents and information clearly posted at the jobsite. Start by displaying your scope of work, along with the contractor's bid, floor plans, and spec sheet in a clear plastic sheet for all trades to reference. This includes detailed pictures and designs for specific tasks, like tile work in shower surrounds and kitchens. Clarity prevents mistakes and delays, ultimately putting more money in your pocket.

Implement a to-do list system by hanging a clipboard on the wall at every project. Encourage your project manager and team to write down any tasks or issues they notice while walking around the site. This practice ensures that everyone is aware of what needs to be done and allows tasks to be completed while the relevant subcontractor is still on-site, preventing unnecessary delays.

Always post safety rules, especially if you expect visits from labor and industries. Post jobsite rules as well, including policies on noise, smoking, safety, and cleaning expectations. A dirty jobsite can lead to injuries, failed inspections, and unprofessionalism. Maintain a clean site to prevent problems from spiraling out of control.

Display all permits in the windows to avoid complaints from neighbors and potential stop-work orders from building inspectors, which can cause significant delays. Post relevant layouts at the jobsite, such as cabinet layouts for kitchen renovations. This information is essential for mechanicals, electricians, plumbers, HVAC technicians, and anyone working on a project with specific layout requirements. Posting layouts helps avoid costly change orders and ensures that everything is placed correctly, preventing issues like unbalanced kitchens or cabinets that don't fit the intended layout.

Display as-builts (existing floor plans from when the property was purchased) and finalized plans (the "after" floor plan you aim to achieve) on all floors. This practice saves time by eliminating the need for workers to go up and down stairs to reference the plans and ensures that framing is done according to the most current information. Include a contact information sheet that lists the owner, permit team, general contractor, project manager, architect, and any other key contacts involved in the project. This allows anyone on-site with questions or updates to quickly reach the appropriate party.

Finally, post design sheets for specs, including design themes for millwork, tile, and special instructions to reduce confusion. For example, if you're working on a craftsman-style house with specific header details, take a picture of the exact millwork you want to be installed and post it at the doorjamb for installers to reference. Similarly, post pictures of the desired tile layout to avoid miscommunications and costly mistakes, such as a straight-line theme being installed as a brick-laid pattern in a mid-century house.

PREPPING THE JOBSITE

Prepping your site will make your life easier as a flipper, and you can begin to create templates and processes that are repeatable for each flipping project. It gives more clarity to everybody on your jobsite. When people know what to do—when it's all at their fingertips—it leads to fewer mistakes, fewer conflicts, and a much smoother, more profitable jobsite.

After everything's been posted, every jobsite should have a key box with its own unique number. I caution you to not use a universal key box code across jobsites. A universal code could lead to security issues, so I always pick a unique code for each jobsite. This ensures that only authorized personnel can access the property and helps maintain the security of your tools, materials, and the property itself.

A picture gallery needs to be set up for every property. We do this on every jobsite—before, during, and after. The reason being, as an operator, we've got a bigger team, projects scattered everywhere, and sometimes I can't drive out there that week. I want to be able to go through, get the photos, see what's happening and what's not, and determine if I should be concerned and get out to the jobsite. Plus, documenting your construction project can actually catch mistakes too.

To set up a picture gallery, designate a specific area on-site where you can display photos of the project's progress. This can be a wall in the main room or a dedicated space in the jobsite office. Print out photos of the property before the renovation began, as well as any architectural renderings or design concepts you have for the finished product. As the project progresses, have your team take photos at regular intervals (daily or weekly) and add them to the gallery. Make sure to label each photo with the date and a brief description of what's shown.

The picture gallery serves several purposes.

- It allows you, as the flipper, to monitor progress remotely and identify any potential issues or concerns that may require your attention on-site
- It helps your team stay motivated by providing a visual representation of their progress and the end goal they're working toward
- It can be used to catch and correct mistakes early on, before they become more costly and time-consuming to fix
- It serves as a valuable marketing tool when it comes time to sell the property, as you can show potential buyers the transformation the property has undergone

By implementing a picture gallery on every jobsite, you'll have a better understanding of each project's progress, even when you can't be there in person. This, combined with the proper posting of paperwork and unique key box codes, will lead to a more organized, efficient, and profitable flipping business.

In one of our projects, we had an electrician install all the recessed lights (can lights) in a property. After the drywall was up and the lights were turned on, we noticed that the lights were not in a straight line. It was a glaring issue, as the first impression of the house was marred by these crooked lights. Upon closer inspection, we found that the lights were off by about an inch on both sides, creating a zigzag effect throughout the property. The electrician adamantly denied that it wasn't his mistake, insisting that the drywallers had moved his can lights and that he wasn't responsible for paying for the fix.

Because we take weekly photos of our jobsites, we were able to pull up the rough-in pictures from before the drywallers started their work. These photos clearly showed that the can lights were already misaligned before the drywallers even set foot on the property. To make it even clearer, we drew a red line through the photos, highlighting the misalignment. Upon seeing this evidence, the electrician laughed and admitted, "Okay, this one's on me." He then took responsibility for the mistake, paid to have it fixed, and compensated the drywallers for the necessary repairs.

Another thing you should do when you are prepping your jobsite is introduce yourself to the neighbors. Let them know who you are and what you're going to subject them to for the next few months. Establish a positive relationship with them up front so that when your teams are ripping things apart, being noisy, and likely leaving messes here and there, your neighbor won't fly off the handle. The last thing you want is a neighbor calling the city on you every day, prompting them to shut your jobsite down or show up more, causing you more issues. So be friendly with your neighbors. I give my cell number out to every one of them, so they have direct access to me or my project manager. We want them to call us, not the city. Plus, if something happens and our contractor does something wrong, we want to be able to get on it right away, correct the issue, and make sure they know not to do that in the future.

VISITING THE JOBSITE

Visit your jobsite at least once a week, preferably on Fridays, to gauge progress and ensure a smooth operation. Check completed work and plan for the next week to avoid over-advancing funds to contractors. Protect yourself from losing money due to unfinished work. During your visit, walk through each room purposefully to catch mistakes, such as incorrect framing or wrong scope of work. Slow down and inspect thoroughly to catch more errors and increase profitability.

Effective project management for real estate investors requires a systematic approach to monitoring progress and controlling costs. Regular documentation through weekly photo updates of the jobsite is crucial, serving as a visual record to verify contractor progress and resolve potential disputes. This should be complemented by weekly contractor updates detailing completed work, issues, delays, and upcoming schedules, keeping you informed about factors that could impact the project timeline.

Personal involvement is key. Conduct regular site inspections to verify contractor reports, document changes to plans or costs, and maintain a to-do list of items that require attention. These site walks provide firsthand insight into the project's status and help ensure that reported progress aligns with reality.

Maintaining up-to-date project reports is essential for financial control. Track the percentage of budget completed for each task and monitor overall budget progress to catch overruns early. Employ a bookkeeper to log expenses and invoices, providing a clear financial picture at all times. This proactive approach to budget management allows for timely adjustments, such as finding trade-offs if over budget or checking comparables to assess if additional costs can be recouped in the sales price.

Finally, use these reports to guide progress payments, ensuring that contractors are paid appropriately for completed work without advancing excessive funds. This careful control of payments reduces financial risk and maintains leverage throughout the project. By implementing these practices, investors can maintain better control over their renovations, minimize financial risks, and increase the likelihood of successful, on-budget project completion.

COST VARIANCES ON JOBSITES

Success in real estate investing isn't just about finding great deals; it's about having the right resources and plans to optimize those deals in ways that others can't. Regularly updating your network, improving your planning skills, and refining your after-plan strategies will make you a more efficient and successful investor. Always be prepared to adapt.

The market, contractor availability, and costs are constantly changing. Regular bidding, maintaining a diverse network, and staying flexible in your approach will help you navigate these changes effectively and maintain your competitive edge. The significant variances in investor pricing and project budgets often stem from three key factors: contractor resources, the after-plan, and investor planning.

Contractor Resources. Having a robust network of contractors is crucial for successful investing. Many investors fail to build a diverse "bench" of professionals, leaving them vulnerable to resource shortages and inflated costs. To mitigate this:

- Continuously expand your network of contractors, especially those specializing in investment properties.
- Regularly bid out projects to multiple contractors to ensure competitive pricing.
- Understand that contractor availability and pricing fluctuate; having more options allows you to adapt.
- Recognize that a lack of resources can lead to project delays and cost overruns.

After-Plan. The desired outcome for a property can significantly impact costs. Investors often make expensive choices when reconfiguring spaces or adding features. To optimize the after-plan:

- Consider multiple layout options to find the most cost-effective solution.
- Balance desirable features with budget constraints.
- Consult with experienced contractors about efficient ways to achieve your goals.

Investor Planning. Proper planning is perhaps the most critical factor in controlling costs and ensuring project success. Many investors underestimate its importance. To improve planning:

- Take an active role in project management; don't rely solely on contractors.
- Develop detailed project plans before starting work.
- Set clear budgets and timelines, and communicate them effectively to your team.
- Anticipate potential issues and have contingency plans in place.

By focusing on these areas, investors can significantly improve their project outcomes. Building a strong network of resources allows for more flexibility and better cost control. This approach enables investors to tackle more challenging projects that others might avoid, potentially leading to higher profits.

HOW TO CONTROL COSTS (EXPECT THE UNEXPECTED)

No matter how experienced you are, unexpected surprises will always pop up. I've been in this business for nearly twenty years and involved in over 3,500 transactions and thousands of flips and apartment projects, and there are still things that catch me off guard. Don't get discouraged by change orders—they're a part of the game. Your job is to control those costs to minimize their impact on your bottom line. Change orders are a big deal because they can quickly eat into your profits, especially on smaller jobs where contractors tend to charge more.

So, what exactly is a change order? As I mentioned back in Chapter 11, a **change order** is a modification to the original scope of work. After the construction contract, estimate, and written scope of work have been clarified, if something unexpected comes up when the walls are opened, that's a change order. The contractor isn't going to absorb that cost, just like they can't expect you to pay for their mistakes.

One way to reduce costs up front is to fix install pricing with trades. For example, I know my flooring guys will install prefinished hardwoods for $2.50 per square foot. That's a fixed cost, and it's up to me to source the materials within my budget. By getting install pricing fixed, my baseline costs are predictable. The same goes for other trades—my plumber charges $50 per fixture, and my electrician charges $25 per electrical fixture. Knowing these fixed costs allows me to be flexible with material selections to stay within budget.

Always make sure your agreements include an option to supply your own materials. If you're working with a general contractor and you have a bunch of change orders that are eating into your profits, you can go to your contractor and say, "Hey, I know you're putting in $3 floors, but I found these for $1.50. They might not look as good, but they'll work for what we need. Can we shave that off the bid?" This gives you room to recoup some of the money lost to change orders. Don't just pay the change orders without pivoting—it's your job to find ways to cut back and substitute materials to keep costs down.

If contractors push back on this because they're charging a percentage markup on materials, offer to still pay them their markup price even though you sourced the materials. They'll be making less overall, but they don't have to go out and get the materials themselves.

Another way to reduce costs is to ensure you have the option to sub in trades with general contractors. In our construction contract, we include a clause that allows us to plug in our own trades. If the general gives me a fixed bid, but I know I can save $3,000 by using my own roofer, or get appliances for $3,000 instead of the $5,000 they quoted, I can substitute those items. If the contractor objects, offer to pay them the same markup they would have made. This creates a win-win situation and sets the tone for a partnership rather than an adversarial relationship.

Change orders also affect the time frame and completion date because additional work is required. When a contractor submits a change order, they must provide a written estimate describing the new scope of work for your approval. They also need to include any adjustments to the completion date. Remember, there are penalty costs associated with delays, so if there's no time change listed, the contractor won't be able to get credit for the extra time.

Change orders can also occur when you, as the investor, decide to upgrade finishes. For example, let's say your original estimate included installing floors at $2.50 per square foot, with an allowance of up to $3 per square foot for prefinished hardwoods. Later, you pull new comps and find that a higher-end finish could increase the value of the property. You contact your contractor and ask to upgrade the flooring spec to a nicer wood, up to $5 per square foot. The contractor needs to provide a written change order stating the new allowance and the corresponding price increase.

Track these changes for budgeting purposes. **Add all change orders to the bottom of your budget, so you know where you really stand.** I've seen clients think they're good on their budget, only to tally up all their receipts at the end and realize they're 30 percent over because they didn't track the changes. The more you keep this information front and center, the less likely you are to make frivolous changes that increase costs.

Additionally, permits are another area to monitor when it comes to cost management. When exploring new markets, consider the potential impact of permit delays on your deals. People often overlook permit deadlines, but these delays can be deal-killers. For example, in Seattle, obtaining a permit might take up to twelve months, which means you would need to acquire the property at a significantly lower price compared to a scenario where the permit process only takes six months. In other words, a seemingly good buy can quickly turn into a bad investment if it comes with major permit hassles.

As you research new markets, the conditions you uncover will dictate the risks you face. To mitigate these risks, there are several strategies you can employ, including proper underwriting, securing access to debt, working with multiple construction teams, prequalifying with permanent financing, verifying your own numbers, and ensuring that you don't overleverage yourself.

It can be tempting to enter a new market and get caught up in the excitement, leading to hasty decisions and purchases when you're not fully prepared. As someone who has seen many investors, including myself, learn real estate investing the wrong way, I cannot stress enough the importance of not overleveraging yourself. Taking on too much debt or committing to projects beyond your means can have detrimental consequences. Remember, we're in this business for the long game, with the goal of maximizing our profits sustainably over time.

By conducting thorough research, understanding the local permit process, and implementing risk-mitigation strategies, you can make informed decisions and navigate new markets with greater confidence. Patience, due diligence, and a commitment to responsible investing will serve you well as you expand your real estate portfolio.

LEGAL CONSIDERATIONS

As you gain experience flipping houses and mitigating risk on the jobsite, you'll also learn some key tactics to reduce your risk on the whole. Having a legal team in place can help reduce the risk that comes with contract writing, permits, and other factors associated with flipping houses.

A key member of your real estate flipping team is a competent and experienced real estate attorney. Many new investors make the mistake of skipping this step or opting for cheap, online legal services. While this may work in some cases, flipping properties carries inherent risks and potential liabilities that require proper legal guidance. **A skilled real estate attorney can navigate the complexities of property transactions, protect your interests, and help you avoid costly legal pitfalls.**

Your legal team should consist of attorneys specializing in real estate law, with experience in areas such as property acquisition, contracts, title issues, zoning regulations, and construction law. They will review and draft legal documents, ensure compliance with local and state regulations, and provide counsel in case of disputes or legal challenges. A good real estate attorney will also help you structure your business entities, such as LLCs or corporations, to minimize personal liability and optimize tax benefits.

When searching for a real estate attorney, look for professionals with a proven track record of working with real estate investors and handling flipping transactions. Ask for referrals from other investors, real estate agents, or industry associations. Schedule consultations with potential attorneys to discuss their experience, communication style, and fee structure. Depending on the complexity of your transactions and the attorney's experience, hourly rates can range from $150 to $500 or more. Some attorneys may offer flat rate packages for standard services, such as contract review or entity formation.

In high-value flips, the role of a real estate attorney becomes even more critical. For example, if you're purchasing a $3 million property with multiple liens from a trustee, your attorney will meticulously review the paperwork to ensure that you're in a secure position and that the transaction is structured properly. They can also help you navigate potential issues related to construction, permits, neighbor disputes, and buyer inspections.

Investing in a strong legal team is essential for protecting your investments, minimizing risks, and ensuring the long-term success of your real estate flipping business. While it may seem like an additional expense, the right legal guidance can ultimately save you time, money, and stress in the long run.

A legal team can draft contracts, like construction contracts, to protect your investment. Legal contracts play a vital role in protecting your investment and ensuring that contractors and other vendors fulfill their obligations throughout the flipping process. A well-drafted construction contract is a powerful tool for holding contractors accountable and minimizing the risk of financial losses or project delays. When working with a contractor, your legal team should draft a comprehensive contract that clearly outlines the scope of work, timeline, payment schedule, and consequences for nonperformance. This contract will serve as a binding agreement between you and the contractor, establishing expectations and protecting your interests.

Working with your legal team to draft robust contracts, particularly for construction work, is a critical step in protecting your investment and ensuring the success of your flipping projects. These contracts provide a legal framework for holding contractors and vendors accountable, minimizing financial risks, and keeping your projects on track. Personally, I recommend flippers get multiple professionals: a contract lawyer, real estate lawyer, construction lawyer, and securities lawyer.

Some of these lawyers' duties may overlap, but make sure to ask about all their services when you start networking to find your team. For many flips, we need different attorneys for different portions of the deal flow. When contractors call to upgrade you, you must control the scope. A construction contract is a legally binding agreement between the property owner and the contractor, outlining the specific details of the work to be performed, the timeline for completion, and the payment terms. When contractors approach you with suggestions for upgrades or changes to the original plan, carefully consider the impact on your budget and timeline before agreeing to any modifications. If you do decide to proceed with an upgrade, avoid relying on verbal agreements.

Verbal agreements can be easily forgotten, misinterpreted, or disputed, leading to confusion and potential financial losses. This is precisely why a well-drafted construction contract is provided at the outset of the project. The contract serves as a road map for how the jobsite should be run, detailing the responsibilities of both parties and the procedures for handling changes or additions to the scope of work. By adhering to the terms of the contract and insisting that any modifications be put in writing, you maintain a clear record of the agreed-upon work and the associated costs.

Relying on verbal agreements can make it challenging to track what was discussed and agreed upon. People's memories can be fallible, and misunderstandings can easily arise. For example, a contractor might casually mention that a particular upgrade will cost "around a thousand dollars," but when the final bill arrives, it's $1,300. These seemingly small discrepancies can add up quickly, eroding your project's profitability. To mitigate these risks, it's imperative to insist on written documentation for any changes to the original contract. This can be in the form of a change order, which outlines the specific modifications, the associated costs, and the impact on the project timeline. By requiring that all changes be put in writing and signed by both parties, you maintain a clear and indisputable record of the agreed-upon work and the corresponding financial obligations.

LLC Protection

Using LLCs for your flips can help provide an additional layer of protection should something go sideways during the flip. Setting up an LLC for each investment property is a smart way for flippers to mitigate risk and protect their personal assets. By creating a separate legal entity for each property, investors can limit their liability exposure and safeguard their personal wealth.

The basic process we follow with each property is to set up an LLC, buy the property, sell the property, shut the LLC down, and repeat the process. With the volume of properties we do, we set up LLCs annually, flip for one year, then shut them down. This is important to consider as you begin to scale your flipping business—your LLC strategy might need to adjust as your portfolio increases.

While an LLC provides a valuable layer of protection, it is not a complete guarantee against all risks, though. Flippers should still exercise caution and due diligence in their business practices. One of the best ways to minimize issues is to deliver a high-quality product. By ensuring that your flipped properties are well constructed, up to code, and free from defects, you can reduce the likelihood of legal disputes or buyer complaints after closing. It's important to note that while setting up an LLC for each property is a common practice among real estate investors, it is not the only option for asset protection.

Other strategies, such as purchasing comprehensive insurance policies or establishing a trust, may also be worth considering. Consulting with a qualified legal professional and a tax advisor can help you determine the best approach for your specific situation and investment goals.

If issues do arise, we take care of them, within reason. The goal is to have contracts in place and written agreements and to avoid personal guarantees. You don't know what the market is going to do, and you could be liable for that money. Instead of being financially free, you'll be financially trapped.

And my final rule: Make sure to disclose, disclose, disclose. Let the buyer know everything that is wrong or could be wrong with the property. This protects us on the deal. We want to list the problems and how we solve those problems. In Washington, it's a "buyer beware" state, so that keeps us in the clear. We've never had to pay out an issue down the road, because we make sure we do the paperwork correctly. Once your team is in place and you are protected legally, you can really home in on your goal to reach financial freedom, which will come from liquidity.

Buyer Beware

Real estate transactions involve complex legal documents that require careful scrutiny to protect your interests. Before closing any deal, it's crucial to thoroughly review all contracts with a reliable lawyer you trust. Legal expertise is essential when navigating clauses and provisions that can significantly impact your goals and obligations. While conciseness is important, it's equally vital to understand the nuances of common real estate clauses to watch for.

- **Contingencies:** Look for clauses that allow for contingencies, such as financing, inspections, or appraisal contingencies, which can provide you with an exit strategy if certain conditions are not met
- **Closing date:** Pay close attention to the closing date and any provisions that allow for extensions or delays, as these can have financial implications and disrupt your plans
- **Title and encumbrances:** Ensure that the contract addresses any existing liens, easements, or other encumbrances on the property and that the seller is responsible for clearing the title
- **Representations and warranties:** Review the seller's representations and warranties regarding the condition of the property, as these can impact your recourse in case of undisclosed issues
- **Allocation of costs:** Understand the allocation of closing costs, such as transfer taxes, escrow fees, and prorations for items like property taxes and utility bills
- **Remedies:** Carefully review the remedies available to each party in case of a breach, such as the ability to seek specific performance, monetary damages, or termination of the contract

While this is not an exhaustive list, it highlights the importance of working with a trusted legal professional to navigate the intricacies of real estate contracts and protect your interests throughout the transaction process.

Verifying the numbers provided by wholesalers is a crucial step in ensuring accurate financial projections and avoiding costly mistakes in real estate transactions. Instead of relying solely on the estimates presented by wholesalers, you should conduct a thorough due diligence process to verify the information independently. First, conduct comprehensive market research to determine the current market value of the property and the potential resale value after renovations.

Consult recent comparable sales, consider market trends, and seek insights from local real estate professionals. Additionally, hire a reputable home inspector to evaluate the property's condition accurately, enabling you to estimate repair and renovation costs more reliably. If you plan to hold the property as a rental investment, research comparable rental rates in the area to verify the potential rental income and ensure that the numbers provided by the wholesaler are realistic. Obtain quotes from licensed contractors for the necessary repairs and renovations to get a more accurate estimate of the actual costs involved.

Factor in additional expenses such as closing costs, holding costs (if applicable), insurance, property taxes, and potential vacancy rates, as these can significantly impact your overall financial projections. Utilize reliable real estate investment analysis tools or software to run your own numbers based on the verified information you've gathered, helping you determine the potential ROI and ensuring that the deal aligns with your investment goals. By taking these steps, you can make informed decisions and mitigate potential risks associated with inaccurate or incomplete information.

Look out for daisy chain deals. In a daisy chain deal, the original deal source (often a wholesaler) finds a property and secures it under contract. Instead of directly marketing the deal to potential buyers, they pass it along to another wholesaler, who then adds their own fee or markup before passing it to yet another wholesaler, and so on. This process can continue through several entities, with each party in the "daisy chain" tacking on additional fees or markups. As the deal moves down the chain, the numbers can become increasingly inflated or distorted from the original, accurate data provided by the initial source.

While there's nothing inherently wrong with multiple parties being involved and compensated in a deal, the concern with daisy chain deals is the lack of transparency and the potential for inaccurate or misleading information as the deal gets further removed from the original source. To mitigate these risks, it's advisable to try to work directly with the main source of the deal, the party that initially secured the property under contract. This allows you to verify the numbers and details directly from the original source, avoiding potential distortions or inflated costs that can occur as the deal moves through the daisy chain. Additionally, it's essential to have clarity on who is in control of the deal and responsible for facilitating a smooth closing process, as well as addressing any unexpected issues that may arise. Open communication with all parties involved, including a commitment to not cut out any legitimate participants, can help ensure a transparent and ethical transaction.

Finally, you never want to close outside of escrow. This should be avoided at all costs. Always close with title insurance. **Escrow** is a neutral third-party service that ensures the proper exchange of documents, funds, and the transfer of property ownership. An escrow company or title company acts as an impartial intermediary, holding funds and documents in a secure manner until all conditions of the contract are met and the transaction can be completed legally and safely.

Closing outside of escrow, also known as a **"private closing,"** means that the buyer and seller exchange funds and documents directly, without the involvement of a neutral third party. While this may seem more convenient or cost-effective, it exposes both parties to numerous risks and potential legal issues. One of the primary risks is the lack of title insurance. **Title insurance** protects buyers against any defects or encumbrances on the property's title, such as undisclosed liens, outstanding mortgages, or ownership disputes. When closing through a reputable title company, the buyer typically receives title insurance, which provides legal protection and financial coverage in case of any title-related issues. Without the involvement of a title company and the issuance of title insurance, the buyer assumes all risks associated with the property's title.

This could lead to costly legal battles, potential loss of the property, or financial damages if any undisclosed issues arise after the transaction is completed. Additionally, closing outside of escrow increases the risk of fraud, mishandling of funds, or misrepresentation of documents. Escrow companies follow strict protocols and procedures to ensure the proper handling and disbursement of funds, as well as the accurate recording of documents with the appropriate government entities.

In contrast, a private closing lacks these safeguards and oversight, increasing the chances of errors, misunderstandings, or even intentional fraud by either party. To protect your financial interests and ensure a legally sound transaction, engage the services of a reputable escrow or title company for all real estate closings. The added security, transparency, and legal protections provided by these professional third-party services far outweigh any perceived convenience or cost savings of closing outside of escrow. If you close outside of an escrow company or title company, your money is not insured.

CHAPTER 13
DESIGN AND THE STYLE CODE

You fail all of the time. But you aren't a failure
until you start blaming someone else.
—BUM PHILLIPS, FORMER PRO FOOTBALL COACH

ALIGNING YOUR DESIGN with the appropriate style of home will maximize value, but note that simply increasing your budget or upgrading specifications doesn't guarantee higher profits. The goal is to optimize design in a cost-effective manner, balancing improvements with potential returns. (Since the design will be the last step in the renovation process, I am placing this chapter here, but don't forget to factor in your finishes into your cost analysis and budget. It is important to consider your desired design as you build out your budget and spec sheet.)

There are several factors to consider when choosing the design elements and style code for your flip project.

THE STYLE CODE

The **style code** refers to the architectural design and layout of the property, such as rambler/ranch, two-story, or daylight basement. It's essential to compare properties with the same style code to ensure an accurate valuation and avoid potential mistakes in your underwriting and budget. If you're evaluating a 2,000-square-foot rambler or ranch-style home, you should focus your comp search on properties with a similar single-level design. Conversely, if the subject property is a two-story house, it's vital to look for comps that are also two-story homes.

Failing to account for style code differences can lead to inaccurate valuations, as different architectural styles can have varying appeal, functionality, and market demand. Properties with distinct layouts and designs often cater to different buyer preferences and may command different price points within the same neighborhood or market.

For example, a two-story home may appeal to families seeking more separation between living spaces, while a rambler might be preferred by buyers prioritizing single-level living or accessibility. These preferences can translate into different perceived values, even among properties with similar square footage or lot sizes. By carefully considering the style code and ensuring that your comparable properties match the subject property's architectural style, you can more accurately assess the true market value and avoid skewed valuations that could result from comparing properties with vastly different designs and layouts.

THE INVESTOR'S DESIRED AFTER-PLAN

Cost variances in real estate investing often stem from the investor's after-plan and initial planning approach. The desired outcome for a property can significantly impact expenses, with choices in layout modifications, architectural design, and renovation scope playing crucial roles. Investor-friendly architects can create appealing designs while keeping costs manageable, whereas custom architects might produce more artistic results at substantially higher prices. The placement of bathrooms, removal of walls, and design of windows can dramatically affect plumbing, framing, and overall construction costs. It's essential to base these decisions on market data rather than personal preferences.

Analyzing comparable properties helps justify investment in high-end features when supported by potential returns. Thorough initial planning helps avoid budget overruns. Developing a clear, detailed scope of work and accurately estimating costs for each aspect of the project can prevent the "TV flip" mentality that often leads to unrealistic expectations. Maintain clarity in your project plans by documenting all specifications in detail. When contractors suggest upgrades, carefully control the scope of work. If you do agree to changes, always get them in writing. Avoid verbal agreements, as they're difficult to track and can lead to budget overruns. Controlling upgrade costs is vital; investors should resist the urge to overspend on small improvements that can quickly accumulate.

Building a network of investor-friendly professionals, including architects and contractors familiar with investment property needs, can contribute to more cost-effective renovations. Flexibility is key, as unforeseen circumstances like city code requirements or structural issues may necessitate plan adjustments. By balancing desirable features with market demands and budget constraints, investors can increase their chances of executing profitable projects.

DESIGNING THE PROPERTY

Design your project according to its architectural style rather than your personal taste. Cohesiveness will lead to a higher selling price, as it makes people feel more comfortable. When buyers are attracted to a specific architectural style, incorporating the wrong specs can create a confusing house, which in turn leads to confused buyers who are less likely to make a purchase.

Cohesiveness is one of the most critical factors to consider when designing a home. A harmonious and aesthetically pleasing look will make people fall in love with the property and make a quick decision to buy. Tying the design elements into the home's architectural themes is essential for achieving this cohesiveness. If you're a flipper who doesn't have a strong design background, you might find it challenging to create a cohesive design. As someone who likes remodeling homes but is not a design expert, I tend to stick to one theme and process, which can sometimes result in a slightly template-like feel that may not capture the highest possible selling price.

To overcome this challenge, I recommend copying the pros. Websites like Houzz, Pinterest, and Remodelista are excellent resources for finding design inspiration. Simply type in the theme and style of the house you're working on, and you'll find a wealth of images to draw from. Use your budget and spec allowance as a guide when sourcing materials and elements. These resources will provide you with the themes you need to accomplish a cohesive and attractive design, even if you're not a design pro yourself. Likewise, try going to Sherwin Williams. They have preloaded paint schemes for mid-century, desert, traditional, craftsman. They're very easy templates. You know that they're going to work, and you can see the colors and how they tie them all together. It makes it very cohesive.

FIVE BASIC ARCHITECTURAL STYLES AND THEMES

The architectural style should dictate the design palate for your property; after all, the property was built intentionally by the original architect.

Because you were not included in the initial design process, you'll need to stick with the integrity of the design.

For me as a flipper, I want to appeal to the masses, trying to stay as neutral as possible. Now, on some of our luxury flips, we do throw in some wallpaper or some extra kind of fun, unique features, because we want to separate the house that way. The right house can be the right property for a louder design. But you don't want to go too off the cuff, because it's going to throw off a couple of your buyers, if not half. So neutral themes work, and neutral works for any type of renovation, any kind of theme. But you still need to tie it all together.

The hard part about designing a theme is that there are hundreds of architectural themes and nuances to select from. It's important to do your research and use whatever avenues for inspiration make sense for your property. I've found that it all boils down to five different styles (which I will go into in the next section). There will be some exceptions to the rule here, as certain locations (i.e., the desert) stray from these five core styles. It's important to match the appropriate theme to the property, and you can ensure you do so by doing your research and knowing what the style for your particular neighborhood is.

Craftsman

Craftsman-style homes are characterized by their distinct architectural features, such as low-pitched gables, overhanging eaves, exposed rafters and beams, and timber-frame wood columns at the front of the property. These elements contribute to an earthy and natural feel, which is the general tone of Craftsman homes.

When designing the interior of a Craftsman home, it's important to incorporate natural woods and a neutral color palette to maintain the style's integrity. Shaker cabinets are a popular choice for Craftsman kitchens, as they feature a simple, clean design that complements the home's overall aesthetic. Box beams running throughout the ceiling are another common feature, adding visual interest and emphasizing the home's structural elements.

Given these characteristics, it's essential to upgrade the millwork package when renovating a Craftsman home. This includes incorporating larger trim and more expensive millwork, shaker doors, and classic tile schemes. For example, instead of using trendy tile patterns like straight set or octagon, opt for more traditional and neutral tile options that align with the Craftsman style.

A key element of Craftsman homes is the importance of bringing nature into the house. To achieve this, choose warm, natural paint colors throughout the interior. Neutral, warm, and inviting colors will help create a cohesive and authentic Craftsman look. Some examples of appropriate paint colors include earthy greens (sage, olive, or muted green tones), warm neutrals (beige, taupe, or light brown hues), or soft yellows (buttery yellow or pale gold tones).

By understanding the key elements and themes of Craftsman-style homes, you can design a renovation that remains true to the architectural style while creating a warm and inviting space. Remember to focus on natural materials, neutral colors, and classic design elements to achieve the desired Craftsman look.

Modern

Modern homes are one of my favorite designs, characterized by clean lines and geometric shapes. They avoid cluttered elements such as arches, ornate columns, and window shutters, emphasizing a clean and minimalistic aesthetic throughout the property. Typical design themes in a modern home include cooler colors, symmetry, and straight set patterns. Minimalistic trim detail is common, which can save money on trim installation, as smaller trim requires less wood. In some cases, window casings are omitted entirely, opting for a simple drywall finish instead. The goal is to keep things symmetric and avoid elements that protrude or disrupt the clean lines of the house.

To prevent the interior from feeling too sterile or white, it's important to incorporate splashes of color and occasional natural wood elements. For example, use a bold, contrasting color on an accent wall or piece of furniture to break up the cool color palette, incorporate natural wood floating shelves or a wood-paneled feature wall to add warmth and texture to the space, or choose flat panel cabinets and doors in a warm wood tone to balance the cool colors and clean lines.

When budgeting for a modern home renovation, keep in mind that certain elements may require a higher investment compared to other architectural styles. For instance, achieving a smooth, clean-lined drywall finish may cost more than a standard drywall job. Similarly, modern homes often feature larger windows to maximize natural light, which can be more expensive than standard-sized windows.

In contrast to Craftsman homes, where the millwork is typically thicker and more costly, modern homes may need more of the budget to achieve a flawless drywall finish or to install oversized windows. It's essential to consider these style-specific costs when planning your renovation budget to ensure you can achieve the desired modern look without overspending.

Mid-Century Modern

Mid-century homes are a twentieth-century architectural style characterized by clean lines, muted curves, minimal ornamentation, large windows, and open floor plans designed to create a seamless flow between indoor and outdoor living spaces. When renovating mid-century homes, it's important to budget for the large windows, which can cost four to five times more per pane than a regular window. Preserving the window schedule is crucial to maintaining the natural light and outdoor connection that define this architectural style. If the property lacks deck or patio space, consider adding these features to enhance the indoor-outdoor flow that is central to the mid-century design philosophy.

Typical design themes for a mid-century home include:

- Cooler colors and symmetry
- Preserving original charm, such as built-in cabinets and window schedules
- Minimalist trim detail
- Splashes of warm color
- Combinations of tiles, such as penny tile or geometric shapes
- Terrazzo flooring
- Natural wood elements to warm up the modern aesthetic

When renovating a mid-century property, focus on restoration rather than complete renovation. Salvage original features like built-in cabinets with old pulls, as long as they are not too worn or damaged. Avoid replacing these unique elements with generic options like shaker cabinets, which can diminish the home's authentic style. Buyers are often willing to pay more for a home that showcases its original mid-century character.

If the property has been well maintained, with light wear and tear, consider updating the existing features rather than replacing them entirely. Duplicating the craftsmanship of these original masterpieces can be challenging, so treat them like works of art and preserve as much as possible. While minimalist trim detail is common in mid-century homes, as it is in modern designs, the color pops tend to be warmer in mid-century properties. Combinations of tiles, such as penny tile or geometric shapes, can add visual interest without overwhelming the space. Terrazzo flooring is a popular choice for mid-century homes, offering a slightly bolder look.

Incorporating natural wood elements is another way to warm up the modern aesthetic of a mid-century home. This design choice was prevalent during the mid-century era and can elevate the overall look of the renovated space, depending on the market and target audience.

Traditional Style

Traditional homes, such as split-levels and two-story houses, are designed to appeal to the masses. While they may have elements of specific architectural styles like mid-century or colonial, they are generally more basic in nature. Understanding how to renovate these properties is crucial, as they represent the majority of the flipping market. When remodeling a traditional home, aim for a timeless style that will last for years to come. Avoid trendy or quickly outdated design choices. Instead, focus on using high-quality items with appealing tones and themes that align with current market trends. But be careful not to overdo it. Remember, traditional homes are designed for the masses, so the goal is to create a comfortable and well-coordinated space without being overly fancy or loud. Incorporate splashes of fun, but do so in moderation to avoid overwhelming the overall design.

Typical design themes for traditional homes include:
- Natural, warm, and inviting colors that appeal to a wide range of people
- Timeless and classic design elements
- White shaker cabinets paired with white quartz countertops
- Accent hardware in brass or black to add visual interest
- Fun, easily replaceable tile that complements the overall design

When selecting key elements like cabinets and countertops, choose options that most people will find attractive and inoffensive. These elements form the foundation of the design and are less easily changed than smaller accent pieces.

To incorporate some personality into the design, consider using accent tiles that are fun and eye-catching but can be easily replaced by the next homeowner, if desired. This approach allows you to create a cohesive theme that can be updated over time without requiring major renovations. When renovating a traditional home, prioritize timeless design choices that will appeal to the broadest possible audience while still incorporating small, fun elements that can be easily changed to suit individual tastes.

Farmhouse

This style was one of the hottest trends in 2021 and 2022. A traditional farmhouse is typically one and a half to two stories tall and features an asymmetrical massing in the front gable. These homes are characterized by simple detailing, open floor plans, and central chimneys, creating a homey and inviting atmosphere that many people are drawn to.

When working on a farmhouse renovation, consider the following common design themes:

- **Warm whites:** Incorporate a mix of whites and blacks throughout the space, opting for warmer white tones rather than stark, cool whites
- **Gridded windows:** Use windows with a grid pattern instead of plain, straight-pane windows to add character and a classic farmhouse look
- **Shaker-style cabinets:** Choose simple yet elegant shaker cabinets for the kitchen and bathroom to maintain the farmhouse aesthetic
- **Natural floors:** Stick with natural-looking oak floors rather than trendy options like bamboo, as this aligns better with the farmhouse style
- **Farm sinks:** Incorporate a farm sink (also known as an apron-front sink) in the kitchen to enhance the rustic, farmhouse feel
- **Classic tile designs:** Use timeless tile patterns like subway tiles with a brick lay pattern in the kitchen and bathroom
- **Accent walls:** Add warmth to the space by incorporating accent walls in earth tones or warm colors
- **Earth-toned accent colors:** When selecting accent colors, opt for warmer earth tones rather than cool hues to create a cozy and inviting atmosphere
- **Mixed hardware finishes:** Farmhouse style often features a combination of brass, black, and stainless-steel hardware throughout the home, creating an eclectic and charming look

By incorporating these design elements into your farmhouse renovation, you can create a space that feels both trendy and timeless, with a warm and inviting atmosphere that appeals to many homebuyers.

KNOW WHEN TO BE THRIFTY

When it comes to lower-grade flips, having a flexible design approach can lead to significant cost savings. Unlike higher-grade flips, where I have specific requirements for flooring thickness, plumbing fixtures, and appliances to achieve a premium look, lower-grade flips allow for more flexibility in materials and finishes.

For these projects, I focus on creating a general tone or theme rather than adhering to exact specifications. This "close enough" design philosophy allows me to shop for deals and take advantage of clearance items without compromising the overall aesthetic of the property. For example, if my comp has a white, penny tile backsplash that costs $10 per square foot, I might opt for a white three-inch by six-inch subway tile at $1.50 per square foot instead. While not an exact match, it still achieves the desired look at a fraction of the cost.

The key to successfully implementing this approach is to thoroughly analyze your comps and determine the price point you're targeting. Are you aiming for a middle-of-the-road price or a premium price? Consult with your listing brokers and get their feedback, as they have firsthand knowledge of buyer preferences and can guide you in making cost-effective choices that will still appeal to your target market.

One tip for finding great deals is to check with big box stores like Home Depot for overstock or clearance items. The pandemic has led to supply chain disruptions, with many stores initially facing shortages and now dealing with excess inventory. Visit their supply desk and inquire about clearance items or odd quantities they're looking to move.

For example, if a store has 752 feet of a particular flooring in stock, it may cost them more to store it than to sell it at a steep discount. In the past, I've seen odd quantities of flooring sold for as little as $.01 per square foot, as the store was eager to clear it out. While prices may not be quite that low now, you can still often find materials at up to 75 percent off if the store has an unusual amount they want to get rid of.

Make a habit of visiting clearance centers and adding them to your vendor list. Develop relationships with store managers and sales representatives at the supply stores you frequent. Let them know that you're an investor and are always interested in buying clearance items. Provide them with your contact information and encourage them to reach out when they have deals available. I regularly receive emails from vendors offering discounted materials they're trying to move.

Case in point, one of my flooring guys recently offered me LVP (luxury vinyl plank) at $.99 per square foot, down from his usual price of $2.50, because the color wasn't popular. We jumped on the deal and used it in all of our apartments, saving 60 percent on our flooring costs. Had I been working on a lower-grade flip, I would have used it there as well. The key is to always ask what they're trying to clear out and if it will work for your project. These savings can add up and significantly boost your returns.

Beyond local suppliers, consider looking into nationwide flooring companies that specialize in blowout deals. For appliances, search for "appliance liquidators" to find warehouses offering mismatched or discounted sets. While you may not get a perfectly coordinated suite, the savings can be substantial compared to buying from a local appliance store.

Don't overlook online resources like Amazon for items such as door handles and faucets. I used to pay $20–$25 per door handle from local suppliers, opting for the higher-priced options for better quality. However, I discovered that I could get comparable handles on Amazon for just $11 each. These small savings of 20–50 percent can make a big difference across an entire project.

Remember, the goal with lower-grade flips is to create an appealing overall look while keeping costs down. By being flexible in your design choices, shopping clearance deals, and building relationships with suppliers, you can achieve impressive returns without sacrificing quality or style.

Keep in mind that pricing can vary significantly between retail-oriented shops and those catering to investors. A cabinet shop with a nice storefront near my office might charge $15,000–$20,000 for a kitchen, while driving forty minutes to the industrial district could yield the same kitchen for around $11,000 installed. Often, the retail-facing shops are buying their materials from the same suppliers as the investor-focused shops. By going directly to the source, you can secure better pricing.

When shopping for materials, always identify yourself as an investor. Many shops offer substantial discounts for investors, as they recognize the potential for repeat business.

Having a clear design and style code in mind at the beginning of your flipping project will allow you to effectively budget and prepare the flip for success. As the saying goes, "Begin with the end in mind," especially when it comes to flipping houses. You will eventually sell the property and a clear vision for the design and finishing touches will help package the home effectively.

CHAPTER 14
SELLING THE FLIP

When you've got something to prove, there's nothing greater than a challenge.

—TERRY BRADSHAW, FORMER FOOTBALL PLAYER, PITTSBURGH STEELERS

WHEN YOU'VE PUT in the hard work of finding a deal, managing the rehab process, and improving your property's value, it's crucial not to fumble at the finish line by rushing your home to market. This is where many flippers trip up, and it's why they sometimes get a bad rap in the industry. They're so eager to cash in on their profit that they list the property before it's truly ready for prime time.

Trust me, I've been there. After months of blood, sweat, and tears (sometimes literally), it's tempting to slap a "For Sale" sign on the lawn and call it a day. But here's the thing: Presenting an unfinished or poorly staged property to potential buyers is like serving a half-baked cake. It might look okay on the outside, but it won't leave the right impression.

I've learned over the years that taking that extra time to really polish your property can pay off big time. It's not just about the repairs and renovations; it's about creating an experience for potential buyers. Remember, you're not just selling a house—you're selling a lifestyle, a dream. So take a breath, step back, and make sure every detail is perfect before you open those doors to the market. Your wallet (and your reputation) will thank you for it.

FINDING THE RIGHT LISTING BROKER

Finding the right broker is a game changer when it comes to selling your flip home, and it's a step that too many investors overlook. Let me tell you, not all brokers are created equal. Each one has their own niche—their own superpower, if you will. In my years of investing across different asset classes, I've learned that using a one-size-fits-all approach with brokers is like trying to fit a square peg in a round hole—it just doesn't work.

I've got a whole roster of brokers—one for flips, another for commercial properties, and a separate one for multifamily deals. Why? Because when your broker really gets what they're selling, they can position your property in a way that attracts the right buyers and often leads to fatter profits. It's like having a secret weapon in your real estate arsenal.

When it comes to hiring an agent or broker to sell your property, investors typically go down one of two paths.

1. **The discount route:** Some folks are drawn to discount brokers who offer reduced listing fees in exchange for volume. And sure, saving a buck always feels good. But let me warn you—don't fall into the cheap trap. You know the old saying "You get what you pay for"? Well, it's especially true in real estate. That being said, depending on what you're selling, a discount broker might make sense. For example, if you're dealing with a straightforward, run-of-the-mill property in a hot market, you might not need all the bells and whistles.

2. **The investment-focused approach:** This is where things get interesting. An agent or broker who understands the investment game can be worth their weight in gold. They're not just there to stick a sign in the yard and host an open house. No, these pros can become an integral part of your business strategy.

I've always paid my brokers the full 3 percent commission, but here's the kicker—I expect them to earn every penny by making my business more efficient. These investment-savvy brokers speak our language. They get the importance of strategic upgrades, they understand the nuances of pricing in different markets, and they know how the cost of capital impacts our decisions.

When your broker can talk cap rates and ROI as fluently as they can describe curb appeal, that's when the magic happens. They can help you price your property to maximize profits, they know how to market to other investors (if that's your target buyer), and they can often get you to the closing table faster. In this game, time is money. A broker who understands the flip business knows that every day a property sits on the market is eating into your profits. They'll work with a sense of urgency that matches yours.

Don't skimp on your broker. Find someone who specializes in your type of deals: someone who can add value beyond just the sale. It might seem like a higher up-front cost, but trust me, the right broker will pay for themselves many times over in higher sales prices, faster transactions, and invaluable market insights. In the world of real estate investing, that's the kind of edge that can take your flipping game from good to great.

EXPECTATIONS FOR THE BROKER

When it comes to working with real estate brokers to list my properties, I've developed a system that goes far beyond just slapping a "For Sale" sign on the lawn. My brokers are involved from day one of the project, right through to closing. I've got a detailed list of expectations that turns my broker into a true partner in the flipping process.

First off, I lean on my broker's expertise to ensure we're on trend with our finish packages. The last thing you want is to renovate a property only to find out your choices are already outdated. My broker provides feedback on our selections, making sure we're creating a product that'll make buyers' hearts skip a beat. Now, here's where it gets interesting. I require my brokers to provide an updated comparative market analysis (CMA) every single month. Why? Because in this business, if you're not on top of market changes, you're already behind. These monthly CMAs are like a health check for our investment. They allow me to review data and make real-time decisions. If I see values creeping up, I might decide to upgrade certain features to maximize our return. If the market's cooling, it might be time to adjust our strategy.

Before we even think about listing, I have my broker request a pre-inspection. This report lands on my desk for a thorough review. It's all about being proactive, folks. We want to address any potential issues before they become deal-breakers. Then comes the pre-listing walk-through. My broker, along with the project manager or contractor, does a final sweep of the property. We're looking for any last-minute tweaks or improvements that could make the difference between a good offer and a great one.

One of my favorite tools in our arsenal is the buyer information pages. My broker creates these detailed sheets that showcase all the improvements we've made to the property. You'd be surprised how many buyers can't distinguish between different finish packages or understand the value of certain upgrades. These info pages are like a highlight reel of our work, justifying our price point and helping buyers see the true value of the property.

Communication is key in this business, which is why I insist on weekly feedback reports. Every Monday, without fail, I get a comprehensive update. This includes feedback from every broker who showed the property, showing counts, and any relevant market activity from the past week. It keeps me in the loop and allows for quick pivots, if needed.

My brokers also handle the nitty-gritty details that can make or break a smooth sale. They coordinate staging (and de-staging when we're headed to closing), get estimates, and work with my project manager on any inspection-related repairs. It's all about creating a seamless experience for the buyer. And speaking of buyers, we don't consider our job done until they're happy. That's why my broker conducts a final walk-through with the buyers and their agent. It's our last chance to ensure everything is perfect and to leave a lasting positive impression.

This comprehensive approach might seem like overkill to some, but it pays off big time. By having my broker deeply involved throughout the entire process, we're able to maximize our profits, minimize our time on market, and build a reputation for quality flips. Remember, in this business, your reputation is everything. A great broker who understands and executes this level of involvement isn't just listing your property—they're elevating your entire flipping game.

PRICING STRATEGY FOR PROPERTY FLIPS

Accurate pricing is crucial when selling a flipped property. It's imperative to set aside personal expectations based on the pro forma or budget overruns and focus on market realities. Overpricing can significantly impede the momentum of a new listing, potentially leading to prolonged market time and opportunistic, low offers from buyers.

When determining the list price, consider the current inventory levels and recent comparable sales. In some cases, it may be appropriate to price 3–5 percent above recent sales, but only if the upgrades and improvements clearly justify the premium. The key is to ensure that the value proposition is evident and explainable to potential buyers.

Once a property is listed, it's essential to maintain price integrity for a reasonable period. Typically, I recommend waiting twenty-one to thirty days before considering a price adjustment. Premature price reductions can be interpreted as a sign of seller anxiety or desperation, potentially weakening your negotiating position.

The goal is to create a sense of urgency among buyers while maximizing return on investment. A well-priced property should generate interest quickly and ideally attract multiple offers. This approach often leads to a more favorable outcome than an overpriced listing that lingers on the market. Rely on comprehensive market analysis, including recent comparable sales, current inventory levels, and broader market trends. Listen to the insights provided by your real estate broker, particularly their comparative market analysis (CMA).

Time on market directly impacts carrying costs and overall profitability. A swift, profitable sale is generally preferable to a protracted selling process, even if the final price is slightly lower than initially anticipated. Pricing a flipped property requires a delicate balance of optimism and realism. By setting a competitive price based on market data and property improvements, you increase the likelihood of a successful and timely sale, which is fundamental to maintaining profitability in the property-flipping business.

STAGING AND PROPERTY PRESENTATION

In our extensive experience of nearly 4,000 flip transactions over the past two decades, we've consistently recognized the value of property staging. We've employed this strategy in approximately 95 percent of our listings, underscoring its significance in our marketing approach. Our typical staging investment ranges from $3,000 to $4,000 for standard properties, escalating to $6,000–$10,000 for our more upscale offerings. In exceptional cases, we've allocated over $25,000 for staging a single high-end property. This investment is justified by the transformative effect staging has on a newly renovated home.

Post-renovation, properties can often feel sterile due to the newness of various elements. Staging with carefully selected furniture and decor serves to warm the space, creating an inviting atmosphere. It plays a crucial role in engaging potential buyers' emotions and helping them envision themselves living in the space. The more vividly a buyer can picture their life in the home, the more inclined they are to submit an offer.

Staging can be particularly beneficial in properties that have undergone lighter renovations. Strategically placed furniture, artwork, and rugs can effectively draw attention away from any remaining wear and tear, presenting the property in its best light. However, it's important to note that not every property requires staging. Homes with straightforward floor plans, well-defined spaces, and prices in the median range may sell effectively based on their inherent features and competitive pricing. Before committing to staging expenses, it's prudent to assess several factors.

- **Evaluate the floor plan:** Is it intuitive and does it make it easy for potential buyers to envision their future living arrangements?
- **Consider the competitive landscape:** What type of inventory are you up against in the current market?
- **Assess your finish quality:** Will your renovations and overall product quality speak for themselves?

While staging has proven to be a valuable tool in our property-marketing arsenal, it's essential to approach each property individually. Analyze the specific characteristics of the home, the target market, and the current real estate landscape to determine whether staging will provide a meaningful return on investment. When used judiciously, staging can significantly enhance a property's appeal, potentially leading to quicker sales and improved offer prices.

MAXIMIZING YOUR FLIP'S APPEAL

In today's real estate market, effective marketing and positioning are crucial for selling flip properties efficiently. While online exposure through major real estate platforms like Zillow, Redfin, and Realtor.com is automatic when listing with a broker, this broad visibility alone doesn't guarantee success. As a broker and experienced investor involved in thousands of flip transactions, I've found that targeted, high-quality marketing efforts make the real impact.

Key elements of impactful marketing include:

- **Professional photography:** High-quality, professional images are essential. They serve as the first impression for potential buyers and can significantly influence their decision to view the property in person.
- **Compelling listing description:** A well-crafted broker's remarks section should highlight not only the property's features but also emphasize the area's attributes and detail the upgrades performed. This information helps buyers understand the value proposition before they even step foot in the home.
- **On-site marketing materials:** Property feature sheets and "silent sellers" placed strategically throughout the home can emphasize

the upgrades and installations, justifying any premium pricing. These materials should clearly communicate the value added through your renovation efforts.

- **Transparency with permits:** Displaying copies of signed-off permits reassures potential buyers about the legitimacy and quality of the work completed. This transparency can be a significant selling point, especially for buyers concerned about potential hidden issues.
- **Strategic open houses:** Weekend open houses maximize exposure to all types of buyers, including those new to the area. These events provide an excellent opportunity to control the narrative about the property's improvements and gather immediate feedback from potential buyers.

Beyond these marketing tactics, the most effective strategy in securing offers—often multiple offers—is good old-fashioned sales communication. We make it a point to follow up with every broker who shows our properties through email, text, and phone calls. This persistent communication serves multiple purposes.

- It allows us to gather detailed feedback about buyers' impressions.
- It helps clarify any misunderstandings about the property or its pricing.
- It provides an opportunity to encourage offers that might otherwise not materialize.

For instance, there have been numerous occasions where a follow-up call revealed that a broker wasn't submitting an offer because they assumed there would be multiple offers, and the list price was at the limit of their client's budget. This conversation often leads to the realization that a full-price offer could secure the property, resulting in a pending sale. While broad online exposure is beneficial, it's the targeted, high-quality marketing efforts and proactive communication that truly drive successful sales in the flipping business. By focusing on these elements, you can effectively showcase your property's value, attract serious buyers, and maximize your chances of a quick and profitable sale.

Your Brand as a Local Flipper

In the real estate flipping industry, establishing a reputable brand is paramount. As a flipper operating in Seattle since 2006, I've learned that a positive reputation is not just beneficial—it's essential for long-term success. The flip industry, unfortunately, has its share of bad actors. Poor construction work, hidden defects, and a general lack of care have tarnished the reputation of flippers in some markets. However, at Heaton Dainard, we've made it our mission to counteract this narrative by consistently delivering quality products that brokers and buyers alike look forward to.

Our approach is rooted in care and education. We encourage all our clients to handle their properties with diligence, emphasizing that attention to detail and quality work often correlate directly with financial rewards. This philosophy has helped us build a brand that, while not universally loved, is widely respected within our community.

In an era of unprecedented housing affordability challenges, we recognize the significant financial commitment buyers are making. It's crucial to ensure they receive a product they truly love. However, it's equally important to set realistic expectations. A flipped home doesn't necessarily mean every single element has been updated. Our process involves evaluating the highest and best use for each property, performing appropriate renovations, and pricing the home accordingly.

We draw a clear line between our responsibilities and those of the buyer. For instance, if a furnace fails months after closing, and it wasn't part of our renovation scope or guarantees, we consider that outside our purview—especially if the buyer conducted their own inspection. However, where we do take responsibility is in the quality of work we've directly overseen. If a licensed contractor we hired performs substandard work, we feel obligated to assist in rectifying the situation, even if the issue wasn't caught during the buyer's inspection.

This approach goes beyond the typical "buyer beware" mentality. We believe that if we hired someone to do the work, it should be done correctly. We're willing to leverage our relationship with contractors to ensure issues are addressed, even post-sale. Our commitment to doing the right thing (when it's reasonable) has been instrumental in building our brand. We strive to deliver the product as marketed and priced, but we're also willing to consider reasonable requests from buyers. In such situations, we always involve the buyer's broker to ensure clear communication about contract expectations and delivery.

Maintaining a logical, fair approach when dealing with buyer requests has paid dividends in terms of our community reputation. We understand that each interaction contributes to our brand image, and we've found that this mindset of integrity and reasonable accommodation has enhanced our standing tenfold.

Building a reputable brand as a flipper requires more than just completing renovations and making sales. It demands a commitment to quality, transparency, and fairness. By consistently delivering on these principles, we've established Heaton Dainard as a trusted name in our market, proving that ethical practices and business success can go hand in hand in the flipping industry.

NAVIGATING BUYER DUE DILIGENCE

The journey from contract to closing is a critical phase in the flipping process, where profits can be secured or lost. Even after a property is under contract, several hurdles remain, particularly if the buyer hasn't waived inspection and financing contingencies.

Inspections represent a significant milestone in the sales process. While it's crucial for buyers to conduct their due diligence, overzealous home inspectors can sometimes create unnecessary alarm over minor issues, potentially spooking buyers.

The 2008–2010 market downturn provided valuable lessons in this regard. During that period of excess inventory and scarce buyers, we focused primarily on cosmetic updates and essential repairs to remain cost-effective. However, this approach often backfired during inspections, with buyers requesting substantial credits for minor issues—sometimes two to three times the actual repair costs. The abundance of available properties meant buyers could easily walk away, jeopardizing our profits.

These experiences led us to adopt a more proactive strategy: We now conduct thorough pre-inspections on all our flips, implement a series of punch lists to identify and address issues, and perform reinspections to ensure all identified issues have been resolved.

This proactive approach offers several benefits.

- It prevents small issues from snowballing into major concerns.
- It reduces the likelihood of unreasonable credit requests from buyers.
- It minimizes the risk of losing buyers due to inspection-related concerns.

As flippers often relying on hard-money loans, time is quite literally money. Every instance of returning to the market can extend our hold times by one to two months, potentially costing thousands in additional interest payments. By meticulously addressing issues up front, we not only preserve our profit margins but also avoid the substantial carrying costs associated with prolonged marketing periods.

The key to successfully navigating the closing process lies in thorough preparation and proactive problem-solving. By anticipating and addressing potential issues before they become obstacles, we can significantly increase our chances of closing deals profitably and efficiently. This approach not only protects our bottom line but also enhances our reputation as reliable sellers in the market. In the flipping business, it's not just about making the sale—it's about seeing it through to a successful, profitable conclusion. Taking the time to properly prepare a property for sale is an investment that pays dividends in smoother transactions and preserved profits.

NAVIGATE APPRAISALS AND CONTINGENCIES

Navigating the appraisal process is a critical step in successfully closing a flip transaction, particularly when the buyer is utilizing bank financing. Almost invariably, lenders require an appraisal to ensure the loan-to-value (LTV) ratio aligns with their requirements, a standard procedure that can nonetheless significantly impact your profit margins if not managed properly. The challenging market conditions of 2008–2010 provided valuable insights into managing appraisal challenges. During this period, characterized by declining values and a glut of inventory, appraisals frequently came in below our selling prices, putting pressure on already tight profit margins typically in the $25,000–$50,000 range.

When faced with low appraisals, we developed a systematic approach to dispute the valuation. This included requesting a formal bank appraisal review, which, while rarely resulting in immediate changes, opened the door for constructive dialogue. We would compile our own set of comparables, providing detailed justifications for why these were more appropriate than those used in the original appraisal. Additionally, we meticulously documented upgrades and their associated costs, highlighting the added value not reflected in the initial appraisal. Throughout this process, maintaining a professional, understanding, and respectful demeanor was crucial.

Experience has taught us that being proactive is far more effective than taking reactive measures. Before any appraisal is conducted, we ensure our team provides the lender and appraiser with comprehensive information. This includes sharing the comparables used to establish our pricing strategy and a detailed list of upgrades with associated costs, clearly demonstrating the property's added value. We also coordinate with the appraiser to have our listing broker present during the appraisal, allowing for an in-person overview of the property, discussion of any offers received, and explanation of our pricing strategy. If multiple offers were received, we present the terms to illustrate the property's market demand.

By providing organized, detailed information up front, we can often prevent appraisal-related issues that might otherwise jeopardize the deal or erode our profit margins. This proactive approach not only helps secure a fair valuation but also demonstrates our professionalism and attention to detail. Navigating the appraisal process successfully is crucial in preserving profits and ensuring smooth transactions. By anticipating potential challenges and providing comprehensive information up front, we can significantly improve our odds of a favorable appraisal outcome. In the flipping business, foresight and preparation are key to protecting your bottom line throughout the entire sales process, from initial listing to final closing.

When selling a flipped property, it's crucial to understand and navigate the various contingencies that buyers may include in their offers. These contingencies can significantly impact the strength of an offer and potentially affect your profit margins. As a seasoned flipper, I've dealt with a diverse range of buyers, including cash buyers, financed buyers, and those involved in tax exchanges. Each type of buyer brings their own set of contingencies to the table, and managing these effectively is key to a successful transaction.

Generally speaking, the fewer contingencies an offer includes the stronger it is considered. In my own practice, when I'm on the buying side, I often write offers with zero contingencies, to demonstrate the strength of my position. However, when selling, it's common to encounter various contingencies from potential buyers.

One of the most typical contingencies is the inspection contingency. This allows the buyer to inspect the property and potentially request additional repairs, which can lead to further erosion of your profit. This underscores the importance of ensuring your flipped properties are in excellent condition before listing. Another common contingency, particularly for noncash buyers, is the financing contingency. This can extend almost to the closing date and allows the buyer to back out and receive a refund of their earnest money if they're unable to secure financing. The shorter this timeline, the better it is for the seller. Title review is another standard contingency, giving buyers time to ensure the title is marketable to their satisfaction.

When negotiating the terms of an offer, I always push to shorten the timelines for these contingencies. The goal is to know as early as possible whether the deal will go through, allowing me to put the property back on the market quickly, if needed. This strategy helps prevent profit loss due to extended loan payments on the property. It's worth noting that cash buyers often present the cleanest offers with the fewest contingencies, which can be particularly attractive in a flip situation where time is of the essence. However, regardless of the buyer type, understanding and effectively managing contingencies is crucial to protecting your profits and ensuring a smooth transaction.

While contingencies are a standard part of real estate transactions, as a flipper, it's in your best interest to negotiate for as few contingencies as possible and to keep the timelines for any included contingencies as short as feasible. This approach helps minimize risk and maximize the likelihood of a successful, profitable sale. Remember, every day a property remains unsold after renovation is completed is a day of additional carrying costs, so efficient management of the sales process, including adept handling of contingencies, is key to maintaining healthy profit margins in the flipping business.

HOW TO NEGOTIATE WITH BUYERS

Negotiating with buyers is a delicate art that can significantly impact your profits in the flipping business. With nearly two decades of experience in negotiating off-market deals, investment purchases, and resales of flips and new construction, I've learned that the single most effective negotiation tool is direct, verbal communication. Phone calls and real-time conversations allow you to gauge the situation more accurately and get a feel for how much a buyer truly wants the property, something that's often lost in email exchanges.

Flipping typically involves expensive debt, so sometimes closing a deal for slightly less money can actually improve your overall profit by reducing holding costs. Always negotiate with logic, taking into account current market activity and the number of potential buyers. In a seller's market, with low inventory and high buyer demand, you can afford to be more aggressive in pushing back on timelines, price, contingencies, and terms. However, even in a buyer's market, you need to be strategic. The longer a property sits unsold, the less profit you make, as returns diminish due to ongoing expenses.

Flexibility is key. If a deal has taken longer than expected to materialize, and a buyer requests additional items during the inspection, it may be wise to be more accommodating to ensure the sale goes through. It's all about balancing the immediate sales price against the ongoing costs of holding the property.

In highly competitive markets, managing multiple offers becomes a crucial skill. Again, verbal communication is paramount in these situations. I encourage my brokers to have extensive conversations with potential buyers and their agents. This approach has often resulted in selling properties for hundreds of thousands of dollars more than initially anticipated. For instance, when dealing with escalator offers—where a buyer offers to beat any other offer by a certain amount up to a maximum price—direct communication can help you negotiate a final price that's higher than your pro forma estimate but still below the buyer's maximum, creating a win-win situation.

The trick to successful negotiation is to remain flexible, informed, and communicative throughout the process. Be prepared to adjust your strategy based on market conditions, the specific circumstances of each deal, and the motivations of individual buyers. Remember, the goal isn't just to get the highest possible price but to close deals efficiently and maintain a healthy profit margin considering all factors, including holding costs and market risks. By mastering the art of negotiation, you can significantly enhance your success and profitability in the flipping business.

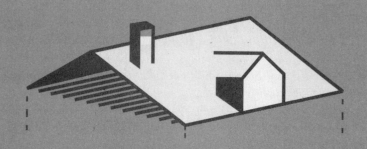

PART 4

SCALING YOUR FLIPPING BUSINESS

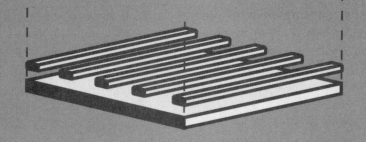

CHAPTER 15
FLIPPING WITH EFFECTIVE TECHNOLOGY

Setting a goal is not the main thing. It is deciding how you will go about achieving it and staying with that plan.

—TOM LANDRY, ORIGINAL HEAD COACH, DALLAS COWBOYS

EVERY INVESTOR NEEDS to utilize technology for their own processes and business size. When you start your flipping business, you likely won't know the areas you can use technology and expand your resources. Heck, you may not even need to streamline the process because you're only completing one or two flips a year. But, if you plan on scaling your business to complete more and more flips, you'll soon learn that technology and vast resources are essential to your success. But the more you scale and grow, the more projects you take on, the more bodies you're going to have working, the more contractors you're going to deal with, the more subcontractors, the more cities and permitting as you expand out—it's hard to keep track of.

You want to do this in steps rather than just hiring right away. Remember, you don't need to grow rapidly in the very beginning, but it is important that you document what you're doing, so as you grow, people will know what to do. Every company and investor has their own pain points inside their processes. Select the technology that works for you, not only in what you're doing day-to-day but also inside your budget.

Again, you don't need to hire up right away, but as you build your fix-and-flip processes, you want to take the time to document it all. As you select your tech, you want to write a detailed SOP (standard operating procedure). That way, when you do hire down the road—maybe not at first, when you're doing two to three projects at a time, but when you get to seven or more projects at a time—you'll have written instructions for every step of the process, making hiring a lot easier.

TECHNOLOGY AND TRACKING

Technology and tracking are the keys to being efficient as an investor. Tracking where you are today and where you are headed can help you better understand your budget for current and future flips. It can also help you better understand the use of time throughout your flips. Technology can help you both track and save time. The more you utilize technology and your team, the more you're going to be able to scale your business.

Integrating technological processes and tools across various aspects of fix-and-flip investing can significantly enhance efficiency, scalability, and profitability. By implementing digital solutions for sourcing and managing contractors, deal underwriting, property acquisition, project management, and financial oversight, investors can streamline their operations and make data-driven decisions.

Using online platforms to find and vet contractors, employing construction management apps for real-time updates, and utilizing real estate analysis software for quick and accurate property evaluations can dramatically reduce manual tasks and minimize errors. AI-driven tools can help identify potential properties, while project-management software can track timelines and budgets more effectively. These technological integrations not only improve communication and coordination among team members but also free up valuable time for strategic planning and business growth. As investors scale their operations, these tools become increasingly crucial in maintaining efficiency, reducing wasted time, and ultimately boosting profitability. By systematically incorporating these solutions, fix-and-flip investors can focus on high-value activities that drive their business forward, leveraging technology to streamline processes and achieve greater success in a competitive market.

The primary goal of implementing technological solutions and organizational systems in fix-and-flip investing is twofold: to enhance efficiency and to facilitate scalable growth. Unlike businesses with standardized products or services, house flipping presents unique challenges for scaling due to the individuality of each project. Every property has its own set of characteristics, renovation needs, and market considerations, making it difficult to apply a one-size-fits-all approach.

To overcome these scaling hurdles, leveraging technology and robust organizational systems becomes crucial. These tools and processes serve multiple purposes.

- They streamline operations, reducing time spent on routine tasks and minimizing errors
- They provide a standardized framework for handling diverse projects, creating consistency in an inherently variable business
- Most importantly, they enable effective delegation, allowing investors to entrust various aspects of the business to team members or automated systems

By establishing clear processes and utilizing appropriate technologies, investors can create a replicable model that adapts to different properties and market conditions. This systematic approach not only improves the management of current projects but also lays the groundwork for handling a larger volume of flips simultaneously.

As the business grows, these systems become even more vital. They allow investors to maintain oversight and control while delegating day-to-day operations, freeing up time to focus on strategic decisions, market analysis, and further expansion opportunities. In essence, the right combination of organizational strategies and technological tools transforms flipping from a hands-on, project-by-project business into a scalable investment model capable of significant growth.

PROPERTY INFORMATION SOURCES

Leveraging technology to gather and analyze property information is crucial for all types of real estate investors. The ability to quickly underwrite properties can significantly accelerate your growth as an investor. In our operation, we typically evaluate over one hundred properties each week. This high-volume approach serves several purposes: It allows us to make timely offers on a wide range of properties, generates the deal flow necessary for our fix-and-flip operations, and helps us identify opportunities that may not fit our investment criteria but could be valuable for our clients as wholesalers and lenders.

This efficient, technology-driven process enables us to increase our chances of finding profitable deals, quickly identify and act on market opportunities, diversify our investment portfolio, and provide more value to our network of investors and clients. By streamlining the property-analysis process through technology, we can optimize our operations and maximize our potential for profit across various real estate investment strategies. This approach not only benefits our direct investments but also enhances our ability to serve clients and partners in the real estate market.

For mobile use, consider specialized apps designed for investors. I personally use PropertyRadar when I'm in the field because it allows for quick property lookups and easy saving of interesting listings. Then, when I'm back at my office, I can conduct a more in-depth analysis using my preferred tools. You don't have to limit yourself to a single resource. You might find it beneficial to use different tools for different situations—a mobile-friendly app for on-the-spot assessments and a more comprehensive platform for detailed analysis when you're at your computer. The key is to find a combination that works efficiently for your investment strategy and workflow.

TECHNOLOGY FOR EVALUATING PROPERTIES (CRMS)

Customer relationship management (CRM) systems are valuable tools in real estate, though their importance can vary depending on your specific business model. A CRM is a software system designed to help businesses manage and analyze customer interactions and data throughout the customer life cycle. In real estate, a CRM can help you keep track of leads, clients, properties, and transactions. It's essentially a centralized database that can help you manage relationships, streamline communications, and organize your business operations.

For fix-and-flip investors, CRMs might not be as critical as they are for other real estate professionals, like agents or wholesalers. This is because fix-and-flip operations often involve fewer long-term client relationships and greater focus on project management. However, CRMs can still be useful in several ways: managing investor clients if you're selling properties to other investors, off-market seller outreach for targeting potential properties, maintaining a contractor database, and tracking your property pipeline.

While CRMs have their place, the most crucial technology for fix-and-flip investors is often project-management software. These tools help you evaluate potential properties, manage rehab timelines and budgets, track contractor performance, monitor project progress, and analyze profitability. But while CRMs can be useful for certain aspects of fix-and-flip investing, particularly as you scale your business, project management and property evaluation tools are often more immediately valuable for managing your rehab projects efficiently. The key is to find the right balance of tools that work for your specific business model and scale.

As an investor, having the right technology and reporting systems in place can dramatically increase your capacity to manage multiple projects simultaneously. In our current operations, we're able to handle fifty to sixty flips at any given time thanks to these tools. This level of efficiency wasn't always possible, especially when I was just starting out.

In my early days as a wholesaler, I often struggled with accurate cost estimation. I would tie up properties with rehab estimates of $40,000–$50,000, only to have investors discover later that the actual costs were closer to $100,000. This discrepancy arose because I lacked proper estimation tools and relied on guesswork or rudimentary pen-and-paper calculations.

For new investors, it's crucial to develop the ability to quickly and accurately estimate rehab costs without immediately bringing in a contractor. This skill serves multiple purposes.

- It allows you to underwrite deals rapidly, giving you a competitive edge in fast-moving markets
- You can provide quick, reliable answers to potential buyers or partners
- Most importantly, it helps protect you from making poor investment decisions based on underestimated renovation costs

As a real estate investor, it's crucial to understand that renovation costs can vary significantly depending on your location. This variability can have a substantial impact on your investment decisions and profit margins.

Let me give you an example from my experience in the Pacific Northwest. Installing a pool in our region costs about 30 percent more than it does in Arizona or California. This price difference isn't arbitrary—it's due to the scarcity of pool installers in our area. We learned this the hard way during the pandemic when pool installations became more popular due to an influx of California relocations. This cost disparity means that, while adding a pool might be a profitable upgrade in California, where it's 30 percent cheaper, it often doesn't make financial sense for us in the Pacific Northwest. The higher cost eats into our potential profits, making it a less attractive renovation option.

The key takeaway here is that you need to customize your rehab calculators to reflect the specific costs in your market. Don't rely on generic national averages or costs from other regions. Instead, research and input local prices for various renovation tasks. What makes sense in one market might be a poor investment in another. By adjusting your rehab calculator to match your local market conditions, you'll be able to make more accurate cost estimates and better investment decisions. This localized approach will help you avoid overestimating your potential profits or underestimating your renovation costs, both of which can be detrimental to your fix-and-flip success.

TASK-MANAGEMENT SYSTEMS

To maximize efficiency, aim to consolidate your tools as much as possible. Using fewer applications can streamline your workflow and improve overall productivity. However, keep in mind that the real estate technology landscape is continually evolving. Stay informed about the latest software developments by following industry trends and engaging with professional networks. For the most current software recommendations tailored to real estate investing, consider following reputable sources on social media or joining online communities focused on real estate investment. These resources can provide valuable insights into emerging tools and best practices in the ever-changing landscape of real estate technology.

Effective task management is essential for overseeing multiple renovation projects across different locations. With projects potentially spread across numerous cities, involving various vendors and staff, it's impractical for an operator to personally visit each site frequently. Task-management software allows operators to:

- Track open, in-progress, and completed tasks.
- Identify and address bottlenecks or issues.
- Manage employee workloads effectively.
- Maintain oversight of multiple projects simultaneously.

When selecting task-management software, prioritize user-friendliness and compatibility with your working style. There are numerous options available, each with unique features.

One popular option is Asana, known for its simplicity and ease of use. It allows users to:

- Load projects with predetermined benchmarks and deadlines.
- Set up preloaded tasks for standard procedures (ordering as-builts, securing jobsites).
- Assign tasks to specific employees.
- Monitor task progress and completion status.
- Facilitate project manager meetings by providing a clear overview of ongoing work.

By implementing these technological tools and processes, real estate investors can streamline their operations, maintain better control over multiple projects, and ultimately increase their efficiency and profitability in the fix-and-flip market.

ACCOUNTING SYSTEMS

As you develop your fix-and-flip business, implementing a robust accounting system is important for maintaining financial clarity and supporting growth. The core function of this system should be its ability to provide regular, up-to-date budget information. This real-time financial reporting is essential for making informed decisions and keeping your projects on track. Your system should allow for frequent updates to project budgets, ideally on a weekly or biweekly basis, ensuring you have the most current financial picture for each renovation project. The ability to generate up-to-date reports on demand is crucial, helping you quickly identify and address any budget overruns or unexpected expenses.

Key financial reports include monthly profit and loss (P&L) statements, showing year-to-date and anticipated profits, and cash flow statements indicating current cash on hand and twelve-month projections. Some investors prefer to manage their own books for real-time tracking, setting regular dates (such as every Friday) to update spreadsheets and reconcile books. This DIY approach can provide immediate insights into project finances.

For newer fix-and-flip operators or those with a small number of projects, one of the first members to bring on to your growing team should be a bookkeeper. This can be a part-time position, where they focus on basic P&L statements for each project, update budgets and financial reports, reconcile invoices, and maintain your financial software system. As your business scales, you may need to employ full-time accounting staff, implement more sophisticated accounting software, and develop more complex financial reporting systems to handle multiple projects simultaneously. In the case of my business, we have three full-time accountants due to the volume and variety of our projects.

The benefits of maintaining organized and up-to-date financial records include better cash flow management, more accurate project cost estimations, the ability to quickly identify profitable project types, easier tax preparation and compliance, and improved decision-making based on accurate financial data. As your business grows, your accounting needs will become more complex. Starting with good habits and systems early on will make this transition smoother and support your business's growth. Regular financial updates and organized bookkeeping are not just about keeping records—they're essential tools for strategic planning and scaling your fix-and-flip operation efficiently.

Using an all-in-one software and budget sheets for tracking your projects can help you live track the renovation—and make adjustments where needed. Renovating a property can be full of surprises, as every wall demolished could create unforeseen projects. It is important for all investors to make sure that they are staying on top of their numbers and reconciling their books every two to four weeks on projects.

Additionally, regular updates to budgets and pro formas are essential as invoices come in and prices change. This allows for accurate profit projections and, for those managing multiple projects, enables twelve-month forecasting to track cash flow and completion dates. While QuickBooks is a popular choice due to its ease of use and compatibility with accountants, beginners can start with a spreadsheet for basic budget tracking and invoicing.

You're going to want to make sure you have a system in place for receiving and paying invoices. It's normal to pay your vendors a down payment of anywhere between 25 and 30 percent. You want to keep track of this amount and each additional invoice that is submitted. For cash flow tracking, you can track what's been paid and what remains in that budget, which will tell you what you can still draw against the construction draws or what liquidity we need to finish out the project. It's essential that these numbers are regularly updated, as it will help you dictate your profit and cash flow. You definitely don't want to run out of cash in the middle of a project.

The importance of maintaining up-to-date financials cannot be overstated. It enables quick adaptation to market changes, such as interest rate fluctuations; helps identify areas to cut costs or adjust strategy;

and facilitates informed decision-making based on current financial status. Regardless of the method chosen, consistent and timely updates to your financial data are crucial for successful fix-and-flip operations. This practice allows for better cash flow management, accurate profit projections, and the ability to pivot strategies when necessary, ultimately contributing to the success and scalability of your real estate investment business.

CHAPTER 16
WHEN TO SCALE

Today I will do what others won't, so tomorrow I can accomplish what others can't.
—JERRY RICE, FORMER NFL FOOTBALL

IN THE BEGINNING, it's generally advisable to concentrate on completing one deal at a time rather than taking on multiple projects simultaneously. This approach allows you to dedicate your full attention to each individual flip, ensuring that you can effectively manage the various aspects of the project, such as renovations, budgeting, and marketing. By focusing on one property at a time, you can minimize the risk of becoming overwhelmed or overstretched, which can lead to costly mistakes or delays.

As you successfully complete each deal and gain more confidence in your abilities, you can gradually adjust your price range and investment criteria to align with your growing experience and financial resources. This measured approach to scaling your business helps to ensure that you maintain a healthy balance between growth and risk management. Your ultimate goal as an investor is to achieve your long-term financial objectives.

Scaling your fix-and-flip business is a crucial next step as a real estate investor to achieve your long-term financial goals. Scaling allows you to access more income streams, which provides more money you can save. For example, when I started my flipping business and became fairly decent at wholesaling, in 2005, my revenue was $2 million. Today, my revenue has ballooned up to $50 million a year. Those are the type of numbers you can see if you approach flipping houses with a scaling mindset.

A SCALING EXAMPLE

Let's look at an example where you work up to just two flips per year.

This comes from one of my online students in Project | RE, our real estate investing education program. This student started with $50,000, does about two flips per year, and aims for a 35 percent return on both flips, to equal 70 percent annual return. Those are the big numbers, but let's break this down.

POWER OF FLIPPING

Case Study with $50,000

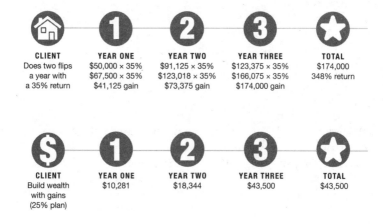

CLIENT	YEAR ONE	YEAR TWO	YEAR THREE	TOTAL
Does two flips a year with a 35% return	$50,000 × 35% $67,500 × 35% $41,125 gain	$91,125 × 35% $123,018 × 35% $73,375 gain	$123,375 × 35% $166,075 × 35% $174,000 gain	$174,000 348% return

CLIENT	YEAR ONE	YEAR TWO	YEAR THREE	TOTAL
Build wealth with gains (25% plan)	$10,281	$18,344	$43,500	$43,500

In the figure above, we see that the $50,000 investment made a $41,125 gain the first year in business, turning $50,000 into $91,125, which you roll into the next flip. Repeat the process to earn a $73,375 gain, which you roll over once more to end three years with about $174,000 and a 348 percent return.

If the same client merely invested with a gains plan, or 25 percent return, they'd end three years with only $43,500, which is $130,500 less than flipping! Instead of choosing one or the other, I'd encourage you to do both (when you're ready). Flip to build cash and reinvest to build investments for your future.

If you use the $43,500 to buy value-add rental properties, and keep that money rolling, it's a way to expedite the entire process. Here is the statement expanded to include formulas for doing one flip per year, two flips per year, five flips per year, and ten flips per year:

One flip per year:
If you start with $50,000 and do one flip per year, aiming for a 35 percent return, your progress would be:
Year 1: $50,000 + (35% × $50,000) = $67,500
Year 2: $67,500 + (35% × $67,500) = $91,125
Year 3: $91,125 + (35% × $91,125) = $123,019

Two flips per year:
If you start with $50,000 and do two flips per year, aiming for a 35 percent return on each, your progress would be:
Year 1: $50,000 + (0.7 × $50,000) = $85,000
Year 2: $85,000 + (0.7 × $85,000) = $144,500
Year 3: $144,500 + (0.7 × $144,500) = $245,650

Five flips per year:
If you start with $50,000 and do five flips per year, aiming for a 35 percent return on each, your progress would be:
Year 1: $50,000 + (1.75 × $50,000) = $137,500
Year 2: $137,500 + (1.75 × $137,500) = $378,125
Year 3: $378,125 + (1.75 × $378,125) = $1,039,844

Ten flips per year:
If you start with $50,000 and do ten flips per year, aiming for a 35 percent return on each, your progress would be:
Year 1: $50,000 + (3.5 × $50,000) = $225,000
Year 2: $225,000 + (3.5 × $225,000) = $787,500
Year 3: $787,500 + (3.5 × $787,500) = $2,756,250

The key points remain the same, which is to aim for a high return through flipping, reinvest the profits to compound the gains, and be disciplined in order to build significant wealth over just a few years of this real estate investing strategy. If you can be highly disciplined the first few years, the compound effect will take over, and that's when you make the real money. If you're only thinking about making an extra $10,000 per year, or even doubling your salary, it's possible you're thinking too small. Think big, but have a plan to match your most ambitious goals and stick with it. Invest in your future with your actions, your mindset, and your resources.

OTHER BENEFITS OF SCALING

Operating a fix-and-flip venture equips you with valuable skill sets, including evaluating properties, sourcing funding, stabilizing, and implementing construction plans to create substantial margins. The question then becomes how you can leverage these skills to expand your business further.

Allow me to share my personal journey as a real estate investor. At the age of 23, back in 2005, I started as a wholesaler. Since then, I have grown my operations to encompass eight different real estate investing businesses. My portfolio now includes a brokerage that services investors by sourcing both on- and off-market properties, as well as a property management company that facilitates the leasing process for clients. Additionally, I have an off-market business and a funding company, Interest Funding, which provides short-term capital and hard-money loans to investors.

And then there's my development business that does fix-and-flip properties, new construction, and apartment syndications where we're turning apartment buildings for long-term wealth and building that up to over 1,000 doors. Scaling over the last twenty years has gotten me to a place where I'm making almost $1 million a year in passive income alone, just through all the different business ventures that I have going on. So as you start to build out your fix-and-flip business, there are naturally going to be other income streams available.

HOW TO SCALE

Here, we're going to cover the three main points of how to scale that fix-and-flip business: First, hire the right team. Second, look for additional income streams in the day-to-day activities that you already have. And third, raise capital and scale your talents as an operator to bring in more capital, which will get you into more projects, which brings in more profit.

The key to scaling is mastering your current business, systemizing it, and then moving to your next lateral business. If you look at my timeline of how I've scaled since getting in the business in 2005, you can see how I systematically added businesses over time, utilizing skills learned in the previous business.

2005

In 2005, as a wholesaler, I wasn't very good for the first six months. There's no way I could just start flipping properties. I had to systemize it, getting everything put together to where the business was running itself with me just managing it. That allowed me to free up time to start buying properties. From buying properties, it allowed me to become a syndicator and developer, because I learned those essential skills of hiring, managing a jobsite, sourcing properties, and then improving them and selling them for a profit.

2008

In 2008, I branched off from the company I was working for as a wholesaler and started my own business. The market crashed and we had to rebuild all of our companies, but we became that business operator. So I went from being a wholesaler to a fix-and-flip operator to then starting my own real estate and business-investment company.

2009

In 2009, because we were sourcing off-market properties and buying properties as flippers, it was hard to get hard money in the door and get funding for your projects.

2010

In 2010, we started our own hard-money company, Intrust Funding. With the skill set that I had built as a flipper, I realized I could start a brokerage and help investors buy properties and execute on the plans with skills I had learned. I started my brokerage at that point.

In 2010, I established Limelite Development and started building homes.

2016

In 2016, I started syndicating larger apartment buildings, where I was bringing in other investors' money, buying value-add apartments, improving them with rehab plans, and then getting a portion of the equity in every one of those transactions.

Avoiding "shiny object syndrome" is crucial when scaling your fix-and-flip business. It's essential to take calculated, lateral steps that lead you into the next income stream, but only after you've mastered your current operations. Prematurely expanding into new ventures can divert your attention and resources, potentially causing your core business to suffer. As a fix-and-flip operator, your primary focus should be on refining your existing business and building a strong team. Systematize your processes and delegate responsibilities to your team members, allowing them to handle 75–80 percent of the day-to-day operations. Your role should transition into managing the remaining 20 percent, overseeing the bigger picture and ensuring smooth functioning. Only when you have a well-oiled machine in place should you consider systematizing the next business venture. Jumping into a new project too quickly can lead to a loss of focus on your fix-and-flip business, causing the wheels to come off and resulting in financial losses.

UPDATE YOUR BUY BOX

As you begin to flip more and more properties, you'll want to revisit your buy box and make adjustments regularly. You might expand for simple flips to studs-down renovations. You might expand your location criteria. With more capital, you might be able to increase your price point criteria. It's important to keep a clear vision of what projects are ideal for you, especially as you widen your abilities (both financially and skill set wise).

Balance a high-yield portfolio. Balancing a high-yield portfolio helps manage risk and ensure steady cash flow, which you can achieve by strategically combining fix-and-flip projects with real estate development. Balancing a high-yield portfolio involves investing in a mix of short-term and long-term projects simultaneously to maintain a consistent income stream. Fix-and-flip projects, along with development, are considered high risk because they involve purchasing a property, adding value through construction or renovation, and then selling it for a profit. My team aims for a 70 percent cash-on-cash return on an annualized (twelve-month) basis from these projects. Basically, what this means is that for every dollar invested into a project, the goal is to earn back the initial investment plus an additional $0.70 in profit within a twelve-month period. This is a high-yield return, which reflects the increased risk associated with fix-and-flip and real estate development projects.

We have over $20 million in projects going on between cosmetic, heavy renovation, and development projects. All of these projects create large returns but at different time periods. Additionally, we sometimes keep our flips as rental properties in order to collect additional cash flow and to keep a certain amount of liquidity in hard-money notes. The real balance is high risk, high reward with low risk, low reward. This is a similar idea to buying stocks and bonds to balance out your overall investments.

For a while, my deal-finders seemed to think I only wanted massive, luxury flips, so that's all they sent me. I'm good at taking on harder flips, but I want a mixed portfolio of easy and hard flips each year, so I hit my numbers before I literally just run out of time. This means communicating often with your deal-finders to make sure they know what you want, what you need, and any changes to your plans. This is something I'd let them know every couple of months or business quarter, so we're always on the same page.

Look to build resources based on new opportunities. There are certain areas that most investors would never touch. While these areas can be considered a "no man's land," the fact that there is less competition means it will be easier for you to win deals. Investing in these "no man's land" areas often involves taking on projects that are more challenging or complex than those in more sought-after locations. These complexities may include issues such as zoning restrictions, extensive repairs or renovations, or navigating local regulations. However, by building the right resources and teams to address these specific challenges, investors can potentially acquire properties at a lower cost and achieve higher margins upon sale.

Typically, in these scenarios, the projects are harder or more complex. But if I can build the resources around what I'm seeing, I can get a better deal. This means examining the market as a whole to see what's not selling or what people don't want to touch. We actually reverse engineer the deal. We'll notice the problem, build the team to fix the problem, then go out and close on the deal because we have the right resources in place. This leads to high margins.

UPDATE YOUR PRO FORMA

Regularly updating your monthly pro forma is crucial for successful project management. This involves not only projecting your expected profits but also forecasting your cash position and return on investment. It's essential to adjust your timeline if unforeseen delays extend your project, as this directly impacts your cash flow, requiring additional payments and potentially reducing your profit margin and cash-on-cash return.

As you scale your business, having accurate and up-to-date financial data readily available becomes increasingly important. Losing track of the status of multiple projects can quickly lead to a snowball effect, which can overwhelm your operation. To streamline your accounting processes, always collect tax information from your vendors before issuing the first payment. This proactive approach saves significant time and costs when closing out your books later. Another key principle to incorporate into your business practices is clearly communicating payment schedules to your vendors. Inform them about your payment process, including when they should submit invoices and when they can expect to receive payment. Providing this information in writing and having them sign it, along with their construction bid, can prevent misunderstandings and ensure that contractors show up to your jobsite as planned.

There's a lot of up-front work when you're setting up your processes and your fix-and-flip business. But organization will reduce lost time. Lost time means lost revenue. The more efficient you can be in getting set up right, the more profitable you'll be down the road. And remember, when you pick your technology, make sure it works for you and your business, not just what I or other influential people in your sphere are using. How do you like to see reporting? How do you like to manage people? And then go out and test drive three to four software programs and see if it works with your daily functions.

Just because you picked your first software doesn't mean you have to use it for the rest of your life. I made that mistake a couple different times where I picked the software, started using it, and then wouldn't get off it. And all it did was create more inefficiencies. Find what the magic formula is by going through this effort. It will help you down the road. And always test this software before you implement it on a permanent basis.

LONG-TERM RELATIONSHIPS

Building long-term relationships with general contractors is a critical strategy for scaling your real estate business efficiently. As these relationships develop, they can significantly streamline your operations and free up valuable time for growth-focused activities. When you work consistently with the same contractors, they become familiar with your standards, expectations, and processes. This familiarity leads to a more systemized approach on jobsites, requiring less direct management from you.

Over time, contractors can anticipate your needs and make decisions aligned with your vision, reducing the need for constant oversight and communication. The reduced management requirement on jobsites is a key factor in scaling. With trusted contractors handling day-to-day operations, you can redirect your time and energy toward strategic business-growth activities. This might include sourcing new deals, exploring new markets, or developing additional revenue streams. A recent evolution in this strategy is bringing long-term contractors in as partners. This approach can be particularly beneficial as you scale other aspects of your business. By offering partnership stakes, you align the contractors' interests more closely with your own, potentially increasing their commitment and performance without the need for constant supervision. This partnership model can also help manage costs as you scale. Instead of hiring additional salaried staff to oversee growing operations, which increases fixed expenses, partnering with contractors can create a more flexible cost structure.

Contractor partners have a vested interest in the project's success, which can lead to better quality work and more efficient operations. Moreover, they often bring their own network of subcontractors and suppliers, which can further streamline operations and potentially reduce costs. Their industry knowledge and connections can be invaluable as you expand into new areas or take on larger projects. By evolving your contractor relationships in this way, you're not just scaling your operational capacity; you're also building a more resilient and adaptable business model. This approach allows you to maintain quality control and operational efficiency while freeing up your personal bandwidth to focus on higher-level strategic decisions and new business opportunities.

As you scale your fix-and-flip business, consider a strategic shift in team management. Instead of expanding your salaried staff, which can significantly increase annual expenses, explore bringing trusted general contractors in as partners. By offering contractors a stake in the deal—typically around 20 percent equity—you can reduce management overhead, lower fixed costs, align interests, and expand your capacity without proportionally increasing your management burden. This approach can dramatically reduce salary expenses—potentially by up to 50 percent or more—while maintaining or even improving project outcomes.

To make this partnership model work effectively, implement robust reporting systems. These should include weekly budget updates, monthly

P&L statements, regular CMAs, photo documentation, and detailed project manager reports. These reports serve to keep you informed, without requiring constant site visits, and highlight potential issues that may need your direct attention. Additional essential reports include year-to-date P&L for closed properties and works in progress, real-time budget sheets, detailed project schedules, and cost spent to date versus completed work ratio.

Pay particular attention to the cost-to-completion ratio. If you've spent $50,000 on a $100,000 budget, ensure at least 40 percent of the work is complete. Aim to keep advanced funds below 75 percent of the total budget to maintain smooth operations and reduce risk. This careful monitoring helps prevent overpayment and keeps projects on track.

By implementing these strategies and maintaining rigorous reporting, you can scale your fix-and-flip business more efficiently. You'll free up time to focus on strategic growth while ensuring your projects remain on track and profitable. Remember, the goal is to expand your operation without proportionally increasing your time investment or financial risk. This approach allows you to leverage the expertise of your contractors while maintaining control through data-driven management, ultimately enabling you to take on more projects and grow your business more effectively.

HAVE A TEAM IN PLACE

Building the right internal team will free up time and allow you to grow your investment business in all different ways. As you grow your fix-and-flip business, you'll need to focus on building a team that you can trust to handle the day-to-day operations, even when you're not physically present. This means hiring individuals with the right skills, experience, and work ethic and providing them with the tools, resources, and guidance they need to succeed. It also means establishing clear lines of communication and setting expectations for regular updates and reporting. By investing time and effort into building a strong team, you'll be able to step back from the daily grind of your fix-and-flip business and focus on strategic growth and expansion. This is the key to scaling your business and achieving long-term success in the industry.

Every operator's team is different in size, but they still need to serve the same function. As a new operator, you're going to start small—maybe with just have one person on your team. As you start to grow, you'll bring in more people to free up your time. But no matter who you have on your team or how big it is, you need to operate several core functions, manage them, and start them early in your process.

Generally, you should consider expanding when you find yourself consistently overwhelmed with tasks, missing opportunities, or unable to provide the level of service your clients deserve. If you're working long hours but still falling behind, or if you're turning down potential deals due to lack of time, it's likely time to bring on help.

Effective scaling requires careful planning and implementation of systems. When hiring, focus on creating detailed job descriptions, clear expectations, and thorough onboarding processes. Develop SOPs for common tasks such as lead generation, property evaluations, and client communications. These documents should outline step-by-step processes that anyone can follow, ensuring consistency and efficiency across your team.

You need progress updates, so create a system where you can get weekly updates of what's going on at the jobsite, what's been completed, and the photo completion. You need to be able to budget and track—where are you at on your budget? Are you over budget? Are you under budget? Do you need to change your game plan? If you're spending way more money on your property, you might need to switch your plan and go for a much more aggressive future market value that could change everything around. So it's really important to develop that system that will help you track that budget.

The goal of hiring and scaling is indeed to buy more time and increase efficiency. However, it's crucial to invest time up front in creating these systems and processes. This initial investment will pay off by allowing new team members to quickly become productive, reducing the need for constant oversight and freeing you up to focus on high-level strategy and growth opportunities.

Include design on your team, so you don't have to manage and pick the specs for every type of house. From 2008 to 2014, I specced out every house—what cabinets, what counters, what colors. I used a lot of templates, in order to systematize, but doing so takes a lot of time, especially as you're scaling your business. Bringing in that resource or that designer will help free up your time and keep your projects moving forward.

You need someone on your team who can give you market analysis, giving you up-to-date information: what's going on in the market, whether you should change your plan, keep with your plan, and then what your financial projections are going to be. Those financial projections are going to tell you how much cash you have and what kind of people you can hire or deals you can buy.

You also need someone on your team with access to funding. Whether it's someone who's working with your banks, getting you the money, or just someone working directly with your lender who can get things funded for you, access to money is key.

So, as you begin to think about scaling your fix-and-flip business, the core people you need on your fix-and-flip team are your project manager, your assistant, a real estate broker, a hard-money lender, a general contractor, and subcontractors you have long-term relationships with. Having a dependable, trustworthy team is going to keep your project moving forward.

The project manager. The core function of your project manager is to get you updates. They're responsible, on our team, for updating all the budgets and contract prices. They go out and do all the estimating based on the scope of work that we made during our underwriting process. If you breezed through the underwriting section, go back and revisit it. Creating that scope of work is essential for being able to scale. The clearer you are on your scope of work, the easier it is for your project manager to take that information and get an accurate bid.

Your project manager should help you get estimates. Personally, I would hire someone as soon as it makes financial sense. They're going to update the budgets based on the estimates coming in, and that way you can have real-time tracking throughout your process. The project manager, as they collect bids, is going to enter in the actuals, which will show you where you are on your cost to date.

Your project manager should do weekly jobsite walks and document with pictures and give you a progress report. Our project managers visit the site a minimum of once a week. Typically, we like to have them drive projects on Monday and Friday—what's starting for the week, what's scheduled in, and then what had been completed for the week—and provide updates, pictures, and a report with all the pertinent information. In addition, they update me on any types of budget issues, change orders, material issues, or even subcontractor issues.

By getting these weekly updates, I can always see a project's progress both visually and in writing and see what's scheduled for the following week. These updates allow me to manage from afar. Pictures are essential, because as I go through the pictures every week, I look for anything that might stand out. If I see something that's framed a little weird or that the spaces look a little off, or even if the jobsite just seems off, that tells me to go drive to the property. Having these reports usually allows me to only have to visit my jobsites maybe four times throughout the duration of the whole project. That saves me a ton of time.

The primary responsibility, for the project manager, is to bid the scope of work with the contractor, schedule the dates with our in-house assistant and the trades of when they're coming out to do the work and do their installs, monitor the timelines for construction, submit invoicing as the work's been completed and they've verified that it's complete, and then update the budget with the assistant. They also check for quality of work. Once the contractors are going through their final part of the project and looking for their final payment, the project manager's doing all the punch list items, making sure the quality's there, making sure all permits are signed off on, and then approving the invoice for paying.

So they handle a lot of the on-site work that eats up a lot of our time as investors. Project manager hiring in our Pacific Northwest market typically costs $60,000–$80,000, but sometimes even up to $100,000 depending on whether the hire has extensive experience in one skill set or another (such as new construction or working on flips).

We used to have a project manager who made nearly $100,000, but we were also able to subsidize costs because he was skilled in doing as-builts, so he could go out and do the as-built, saving me about $500 per project. Multiply that by thirty projects, and that ends up being about $15,000 right off the top. So depending on what their skill sets are will depend on how much you're paying them. Currently we pay our project managers $90,000 a year, but they also get to invest with us or through us.

Listing and construction assistant. We've merged our construction admin role with our listing assistant position. This dual-role strategy arose from the practical reality that our current business volume doesn't warrant a full-time construction assistant, especially given the cooled market and reduced project load. When building your team, explore multifaceted roles that align with your business needs and candidate skills. For instance, a construction assistant with bookkeeping aptitude could handle both responsibilities. In our case, we found someone with extensive experience in property listings and prep work, creating a synergistic role that spans both construction management and listing preparation. This team member now oversees the entire life cycle of our projects. They handle listing prep, including crafting marketing descriptions, coordinating with stagers and photographers, and arranging property cleaning. Simultaneously, they manage construction-related tasks throughout the project's duration. This approach not only maximizes efficiency but also ensures a cohesive workflow from property acquisition to listing. By embracing such adaptable strategies, you can build a lean, efficient team that meets your current business needs while positioning you for future growth. How might you apply this flexible thinking to your own team structure?

This position's primary responsibility is to order specialty items. Typically, we have our general contractors and subcontractors source all materials with the allowances and specs we give them. We do that because it helps us scale. Not having to track things down saves us time. Always think about that as you're making your processes.

We typically have our subs buy the materials, but for specialty items like light fixtures, maybe appliances, or just some general ordering that we don't want to give over to the general, we have this person order all those things. They also schedule subcontractors. So as our project manager is creating the schedule and getting things bid out, our construction assistant then handles the communication of when they should be starting and stopping. We like to have them do it inside the office, because our PMs are always running around at different jobsites. They may forget to call someone, whereas this person in the office is hyperorganized. We go through the budget and the projects every week, and then this role builds that schedule based on our weekly meeting.

The construction admin also follows up with all vendors. They help with pricing out appliances, cabinets, countertops, and any items that we're subbing into the project outside the general contractor's scope of work. Many times, we're trying to save money on appliances, garage doors, roofs, and other items in our plan that we can easily sub in that won't affect the schedule.

The good news is a lot of those things don't have to be done in the very beginning, like the general contractor getting started on all the rough-ins. Our construction admin can get numerous different bids for us, which saves us money on average. Typically, when we're getting three bids over one bid, we're going to end up saving about 5–10 percent on that item. So by having this person, not only is it an expenditure, but it saves us money and helps pay for that position. So look at it as you're hiring that position—don't just think about the cost. Where's the benefit? How much are they saving you? The cost against your bottom line might be a lot less than you expected.

They also prepare the listing presentation. So as they go through the project, they've worked on it with the PM and helped schedule all the trades. As it gets to completion, they're working with the project manager on the final punch list and doing the final walk-through and scheduling the photographer and cleaners. By having this person also assist with the project manager, it helps get a second pair of eyes on each project.

The last thing we want to do is list a property, get it on the market after we worked on it for six to twelve months, and then for it to have a bunch of flaws. No person is perfect. So by having the construction admin, who understands the project and also brought people out to the site, do the walk-through, it allows them to double-check with the project manager and help with the punch list as well.

Having this listing admin handle the scheduling and ordering of materials also frees up time for my project manager, so they can really focus on the budgeting and the reporting of the project rather than going backward and just ordering up materials.

Once the property is sold, this assistant also handles all the de-staging and gets the formal handoff to the next potential buyer. They meet them there, hand them the keys, provide any kind of warranties, and generally make the handoff a lot smoother. The smoother your handoff is to your next potential buyer, the fewer headaches you're going to have down the road. Those headaches down the road will eat up your time, which will eat up money. So by preventing those, it's just going to allow you to scale even further. In addition, they do the final clean, making sure it's ready for delivery.

This role also performs a weekly walk of properties on the market. So not only do I get reports from my project manager telling me the status of current projects, but I also get reports from those projects on the market—is the yard in good shape? Are the beds fully weeded and cleaned? Is the house clean? Are the temperatures in the house good? We want to make sure that the property's being marketed well. All those are little details that can slow down your project, which will slow down the sale, which will slow down your cash. Again, the more cash we have, the more we can redeploy it and the faster we can scale. Having a property ready for market at any given time will help sell it quicker.

When you're hiring an assistant for construction or listing, your typical cost, at least for us, is $40,000–$80,000. The lower end will be for someone performing more basic functions, like scheduling contractors and ordering out materials. On the higher end is someone doing a combination of two jobs, like we have this person doing.

Don't forget, you can also hire these people hourly, usually between $20 and $25 an hour, and you can use them part time as you scale your business and then roll them into full time. They must be detail oriented since, as operators, we run multiple businesses and have our hands in all different fields. We're constantly trying to bring all the pieces together, which makes us, as operators, a little bit disorganized. So this person being a central hub and collecting information and reporting it so I can manage from their information is essential.

This person should have at least two years experience in construction and real estate and, as I've mentioned before, be meticulously organized. And if they have any sort of design background, that's always preferred, because I don't want my construction admin assistant asking me details on every spec. If I give them a rough theme, I want them to be able to source that theme and just get it ordered, so I don't have to think about it. The fewer questions the better.

Real estate broker. Leveraging a real estate broker effectively can be a game changer for fix-and-flip operators looking to scale their business. While many investors focus on commission discounts, the true value lies in the additional services and expertise a skilled broker can provide. When scaling your operation, time becomes your most precious resource. A well-utilized broker can save you countless hours and provide invaluable insights throughout the investment process.

Here's how to maximize this relationship:

- **Comparative market analysis (CMA):** Have your broker provide a CMA for every potential investment. This not only saves you time but also vests the broker in the deal, potentially leading to higher sale prices.
- **Property evaluations:** Let your broker drive and evaluate comparable properties, saving you hours of legwork and providing detailed reports on spec levels.
- **Regular project oversight:** Have your broker visit projects bimonthly. Their fresh perspective can catch issues that project managers or contractors might miss, preventing costly mistakes.
- **Design input:** Involve your broker in design decisions. Their market knowledge can inform choices on finishes, colors, and features that appeal to buyers.

- **Presale coordination:** Task your broker with coordinating cleaning, staging, pre-inspections, and final punch lists. Their buyer-oriented viewpoint can identify improvements that increase marketability.
- **Specialized knowledge:** Work with investment-focused brokers who understand your specific "buy box" and can assist with underwriting and deal packaging.

By integrating a broker deeply into your process, you're not just saving time—you're gaining a valuable team member invested in your success. This approach allows you to focus on high-level strategy and business growth while ensuring each project receives thorough attention. As you scale, this broker relationship becomes increasingly crucial. It provides a consistent, reliable system for evaluating, improving, and selling properties across a growing portfolio. The broker's involvement from acquisition to sale creates a seamless workflow, reducing your personal time investment per project and allowing you to take on more deals.

Hard-money lender. Consistent access to funding is the lifeblood of real estate investing. During market downturns, like 2008–2010, lack of available capital significantly hindered growth for many investors. A dependable lender can be the difference between completing ten or fifty homes annually. With reliable funding, you can take on more projects simultaneously, dramatically increasing your business's scale and profitability. Long-term relationships with lenders often lead to better terms.

While many lenders require 20–25 percent down, a strong track record can reduce this to 5–10 percent, freeing up more of your capital for additional investments. A lender familiar with your business can also process loans more quickly and efficiently, allowing you to move faster on deals. While it's tempting to always chase the lowest rate, the value of a long-term relationship often outweighs marginal rate differences. Stick with one primary lender for an extended period (five to seven years) to build trust and demonstrate reliability. Always be aware of market rates, but avoid constantly switching lenders for small savings.

Keep your lender informed about your business plans and successes to build confidence in your operations. Similarly, maintaining long-term relationships with general contractors and subcontractors is crucial for efficient scaling. Long-term contractors learn your preferences and standards, reducing the need for constant oversight. Established relationships can save hundreds of hours annually in meetings and explanations, allowing you to focus on business growth. Sometimes paying slightly more for a trusted contractor is worth it for the consistency and time savings.

Long-term contractors can integrate seamlessly with your business processes, further improving efficiency. While these contractors aren't on your payroll, treating these relationships as integral parts of your team is key to successful scaling. The time and hassle saved through these established relationships allow you to focus on strategic growth, potentially offsetting any marginal cost increases. As you scale, the efficiency and reliability gained from these partnerships become increasingly valuable, enabling you to take on more projects and grow your real estate business more effectively.

GETTING BACK YOUR TIME

As your fix-and-flip business grows and you've established a core team, you'll find your operations becoming more streamlined. Your team will be handling essential tasks, like jobsite inspections and reporting, while you focus on managing through data-driven insights such as budget reports, CMA values, and pro forma cash flow projections. This improved efficiency will inevitably free up your time, presenting opportunities for strategic expansion.

To scale your business effectively, consider leveraging this newfound time to explore complementary revenue streams that align with your existing operations. These additions can significantly boost your profitability without requiring extensive new systems or workload. Here are three logical steps to consider:

1. **Wholesaling:** Utilize your deal-sourcing skills to find properties you can contract and then sell to other investors. This leverages your market knowledge and network without the need for renovation work.
2. **Broker services:** If you're licensed or have a team member who is, offer real estate services to other investors or clients. This can include helping clients buy or sell properties, capitalizing on your market expertise.
3. **Joint venture (JV) operations:** Partner with other investors or contractors on projects. This allows you to expand your reach and take on more deals without necessarily increasing your personal workload.

As you implement these additional revenue streams, focus on systematizing each process. Delegate tasks to your team members, allowing them to take ownership of specific areas. For instance, a team member could manage the wholesaling pipeline and another could oversee broker services while you focus on cultivating JV relationships.

The key to successful scaling is to view these additions not as separate entities but as integrated parts of your overall business strategy. Each new revenue stream should complement and enhance your core fix-and-flip operations. The goal is to increase your income while gradually making your role more passive. As these additional revenue streams grow, you'll have the resources to hire more specialized team members, further systematizing your operations. This cycle of growth, systematization, and delegation is the path to scaling your business effectively, potentially doubling your income while simultaneously reducing your direct involvement in day-to-day operations.

CONCLUSION

*I've missed more than 9,000 shots in my career.
I've lost almost 300 games. Twenty-six times I've been
trusted to take the game-winning shot and missed.
I've failed over and over and over again in my life.
And that is why I succeed.*

—MICHAEL JORDAN, FORMER NBA PLAYER

WHEN I STARTED this business, I never anticipated reaching the level of success we've achieved, with over $1 billion in sales and numerous investor and lending opportunities. I lacked any special training, substantial initial capital, or established infrastructure (and many can relate to starting at zero). However, what I did have was a determination to work hard and build a successful business. This was my North Star, and I was able to focus on this despite the many storms that come from this business, including the 2008 market crash. Despite witnessing others abandon their ventures, I decided to push through and focus on creating a recession-proof business model.

As our earnings consistently reached seven figures, we strategically reinvested back into our business. Specifically, we focused on reinvesting in the Seattle real estate market, which propelled us from eight doors to nearly 1,000 doors in just fifteen years. While our local market has a lot of challenges due to its expense and complexity, the methods we employ can be adapted to thrive in any high-demand market. These investments generate an additional $50,000–$60,000 per month in cash flow, which is the net amount of money generated by a property after subtracting all operating expenses and debt service from the gross rental income. It's important to note that our success comes from our core flipping skills, which I've broken down in this book. If you're willing to put in the work, I believe you can achieve similar results.

Exponential growth in the context of flipping houses refers to the compounding effect of successfully reinvesting profits from one house flip into subsequent projects, thereby accelerating wealth accumulation over time. When executed effectively, each successful flip not only generates a profit but also provides additional capital to undertake larger and more profitable ventures, leading to exponential growth in wealth.

Initially, a house flipper like yourself might start with a modest investment, purchasing a distressed property at a below-market price. Through strategic renovations, improvements, and aesthetic enhancements, the property's value is significantly increased, allowing the flipper to sell it at a higher price than the purchase and renovation costs combined. The profit generated from this first flip can then be reinvested into the acquisition of additional properties or into more extensive renovation projects. With each successive flip, the flipper gains both experience and resources, enabling them to tackle larger and more lucrative opportunities.

As the flipper's portfolio expands, the pace of growth accelerates due to the compounding effect of reinvested profits. With a larger capital base, they can pursue multiple projects simultaneously, further increasing the potential for profit generation. Moreover, successful flips can also lead to networking opportunities, access to better financing options, and improved market credibility, all of which contribute to exponential growth.

If, like me fifteen years ago (and still to this day), you are willing to put in the work, you can learn how to do your first flip and then scale your business to make real money, possibly even generational wealth for your family and future legacy. Flipping isn't the easiest thing in the world, but if you are willing to put in the work, it's the type of business that grows at an exponential pace. You will learn a lesson on every project and within every market, so once you have a pile of lessons learned, you'll know how to handle future situations in an economic manner. This is why we create systems. This is how you scale to six figures, then seven figures, and beyond.

FOUR SIMPLE RULES TO GET STARTED

We've covered a ton of information, which I know can be overwhelming. Here are four simple rules to create your own detailed plan to get started:

1. **Start small and build systems**. Yes, the bigger fixes pay more, but they can also derail newer investors in the industry. If you go for the short-term money, you won't make the long-term money. It's a vicious cycle that often comes from ego. If you're willing to learn

the right steps, such as those detailed in this book and on your first few flips, then you can build a system to make more money than you've ever dreamed of. But you can't do that if you're treading water in a deal beyond your current capabilities.

2. **Stick to your buy box.** A buy box is a flipper's defined lane or lanes of investment that they can execute on (meaning what can you afford with the capital you have and resources available to implement the plan). About 95 percent of the time I've gotten in trouble on a deal, it's because I got blinded by the numbers. I was a deal junkie, and I ignored my buy box. I couldn't get past how cheap a property appeared to be. But, just because a property is cheap, that doesn't mean it's a great deal. You have to define and understand your buy box, so you know whether or not the deal fits what you've committed to doing in your business. Yes, your buy box can change, and it will with time, but don't force a deal into your buy box if it could derail your business. An example of this is finding a cheap house in a neighborhood where it's hard to sell deals. I see people doing this all the time, and they wonder why no one will buy their deal. The same is true for your experience level and resources.

3. **Don't overleverage yourself.** This was perhaps the defining lesson I learned back in that 2008 deal. Investors get greedy because they want to bring in as much capital as they can. They can get you into big trouble. Too much debt can sink you. Be realistic about your goals and your deals. Just because you have access to money doesn't mean you have to spend it.

4. **Avoid problem properties in the beginning.** Avoid unknown timeline properties, meaning properties where permit timelines and seasonal delays can add additional time to a project. For example, my box includes avoiding ECA (environmental critical areas)—properties that have wetlands, special inspections, or structural hillside changes. There are so many hidden costs in these types of deals. If you've found a home in the market with these types of issues, and it's been on the market for months or years, there's a reason for this. It's not impossible to make it work, but it's significantly harder to control your game plan on these types of deals. There's too much out of your control. Anytime there is environmental impact (a swampy yard or wetlands), it can cause massive issues and time delays. Much like an eroding hillside, time delays erode your cash-on-cash return and kill profit

on deals. Properties with unknown timelines and expenses can drown in holding costs and construction overruns.

For the most part, flipping is a busy business, but if you have a squeaky wheel that takes too much cash and too much time, it can screw up your scalability when flipping multiple deals. Focus on categories you understand and can manage without too many added difficulties. These properties eat up resources.

Flipping homes is one of the most profitable avenues in real estate investing. Not only can it expedite your path to financial freedom, renovating homes for profit can also be personally rewarding, improve your local community, and (I will even admit) fun. Despite its attraction, however, the risks involved should not be downplayed. The purpose of this book was to help you create systems and strategies that mitigate risks and set you up for success. Creating system behind each step in your business model not only allows you to grow and scale faster, but it will also make you bulletproof in all market conditions. Go out there and get to flipping!

ACKNOWLEDGMENTS

I NEVER THOUGHT I would achieve the success I have today. I could not have undertaken this journey without all the business professionals I have worked with over the past nineteen years. Each experience, win or lose, has helped shape who I am today.

Will Heaton—We started this business when we were just two 20-somethings with a lot of ambition. I never could have dreamed we could have turned it into what we have today. Thank you for getting me started in the business and continuing to be my sounding board and best friend after all these years.

Nick Weaver—We have made it a long way from working at Red Robin. We have grown up together in this industry, and I am so appreciative you have been here along the way.

Ryan Burgess and Megan Halter—You are more than just the incredible talent behind our fix-and-flip company. You look after every project and every home we create like it's your own. I truly believe that it is the heart you both bring that has made this business a success.

On the Market Podcast and BiggerPockets—I am still in awe of and humbled by the incredible opportunity you have given me. Connecting with other investors and being able to give back through education has been one of the most rewarding experiences of my life. Dave Meyer, Kailyn Bennet, Henry Washington, and Kathy Fettke: You are some of the people I look forward to talking with every week.

Huge thank-you and shout out to the BiggerPockets publishing team—Katie Miller, Winsome Lewis, Savannah Wood, and Kaylee Walterbach. Thank you for guiding me through this process. I am definitely more of an investor than an author. Thanks for teaching me your ways!

Mark Karins—You have been an amazing mentor for me, teaching me about business, how to conduct myself, and how to communicate with business professionals.

For the incredible team of employees and brokers that have supported my journey over the years—my team at Heaton Dainard is the foundation to my success. My broker community and long-term relationships have given me the support to excel. Thank you to all the general contractors, subcontractors, and vendors who have put in countless hours of hard work to help me take these homes to the finish line.

Lenders, my main lender Intrust Funding, and especially Sandy Davis— Thank you for believing in me when I was a broke 25-year-old kid.

My Heaton Dainard, Intrust Funding, and ProjectRE clients—Thank you for choosing and trusting me. Every project we have helped you with has taught me a lesson in life.

Brad Holcom—You may have paved the way for a new chapter in my life.

My students—Watching you all crush it out there is one of my greatest joys.

My family—Thank you for moving every two to three years for my owner-occupied flips! You are my happy place and motivate me every day.

My two children, Bianca and Jameson—You have taught me to never forget how blessed I am, to be present, and to cherish each day. I love you guys.

ABOUT THE AUTHOR

AT THE AGE of 23, James Dainard began his real estate career while completing his business degree at the University of Washington. Over the past eighteen years, James has become the foremost expert real estate investor in Washington, with an unparalleled reputation. James specializes in value-add acquisitions and has been involved in over 4,000 renovations, from fix-and-flip, ground-up development and construction, and apartment turns. James is an active investor in the Pacific Northwest, who has grown his real estate portfolio to nearly 1,000 properties. As a real estate broker, James has completed over 3,000 real estate transactions totaling over $1 billion in sales. James's success has garnered numerous accolades, including his companies winning Puget Sound's Fastest Growing Companies, Washington's Fastest Growing Private Companies, Inc 500, and being selected by the *Puget Sound Business Journal*'s "40 under 40" list. James is a cohost of the Bigger Pockets *On the Market* podcast and an active contributor on the BiggerPockets YouTube channel.

He is a licensed broker and managing partner of six real estate investment companies that work together to maximize profit for his investors: Heaton Dainard, a full-service real estate brokerage; Buck Buys Houses, an off-market property acquisition company; Intrust Funding, a hard-money lender; Limelite Development, a development company that specializes in fix-and-flip, townhome, and single-family ground-up construction; Converse Capital, a syndication investment company; and ProjectRE, a real estate educational platform.

WHAT'S IN YOUR TOOL KIT?

AT THIS POINT, it's a good idea to start thinking about what tools are currently in your tool kit. Things like a tape measure, public picture storage, walk-through sheets, pro forma, flashlight, hand sanitizer, construction contract, and proof of funds are all necessary items for the serious investor.

Tape measure: Let's say you're upsizing a three-bedroom, one-bathroom to a three- bedroom, two-bath, but when you did your walk-through, you referenced where the second bathroom would go. Then you buy the property, but you didn't measure the space, and it's actually a foot too short to be up to code. Now you have to rethink the entire project to find a new value-add.

Public picture storage: Using something like Google Drive to store photos and video walk-throughs to share with collaborators is key on any deal. You need to document all of your photos and keep them in a central location, so everyone is on the same page when it comes to managing the deal.

Walk-through sheets: Walk-through sheets help you keep track of damages, repairs, future plans, and everything in between. Again, this helps with future communication to make sure everyone is running a smooth, efficient operation.

Pro formas: A pro forma is a preliminary bill or estimated invoice used to request payment from a committed buyer. It will include a description of the goods or services, the total payout amount, and other details. This might include JV agreements and similar documents.

Hand sanitizer: This may sound crazy, but I've had so much random stuff fall on me to the point that I have to essentially bathe in hand sanitizer on-site. It's ridiculous, so keep some in your tool kit. Believe me, you'll regret not having it. It's almost as important as a proof of funds letter.

Permit, floor plans, and spec folders: Keeping a copy of plans and permits in a protected folder is a great way to help answer questions as trades and subcontractors come through.

Safety information and contact forms: Contact information for owner and staff working on project and all safety policies should be posted.

Lockbox: Each jobsite should have its own lockbox with its own unique code to help with access for trades and staff. Installing a backup access plan is a good idea.

Wireless cameras: To ensure site safety and security, a wireless camera system is recommended.

 You can find a printable version of this Tool Kit at www.BiggerPockets.com/FrameworkBonus.

GLOSSARY
KEY TERMS IN FLIPPING

1031 exchange: A tax-deferral strategy that allows investors to sell a property and reinvest the proceeds into a like-kind property while deferring capital gains taxes.

The 70 percent rule: A guideline stating that real estate investors should pay no more than 70 percent of a property's after-repair value (ARV) minus the cost of necessary repairs. It serves as a quick filtering process to evaluate potential deals.

After-repair value (ARV): The estimated value of a property after all planned renovations and repairs have been completed.

BRRRR: An acronym for "buy, rehab, rent, refinance, repeat"; a real estate investment strategy that involves purchasing a distressed property, renovating it, renting it out, refinancing to pull out the initial investment, and then repeating the process with another property.

Buy box: A set of criteria that defines an investor's preferred investment properties, including factors such as price range, location, property type, and desired returns.

Cash flow: The net income generated by a rental property after all expenses, such as mortgage payments, property taxes, insurance, and maintenance costs, have been paid.

Cash-on-cash return: The annual return on investment calculated by dividing the total profit from all deals by the total cash invested over a twelve-month period.

Cents on the dollar: A marketing term indicating that a property is being purchased at a significant discount compared to its actual value.

Comparables (comps): Recently sold properties similar in size, location, and features to the property being evaluated; used to estimate the ARV and inform the investor's decision-making process.

Contingency: A clause in a real estate contract that specifies conditions that must be met for the sale to be completed, such as a satisfactory home inspection or the buyer securing financing.

Distressed property: A property that is in poor condition, often due to neglect, damage, or the owner's financial difficulties, which may be available for purchase at a discounted price.

Due diligence: The process of thoroughly investigating a potential real estate investment, including evaluating the property's condition, market value, and potential risks or liabilities.

Earnest money: A deposit made by the buyer to demonstrate their commitment to purchasing a property; typically held in escrow until the closing date.

Equity: The difference between a property's market value and the outstanding mortgage balance, representing the owner's financial stake in the property.

Escrow: A neutral third party that holds funds and documents related to a real estate transaction until all conditions of the sale have been met.

Fix-and-flip: A real estate investment strategy that involves purchasing a property, renovating it, and then selling it quickly for a profit.

Forced appreciation: The increase in a property's value due to improvements made by the owner, such as renovations or additions.

Future market value (FMV): The estimated value of a property after the planned renovations have been completed.

Hard-money lender: A type of lender that provides short-term, high-interest loans to real estate investors, typically secured by the property being purchased.

Joint venture (JV): A partnership between two or more parties working together on a real estate deal, often with one party providing a skill set and the other providing liquidity.

Lien release: A document that confirms a contractor or subcontractor has been paid in full and waives their right to place a lien on the property for nonpayment.

Off-market property: A property that is not listed for sale on the Multiple Listing Service (MLS) or other public platforms, often requiring investors to proactively search for and approach potential sellers.

Punch list: A list of minor repairs, touch-ups, and incomplete items that need to be addressed before a renovation project can be considered complete.

Return on investment (ROI): A metric used to evaluate the performance of an investment, calculated by dividing the net profit by the total cost of the investment, expressed as a percentage.

Scope of work: A detailed description of the specific repairs, renovations, and improvements to be made to a property during the flipping process.

Soft-money lender: A type of lender that offers more flexible terms and lower interest rates compared to hard-money lenders, but with more stringent qualification requirements.

Staging: The process of preparing a property for sale by decluttering, cleaning, and strategically arranging furniture and decor to make the space more appealing to potential buyers.

Wholesale: A transaction where someone sells the rights to a property rather than the actual property itself, acting as a middleman in the deal.

Wholesaler: An individual or company that specializes in finding distressed or off-market properties, securing them under contract and then selling the contract to an investor for a fee.

Zoning: Local laws and regulations that dictate how a property can be used and developed, such as specifying whether a property can be used for residential, commercial, or industrial purposes.

 You can find a printable version of this Glossary at www.BiggerPockets.com/FrameworkBonus.

Real Estate Partnerships: How to Access More Cash, Acquire Bigger Deals, and Achieve Higher Profits by Ashley Kehr and Tony Robinson

Real estate investing can be a complicated puzzle—you need time, money, experience, and connections to start and scale your business effectively. Rather than hustling to provide every component on your own, finding a real estate partner can help fast-track you to the portfolio of your dreams.

www.BiggerPockets.com/ ReadREPartnerships

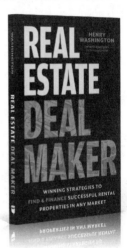

Real Estate Deal Maker: Winning Strategies to Find & Finance Successful Rental Properties in Any Market by Henry Washington

The two biggest problems in real estate are finding properties and funding deals— and the solution to both starts here. Are you ready to master the art of finding remarkable properties and securing the funds to seal the deal? Look no further.

www.BiggerPockets.com/ReadDealMaker

Scaling Smart: How to Design a Self-Managing Business by Rich Fettke and Kathy Fettke

Are you ready to create passive income, free up your time, and grow your business without sacrificing your sanity? In *Scaling Smart*, RealWealth founders Rich and Kathy Fettke distill more than twenty years of business strategy into an approachable guide to scaling a successful enterprise.

www.BiggerPockets.com/ ReadScalingSmart

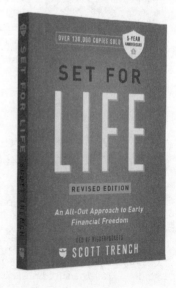

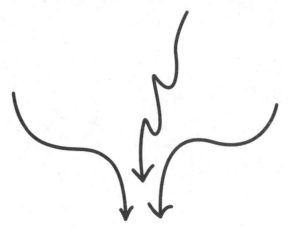

Follow us on social media!

Continue your learning and start taking action with
a FREE BiggerPockets webinar! Join Dave Meyer and follow
his steps to get your first rental property in the next 90 days.
Head to www.BiggerPockets.com/90dayweb.

Looking for more?
Join the BiggerPockets Community

BiggerPockets brings together education, tools, and a community of more than 2 million like-minded members—all in one place. Learn about investment strategies, analyze properties, connect with investor-friendly agents, and more.

Go to **www.BiggerPockets.com** to learn more!

 Listen to a **BiggerPockets Podcast**

 Watch **BiggerPockets on YouTube**

 Join the **Community Forum**

 Learn more on **the Blog**

 Read more **BiggerPockets Books**

 Learn about our **Real Estate Investing Bootcamps**

 Connect with an **Investor-Friendly Real Estate Agent**

 Go Pro! Start, scale, and manage your portfolio with your **Pro Membership**